GOD'S GREAT PLAN FOR THE WHOLE WORLD

The Biblical Story of Creation and Redemption

Phillip A. Ross

Marietta, Ohio

Copyright ©2019 Phillip A. Ross
All rights reserved.

ISBN: 978-0-9820385-7-4
Edition: 2019.10.7

Published by

Pilgrim Platform
149 E. Spring St., Marietta
Ohio, 45750
www.pilgrim-platform.org

Biblical quotations are from the English Standard Version, Standard Bible Society, unless otherwise cited. KJV indicates the King James Version, in public domain.

Printed in the United States of America

BOOKS BY PHILLIP A. ROSS

The Work At Zion—A Reckoning, Two-volume set, 772 pages, 1996.

Practically Christian—Applying James Today, 135 pages, 2006.

The Wisdom of Jesus Christ in the Book of Proverbs, 414 pages, 2006.

Marking God's Word—Understanding Jesus, 324 pages, 2006.

Acts of Faith—Kingdom Advancement, 326 pages, 2007.

Informal Christianity—Refining Christ's Church, 136 pages, 2007.

Engagement—Establishing Relationship in Christ, 104 pages, 1996, 2008.

It's About Time! — The Time Is Now, 40 pages. 2008.

The Big Ten—A Study of the Ten Commandments, 105 pages, 2001, 2008.

Arsy Varsy—Reclaiming The Gospel in First Corinthians, 406 pages, 2008.

Varsy Arsy—Proclaiming The Gospel in Second Corinthians, 356 pages, 2009.

Colossians—Christos Singularis, 278 pages, 2010.

Rock Mountain Creed—The Sermon on the Mount, 310 pages, 2011.

The True Mystery of the Mystical Presence, 355 pages, 2011.

Peter's Vision of Christ's Purpose in First Peter, 340 pages, 2011.

Peter's Vision of The End in Second Peter, 184 pages, 2012.

The Religious History of Nineteenth Century Marietta, Thomas Jefferson Summers, 124 pages, 1903, 2012 (editor).

Conflict of Ages—The Great Debate of the Moral Relations of God and Man, Edward Beecher, 489 pages, 1853, 2012 (editor).

Concord Of Ages—The Individual And Organic Harmony Of God And Man, Edward Beecher, D. D., 524 pages, 1860, 2013 (editor).

Ephesians—Recovering the Vision of a Sustainable Church in Christ, 417 pages, 2013.

Galatians: Backstory/Christory, 315 pages, 2015.

Poet Tree—Root, Branch & Sap, 72 pages, 2013.

Inside Out Woman—Collected Poetry, Doris M. Ross, 195 pages, 2014 (editor).

God's Great Plan for the World, 306 pages, 2019.

John's Miracles—Seeing Beyond Our Expectations, 180 pages, 2019.

"We are storytelling animals, and cannot bear to acknowledge the ordinariness of our daily lives." –Stephen Jay Gould

*For John Saggio and the
great conversation*

*And for my grandchildren: Brielle,
Clark, James, Isaac, and Simon;
and their children*

Table of Contents

Preface..i
Adamic Humanity..1
Noaic Humanity...43
Abrahamic Humanity..56
The Word Into The World...................................83
Tabernacle...119
King And Temple..146
Ancient Kingdom..168
The Prophets...187
The Advent..221
The Christ...238
Appendix...281
Alphabetical Index..299
Scripture Index..305

PREFACE

The idea for this book has emerged after decades of biblical teaching and preaching, culminating in the observation that most Christians with whom I am familiar do not have an understanding of the overall story, trajectory, or context of the Bible. Rather, they understand the Bible as a collection of stories at best and a selection of random verses at worst. People often ask, "What is your favorite verse?" as if the main feature of the Bible is the beauty, depth, and wisdom of various verses that provide inspiration and/or guidance for those willing to ferret them out.

Such a perspective is certainly better than biblical disbelief or apathy, but it fails to garner the main thrust or point of the long, biblical metastory. Granted that the main features of this long, overarching story are difficult to discern amid the cacophony of details and spiritual oddities that populate the pages of the Bible. The Bible is concerned about long periods of time, while our concern is daily living. It is very easy to get distracted from the arduous pursuit of discovering God's ultimate purpose in providing God's take on our history. What is God's point, purpose, or lesson of the overall story of the Bible?

One of the difficulties of such an approach is that each of us as individuals are caught up in the particularities of our own culture and time. In addition, each particular culture is similarly caught up in its own historical and epochal struggles. God's great story is genuinely multicultural and multiepochal in that God provides an eternal perspective, or as close to such a perspective as is possible.

In addition, this book has been written in the twilight of my own pastoral career and a lifetime of biblical study with more than two dozen of my own books in print, books about the Bible. Thus, this book is the culmination of a long conversation about the Bible, and assumes familiarity with my work, as well as with biblical and Christian theology and history. I have occasionally footnoted references to other works, mine and others, that impact various ideas discussed here, should the reader want more detail. Of course, I assume some familiarity with the biblical stories and the history of their interpretation.

This book is dedicated in part to John Saggio, whom I have never met, but who sent me a copy of his gargantuan, self-published book, *The Destiny of Israel and the Twilight of Christianity*, subtitled: "In Quest of the Meaning and Significance of the Hebrew and Greek Scriptures" (www.TwilightofReligion.com). Saggio taught philosophy at Mesa Community College, and inscribed in the book he sent to me,

> "To: Phillip A. Ross, Having thoroughly, carefully and completely read '*Conflict of Ages*,' I thought you would appreciate a complimentary copy of this volume, hoping you will follow your advice at the end of your preface to 'Conflict of Ages,' (which reads) 'May the Lord bless you as you read this book. Please consider it carefully and prayerfully. And if you make it all the way through it, join the conversation.' Thus, with the volume now set before you, I join the conversation."
>
> January 1, 2017
> John Saggio

Saggio's book is a thorough defense of Preterism,[1] making the case from both the Old and New Testaments that all biblical prophecy has been completely fulfilled. I agree with Saggio's conclusion that the advent of Christ fulfilled the Old Testament, but I take exception with his idea that the destruction of the Temple and Jerusalem in A.D. 70 fulfilled the New Testament. He speculates that the era of the Bible is over, and that it is time to get

---
1 https://wiki2.org/en/Preterism

beyond Christianity. His biblical scholarship is indisputable, but his conclusion about Christianity lacks the essential teaching or lesson of the Bible, and denies the reality of the Holy Spirit. Consequently, this book has been written with Saggio in mind. And again I offer the same invitation: May the Lord bless you as you read this book. Please consider it carefully and prayerfully. And if you make it all the way through it, join the conversation.

Modern scientists propose that the earth is millions of years old and that humanity is hundreds of thousands of years old. If that is true, they have a lot of explaining to do about the paucity of cultural evidence. Given the explosive presence of humanity on the earth over the past five thousand years, it would seem that if humanity were much older than that, there should be an abundance of evidence because humanity has left such a massive footprint over the last five thousand years. Where are all the bones of the previous generations? And where are their cultural remains—buildings, roads, etc. Even without the development of language and writing, the human propensity for reproduction should have left some significant remains. A mere piece of a bone here and there hardly explains humanity's potential for explosive growth that we have seen over the past five thousand years. Even if they are right, something significant changed about five thousand years ago with the development of written language. And the Bible, being a book, is about that change.

But I'm not going to explore prehistory in these pages. Human history may or may not extend back as far as modern scientists imagine. My concern here begins with the written pages of the Bible. My intention is to briefly sketch the grand arc of the Biblical narrative as it is presented in the Bible. If there is a grand story, there must be a grand point, purpose, or lesson. And while the biblical story begins with the Creation Story in Genesis, the Bible as a compendium of literature does not begin there. If we are going to understand the biblical story, we must first posit that there is an actual biblical story, a comprehensible and overarching narrative that runs from Genesis through Revelation.

However, if there is such a narrative, we must also assume that someone intentionally wrote or arranged the various sub-stories into a comprehensive whole. It must necessarily be a "someone" because only persons tell stories. Such a story may involve more than one person, and of course, the Bible does. There are many biblical authors. Nonetheless, there must still be one single person or group who arranged the various stories into a comprehensible whole, or who thought that they were doing so. Traditional Christianity understands that Person to be the Holy Spirit. God Himself is the ultimate author of the Bible, and in order to get at the grand narrative, we must posit, assume, or believe this to be the actual case of the matter. The Holy Spirit is the holistic narrator—and the editor.

The Bible, of course, comes in two testaments, an old one and a new one. This division is both essential and problematic. It is essential because the story is not complete without them both, and it is problematic because upon casual observation there appears to be many contradictions and complications between them.

Nonetheless, we begin with the Old Testament as we currently have it, in it's current Protestant form. It presents itself as a whole, from Genesis to Malachi. The thirty-nine books have a common thread. But it is important to understand that it did not historically begin in the form we have. Its actual beginnings are shrouded in the fog of history, of course. And the truth be known, we only have a few fragments of copies that date back to the origins of writing during the early Babylonian period. Most of the extant manuscripts are of a much later date. However, my intention here is not to delve into the origin and authenticity of early manuscripts, but to examine the plain reading of the Old Testament story as it presents itself today. To do that we need to know that it wasn't always as it is today.

The earliest whole manuscript copies of the Old Testament extant today originate from the era of the Second Temple, following the Babylonian captivity of Israel. And the best scholarship suggests that the Old Testament literature was put into the basic form that we have today by ancient Israelites during their Babylonian captivity, and continuing into the Second Temple era. This is important because it provides a point of reference for understanding the overarching narrative as it was assembled by those who built the Second Temple, the Temple that Jesus encountered. This is important because the New Testament is about Jesus and His relationship to the Old Testament or Second Temple Judaism.

Much earlier, ancient Israel came to a crossroad experience as the destruction of the Temple by Nebuchadnezzar in 587 B.C. left the Jews with a bitter experience to reckon. The story of the destruction of the Temple and Jerusalem that led to the Babylonian Captivity is a central element of the Old Testament. How could God have allowed such a failure to happen to His chosen people? During their Babylonian captivity they regrouped and set out to understand what had happened to them, and why God had not protected them. They combed through their religious literature for guidance and direction, and produced the Tanakh.[2] Why the Tanakh? Why include these first five books of the Torah? First, they recognized certain similarities between Adam and various other biblical heroes.

For instance, God spoke to Adam, and God also spoke to Moses. God promised Adam that he could eat from the Tree of Life if he would not eat from the Tree of the knowledge of good and evil. Similarly God promised to lead Moses to the Promised Land if he would not break the Ten Commandments. Adam was to instruct Eve, and Moses was to instruct Israel. Eve rejected God's Word in the story of the Fall, and Israel rejected God's Word in the story of the Golden Calf. God then banned Adam and Eve from the Garden, and God banned Moses and his generation of Israelites from the Promised Land. They wandered in the desert for forty years, and only after Moses and that generation had died did they move into the Promised Land. Similar comparisons exist between Adam and Abraham, Adam and Joseph, Adam and Joshua, etc.

---

2   Tanakh: an acronym of the first Hebrew letter of each of the Masoretic Text's three traditional subdivisions: Torah (*Teaching*, also known as the Five Books of Moses), Nevi'im (*Prophets*) and Ketuvim (*Writings*)—hence TaNaKh. The form of this text, authoritative for Rabbinic Judaism, is known as the Masoretic Text (MT), and is divided into twenty-four books, while the Protestant Bible translations divide the same material into thirty-nine books.

Part of the purpose of putting the story together as they did was their effort to explain Israel's failure and the subsequent destruction of their Temple and Babylonian captivity. They never doubted God's sovereignty, so they focused on Israel's failure. Genesis 1-3 provides the first iteration of this foundational story. There we find the essential biblical story in three movements: the call, the fall, and the hope. God created a people and gave them everything they needed (Adam and Eve in the Garden). But they rejected God's order (sin and the Fall). Yet, God provided hope for their redemption (the Protevangelium[3] in Genesis 3:15). This story is repeated in cycles of epochal history throughout the pages of the Old Testament.

The biblical story of human failure is not without the hope of human renewal. In fact, the story is essentially a story of hope, of a hope that has guided Israel ever since the Fall. From the very beginning God had promised that one day the seed of the woman would triumph over the serpent (Genesis 3:15). The overarching narrative of the Old Testament is the story of Israel's continual failure regarding their triumph over sin, and the point is that they could not do it themselves. Rather, God would need to do it for them by sending a savior. God has called humanity to be what we in and of ourselves cannot become apart from God Himself. The Old Testament is the story of humanity's best efforts and ultimate failure; and the New Testament is the story of God's provision in spite of our failure.

Thus, the Old Testament begins with the hope of humanity, Adam, who was created by God in perfect goodness, but who was waylaid by the serpent and banished from the Garden. Central to this story is the fact of the existence of the serpent in the Garden. The serpent was already there as Adam and Eve worked the Garden, and they would need to displace him. After the Fall, God cursed them all and banned them all from the garden, actively putting enmity or strife between the serpent (a previous resident in the Garden) and the woman or humanity. The serpent would

---

3   Several of the early Church fathers, such as Justin Martyr (160 A.D.) and Irenaeus (180 A.D.) regarded this verse as the first messianic prophecy in the Old Testament.

crawl beast-like and eat dust (Genesis 3:14), and Adam would one day return to the dust (Genesis 3:19). It sounds like God called humanity to rise out of a beast-like existence by mastering sin.[4] This long story found its culmination in the destruction of the Temple in 587 B.C. and their subsequent Babylonian capture. And we find that the end of the Old Testament in the closing chapter of Malachi we are left with the hope for a coming savior to rescue God's captive people once again.

The overall shape of the Old Testament as we have it today was formed by the experience and worldview of the Jewish priests in Babylonian captivity and the subsequent Second Temple Jewish establishment. I'm not saying that the story of the Old Testament is nothing more than a man-made product of Jewish production, but rather that it issues out of the failure of humanity represented by the Jews to actually become what God has created humanity to become, based on the test case of ancient Israel. This process of failure has been, and continues to be, corrected in fits and starts by God's Holy Spirit through the ages. This pattern of repeated failure (call, fall, and hope) is the engine of human growth, maturity, and progress. This vision is necessarily postmillennial in character, and evinces an eschatology of hope. The Old Testament provides a story of God forging a kind of human character that is able to endure the hostilities of earthly existence.

NEW TESTAMENT

The New Testament was birthed out of the angst and ashes of the failure and destruction of the Second Temple in A.D. 70 by Rome. The importance of the advent of Jesus Christ becomes more clear after the destruction of the Temple and the kingdom of Israel. The story of Jesus Christ is best read in the light of A.D. 70 because without the destruction of the Temple and the kingdom the primary meaning of the story of Jesus Christ would not exist as we know it. It is necessary to see that Christianity rose from the ashes of ancient Jerusalem. Christ came to provide what we in and of ourselves cannot accomplish.

---

4   See Appendix: Sin, p. 289.

In addition, in the light of Hebrews 7 we see that Jesus Christ is not just another character in the Old Testament mold, like John The Baptist was. Jesus Christ transcended the priestly establishments of both Aaron and Levi. Jesus Christ was a priest in a completely different tradition, that of Melchizedek, of whom little is known still today. The meaning and implications of this fact are extremely important, as well as mind-boggling.

Much of what we think we know about the Bible we learned in Sunday School, and has been derived from various over-simplified biblical stories built on moralistic platitudes. Of course there is nothing wrong with biblical morality or with teaching children biblical morality platitudinously, that is to say—simply. Such teaching is good for children, however, when we become adults we need to give up our childish ideas and expectations. But that does not mean that we should throw out the proverbial baby with the bath water. Rather, we need to see the old stories with new eyes. There are important details in the stories—contextual and linguistic nuances still being uncovered.

The biblical story that I'm going to tell you in these pages is not the only true biblical story available. The Bible is a complex book, with many authors who cover many themes over thousands of years. The truth is that there are many true stories and perspectives that the Bible provides. Some of those stories and perspectives provide harmony for one another, and some of them don't. While many people think that the Bible is full of contradictions, conflicting stories or facts are not so much contradictory as they provide real truth from different perspectives. When you see something in the following pages that is unfamiliar, don't simply reject it. Rather, search the Scripture yourself to see if what I'm saying is part of the Bible.

The perspective you will find in these pages is thoroughly biblical, yet thoroughly contemporary in that it issues out of the compendium and mindset or worldview of contemporary data. Just as, for instance, medical science has discovered that the truth of the human body is far more complex than our ancestors believed, so the truth of the Bible is also far more complex than our ancestors believed. This is not to say that everything previous generations have believed about the human body or the Bible is wrong—it's not. We cannot escape our own worldview, nor can anyone adequately understand the worldview of a different era. We always see things from our own perspective, our own time, our own place in the world and in society.

People often find that the perspectives of previous eras are inadequate to the realities of their own time. It's not that the truth of the Bible or the truths in the Bible have changed—they haven't. The Bible continues to be what it has always been. Rather, the abilities of modern science and research are able to penetrate deeper into biblical truth(s) because we have more data. The simple answers of previous generations are not satisfying to modern minds, but that doesn't mean that those simple answers are wrong. Rather, it means that we can now dig deeper into those same answers and find ever more complexities that produce ever more meaning, and that meaning connects with contemporary people.

This research phenomena is not new, but it has always been the case that each new generation must determine the veracity of the Bible for itself, in its own ways, based on its own methods, procedures, and data. This is what the reformers of the sixteenth century meant by their motto: *semper reformanda*. The church must be in continual reformation, always working to discover the full truth of the Bible, and articulate that truth in ways that speak meaningfully to the existing people of the era in which they live.

Many scholars will no doubt fault me for using Wikipedia as a resource because it is not always reliable. But may I remind those scholars that it is not always unreliable, either. I use it because my intention is not simply to appeal to scholars but to appeal to ordinary people. This book is not a work of scholarship, but a work of revelation. It is an effort to reveal biblical elements and perspectives in a way that ordinary people can appreciate today, and encourage those same people to reevaluate what they have been taught about the Bible by looking at it with new eyes, without the old, tired Sunday School platitudes.

The task before me here is to review the long story of the Bible in a way that both honors the faithful perspectives of Christians of previous eras, and yet speaks biblical truth in a way that makes it real and true for people today. Pray for my success in this endeavor by praying that you will be open to receiving information that has always been there, but has been overlooked for whatever reasons. The metastory of the Bible that you will encounter in these pages is not really new, but is actually quite old. I say *really* because you may not be familiar with it in the way that I will lay it out. Christian scholars have been saying since the beginning that Christians need to read the New Testament in the light of the Old, and the Old in the light of the New. That's what I'm trying to do. I'm shining the light of Christ back into the Old Testament, and then bringing those discoveries back into the New Testament.

Thanks to my wife, Stephanie, to Ray Foss for our many conversations and collaborations, and to Richard Brewer for proofreading. Whatever errors or misstatements you find in these pages are entirely of my own making. Please help me correct them by alerting me to them, and/or correcting them in your own mind and work.

I am grateful that the Lord has kept me out of the limelight, which has given me the opportunity to be and to think like an ordinary person, without trying to appeal to the desires of my readers or to try to appease my critics. I have no desire to please anyone other than God, and myself, of course. I'm trying to make sense of the Bible in the twenty-first century in a way that will appeal to twenty-first century people, and honor the traditional truths of Christian faithfulness. Lord, have mercy.

ADAMIC HUMANITY

In the beginning God... —Genesis 1:1

In the beginning was the Word, and the Word was with God, and the Word was God. He was in the beginning with God. All things were made through him, and without him was not any thing made that was made. In him was life, and the life was the light of men. The light shines in the darkness, and the darkness has not overcome it.
—John 1:1-5

It's about character. God is the first or prime character of this ancient story. The story is about God's character, and His love and concern for our world. God's story takes place in a world of words and stories. According to John, it all began with "the Word" (John 1:1). This well-known but too often ignored idea has significant consequences to our understanding of the Bible. In the following pages we will explore the Bible in the light of the foundational idea of the *Word* or λόγος.[1] It will reveal that the character of God has come into this world through the medium of, but in no way limited to, words and stories. Words are the building blocks of ideas and stories, and the idea of God has given birth to a world of words, and those words, His

---

1 Logos: A Greek technical term in Western philosophy for a principle of order and knowledge. Logos is the logic behind an argument.

Word, have brought about a *uni-verse*, a unified story issuing from a reality in which the character of God has manifested. It's not just that God's character has manifested in the story, but it has actually manifested in the world. Ideas have consequences, impacts, outcomes. The Bible begins with the story of God's impact in the world.

"In the beginning God created…" (Genesis 1:1). But what exactly did God create? When we take John's insight (John 1:1) into account we see that the creation under consideration includes some sort of ideation, of forming and relating ideas to reality. This ideational process is apparent throughout the story of creation because the text refers to it many times with the phrase: "And God *said…*" (Genesis 1:3, 6, 9, 14, 20, 24, 26, 29). Each instance of God speaking resulted in various aspects or parts of creation or ideas about creation coming into existence. While I don't want to deny that God actually created such things in the physical world, the point I'm making here is that God was also creating the language that faithfully corresponds to the world He created. The point of the story is the power and integrity of God's Word to create. But to create what, exactly?

Regardless of whether the text indicates the *ex nihilo* creation of various objects in the world that we see, or the creation of language that reflects the integrity of God's description of the things in the world, the same point persists: God's Word, His description of things is true and powerful, and can be trusted. From this, consider that the story of the Genesis creation is the story of the fusion of language to humanity, of language to the creation of a human habitat, which will come to a critical juncture with Jesus Christ, who is the Word made flesh (John 1:14). This is a major controlling theme throughout the biblical story. The human habitat that God created is not just a garden on earth, but also includes the language or linguistic structures needed to thrive in the garden.

Jordan Peterson in his widely popular book, *12 Rules for Life*,[2] speaks of something similar:

---

[2] Random House Canada, 2018, p. 236.

> "At the beginning of time, according to the great Western traditions, the Word of God transformed chaos into Being through the act of speech. It is axiomatic, within that tradition, that man and woman alike are made in the image of that God. We also transform chaos into Being, through speech. We transform the manifold possibilities of the future into actualities of past and present.
>
> To tell the truth is to bring the most habitable reality into Being. Truth builds edifices that can stand a thousand years. Truth feeds and clothes the poor, and makes nations wealthy and safe. Truth reduces the terrible complexity of a man to the simplicity of his word, so that he can become a partner, rather than an enemy. Truth makes the past truly past, and makes the best use of the future's possibilities. Truth is the ultimate, inexhaustible natural resource. It's the light in the darkness."

The Hebrew text in Genesis 1:1 says that God created "the heavens and the earth." There are two aspects involved here: 1) the words themselves as objects or ideas of the mind, and 2) the realities that the words refer to, which in this case we can best understand to mean simply *land* and *sky*. Note, however, the use of the definite article (the), which indicates a particular instance, *this* land and *this* sky, the land and sky of the reader's immediate experience. The addition of the definite article means that God did not mean land and sky generically or generally, but specifically.

Should we understand this as literal history? Or is this literature about something historically significant to this people's particular experience? Is it mythic? Is it a story that illuminates a truth that is deeper than immediate experience? Is it a reference to the literal heavens and earth, to air and dirt, or to our awareness and experience of what we see, the idea of air and dirt as such ideas occur in our minds? The early Hebrews would have understood Genesis 1:1 to mean two simple things: 1) that God had provided their particular human habitat, and 2) that their human habitat was not a product of chaos, as the competing Babylonian texts taught. The order into which the human habitat fit was God's order, an order not of human conception, or making. It was not the order of the false gods of Babylon, but an order that would tame the chaos of primitive life.

However, just because the early Hebrews would have had a literal understanding of these words does not mean that the text was then or is now limited to such an understanding. There are many ancient myths that were not intended to be interpreted literally. Myths generally provide for significant complexity, abstraction, and analysis. Ancient peoples were not ignorant.

Believing that God is the ultimate author of the text allows each generation of readers to discover additional revelation that issues out of their contemporary understanding of the text, not in contradiction to the original understanding, but at a deeper level that is in harmony with the original meaning. Because the biblical God is the God of history, our understanding of God's Word increases over time as history accumulates, as language increases in articulacy. As human understanding accumulates we are able to see more detail and granularity of God's revelation. The light of God's revelation increases over time for those who have eyes to see and ears to ear, those who have the interest to dig into it. The underlying literary idea of this text is that humanity has been fit into the order that God has made. It is not for us to fit God into the order that people make. The eternal question is: who does the leading and who does the responding? Does God follow our lead? Or do we follow God's lead?

The early Hebrews would have known nothing of our modern debates about creationism and the highfalutin orbits into which we modern people have cast these few words of Genesis. This does not mean that the current creation/evolution debates are off base regarding the substance of their arguments, it only means that the intention of the biblical creation story, its literary meaning and intent, was not to convey specific information about the origins of the farthest reaches of time and space. Rather, the biblical story from start to finish is about human life on earth.

We are not (humanity is not composed of) earthly beings learning how to live in heaven after we die; rather, we are heavenly beings learning how to live on earth before we die. This change of perspective dwarfs that of Copernicus in terms of its importance and application. Copernicus was outwardly focused, looking outward to the heavens and the solar system, and he imposed that outward perspective on the biblical creation story, as did those who followed his line of thinking, his worldview—in the church and out. Of course, he was correct in his observations from his perspective, but wrong in his encouragement of the idea that the creation story is primarily about the place of the earth in the heavens (the location of the earth in space), and not about the place of humanity on earth (or in the universe). The creation story is about a particular sequence of time on earth, the beginning of such a time sequence, the beginning of history as we know it. The human habitat, which is what God created in the story, was and is composed of land, sky (air), and sea. These three things or areas of the earth comprise the physical habitat of humanity. The living creatures live on land, in the seas, and in the air.

The opening words of Genesis simply acknowledged that these things were and are the provision of God, and are for the flourishing of humanity on earth. And with the creation of Adam, something new was added—not just a new kind or species (*homo sapiens*), but a new world order centered in or on the kind, *homo*, who were graciously endowed with *sapience*.[3] To indicate the emergence of this new order, the story tells us that God did not create Adam from the existing order of animals that preceded him, but created Adam afresh from dirt, from inanimate matter. Adam (humanity) was quite different than the other creatures of the earth. Something unique was added to Adam that the other creatures did not have. God breathed life—sapience—into him. The breath of life is the introduction of sapience in that breath is the engine of language, words, and stories,

---

3   From Latin *sapiēns*, present active participle of *sapiō*, to discern or be capable of discerning. Wisdom or sapience is the ability to think and act using knowledge, experience, understanding, common sense, and insight. Wisdom has been regarded as one of four cardinal virtues; and as a virtue, it is a habit or disposition to perform the action with the highest degree of adequacy under any given circumstance with the limitation of error in any given action. This implies a possession of knowledge, or the seeking of knowledge to apply to the given circumstance. Source: https://en.wikipedia.org/wiki/Wisdom

and these are the tools of understanding and wisdom (sapience). And the human story has become the most important thing on earth. The novel ingredient that God gives and humanity brings to the world is understanding—knowledge, wisdom. The creation story is as much about the creation of the structure of human knowledge and wisdom as it is about the creation of stars and dirt.

Does this mean that God did not create the universe *ex nihilo?* No, it just means that these opening words of Genesis point to the terrestrial not the celestial. If anything, they indicate that the God of the celestial realm put His attention on *this* particular terrestrial realm—earth—and breathed into or shared with Adam something unique, something that God also has—sapience. The object of these words was the earthly habitat, not the heavenly domain.

The creationism debate that has developed in response to the advancements of science and technology over the past few centuries moves away from the simple intended meaning of these few words at the opening of Genesis by overlooking or ignoring the significance of what God shared—His breath, His Spirit, His Word, His sapience. So, rather than imposing our debate on God's opening words of Genesis, let us endeavor to hear God's debate at that time with ancient Mesopotamia. The Genesis story was written to set the record straight, to correct the errant myths of Mesopotamia.

> "Mesopotamian religion has historically the oldest body of recorded literature of any religious tradition. What is known about Mesopotamian religion comes from archaeological evidence uncovered in the region, particularly numerous literary sources, which are usually written in Sumerian, Akkadian (Assyro-Babylonian) or Aramaic using cuneiform script on clay tablets and which describe both mythology and cultic practices. Other artifacts can also be useful when reconstructing Mesopotamian religion. As is common with most ancient civilizations, the objects made of the most durable and precious materials, and thus more likely to survive, were associated with religious beliefs and practices. This has prompted one scholar to make the claim that the Mesopotamians' 'entire existence was in-

fused by their religiosity, just about everything they have passed on to us can be used as a source of knowledge about their religion.' While Mesopotamian religion had almost completely died out by approximately 400-500 CE after its indigenous adherents had largely become Assyrian Christians, it has still had an influence on the modern world, predominantly because many biblical stories that are today found in Judaism, Christianity, Islam, and Mandaeism were possibly based upon earlier Mesopotamian myths, in particular that of the creation myth, the Garden of Eden, the flood myth, the Tower of Babel, figures such as Nimrod and Lilith and the Book of Esther. It has also inspired various contemporary Neo-pagan groups."[4]

We still hear the contemporary case for the modern preference of the ancient world myths in the text of this quotation when it asserts that

"many biblical stories that are today found in Judaism, Christianity, Islam and Mandaeism were possibly based upon earlier Mesopotamian myths."

This perspective suggests that the biblical stories emerged out of the Mesopotamian myths, which is the most popular academic thesis among scholars today. However, the larger story conveyed by the Bible, taken at face value, reverses this position by suggesting that the Mesopotamian myths are faulty fragments left over from the original creation story of humanity on earth, the biblical story that had been corrupted by sin. This larger part of God's story is played out in the first three covenantal eras of biblical history: the Adamic era, the Noahic era, and the Abrahamic era. The first two of these eras or ecological periods were so different from the contemporary era that it is difficult to know anything of significance about them. The most valuable and accurate information available comes from the Bible, rightly understood. My intention here is to suggest a basic outline for this larger, older story.

In opposition to the Mesopotamian myths, the Bible presents the idea that the original, natural foundation and order of the

---

4   Source: https://en.wikipedia.org/wiki/Ancient_Mesopotamian_religion

earth was well-ordered and predictable, not chaotic as the Mesopotamian myths portrayed it. God's argument was that there was an original celestial order into which the order of the human habitat fit, or out of which the new human world order emerged by the breath of God. God had created or established the original order of the world, of the heavens and the earth. What God created or established in Genesis 1 was as much about the new human world order itself, the order that human language would bring about, as it was about the things that were ordered. Before the creation of Adam, the story is about the creation of crawlers, swimmers, flyers, seasons, earth, sun, moon, stars, etc., being put in order by God. Once Adam is on the scene, his first job is to name the creatures God created, and by naming them Adam was creating a linguistic catalog of resources. God supervised Adam's naming, which created a taxonomy, a structure of language for application in the world. We might think of it as a mental or linguistic structure that exists in the abstract world of thought. Plato called them *Forms*.

> "The theory of Forms or theory of Ideas is Plato's argument that non-physical (but substantial) forms (or ideas) represent the most accurate reality. When used in this sense, the word *form* or *idea* is often capitalized. Plato speaks of these entities only through the characters (primarily Socrates) of his dialogues who sometimes suggest that these Forms are the only objects of study that can provide knowledge; thus even apart from the very controversial status of the theory, Plato's own views are much in doubt. However, the theory is considered a classical solution to the problem of universals."[5]

Consider the possibility that the order itself, the intellectual catalog, as distinct from the things created, is the new habitat that emerged with Adam, the homo sapien. It is an intellectual habitat, but much more than that because ideas will actually change the real world. The biblical story of the creation of Adam is the story of *logos* (λόγος) being fused to humanity[6], or *logos*

---

5   Source: https://en.wikipedia.org/wiki/Theory_of_Forms
6   See Appendix, p. 283.

emerging out of humanity in consequence of God's breath. John calls it *the Word*,

> "In the beginning was the Word, and the Word was with God, and the Word was God" (John 1:1).

More than the mere creation or development of human language, we find the first concern of the Bible is the integrity of God's Word, and the importance of the reflection of that integrity in human language. The issue is that God's Word is of a higher order by at least one and likely many degrees or levels. The Bible teaches that God's Word uniquely and perfectly corresponds to reality, the reality that God created, where reality is understood to be the correctly integrated nexus of the objective world and subjective description. In contrast, human language fails in many ways to accurately comport with or correspond to God's reality. We could say that God's Word, as God understands it, has integrity with reality, and human language pales in comparison. The biblical story is the story of God's Word coming to human flesh, and the attendant difficulties involved in holding God's perfection and human perception together, holding divinity and humanity in union.

The story of Creation is the story of God's world manifesting on earth. Christians have struggled with questions about the existence of God for centuries, and several proofs have been suggested over the ages. But, as valuable as those proofs are, a better approach can be found by asking, not whether God actually *exists*, but whether God is *real*. As an analogy, God is as real as geometry, as real as a straight line or a perfect circle. Is there such a thing as a straight line? Do straight lines *exist*? Modern science necessarily argues that there is no such actual thing, and uses electron microscopes to prove the point. Everything is actually composed of swirling atoms dancing in time. Thus, there is no such thing as an actual straight line. Straight lines are intellectual constructs. But are they *real*?

Common sense argues that the idea of straight lines (and the whole of geometry) is demonstrably obvious (self-evident) and immanently practical. The world that we know and live in, our human habitat, would not exist apart from our knowledge and application of geometry. Therefore, whether or not straight lines actually exist, they are undeniably real in the sense of being capable of being treated as fact, and coinciding with reality. Well, God is as real as straight lines. That is, God is demonstrably obvious and immanently practical. God is also capable of being treated as a fact, and coinciding with reality. This second sense does not mean that God is material in nineteenth century understanding of material. Rather, God's materiality corresponds to the materiality of a quantum physics view of our world of experience.

REVIVAL

As children of the Great Awakenings, contemporary people commonly tend to think that the Bible is about helping people get "saved" so that they can get into God's celestial kingdom when they die, and there is an element of truth to such thinking, even though the actual truth of that idea is not what people usually think it is. God's plan has always been to replicate heaven on earth, to do things on earth as they are done in heaven (Matthew 6:9-13). In the Lord's Prayer we see that God has a prior and more fundamental perspective that is easily overlooked. We are not merely human beings endeavoring to live by heavenly precepts, but we are actually heavenly beings endeavoring to live together in this terrestrial habitat. Consequently, our most primal identity belongs to God's eternal and celestial kingdom, and our human identity is but a temporary measure established for this short life in the terrestrial realm that we call *earth*. Too often Christians are consumed with the idea of getting into God's heaven, while God through His story in the Bible has always been working to bring heaven to His people on earth. We're focused on getting out, while God is focused on getting in.

The opening words of Genesis tell us that the origin of humanity belongs to God, that we and this world are not the consequence of chaos, nor of some evil god of history or of our imaginations. Rather, human *being* (the verb not the noun) can be most fully engaged when lived in conformity with the God-given supernatural order of the world. Furthermore, that supernatural order has been established by God, and while it has much "wiggle room" (grace), there are limits beyond which become harmful for the flourishing of human life. The story of the Bible is the story of God's order on earth, a metanatural or supernatural order that is in the process of being reclaimed, remodeled, reformed, reordered in the world through God's people. Eventually God's order will dominate this world to provide maximum human flourishing and health for the whole planet, and even now that new order is more prevalent than ever before in history. But there is still a long way to go before God's mission is completed.

According to the Bible the earliest beginning of the earth was without God's order. It was desolate, formless, vacuous, much like our photos of the surface of Mars—except that the earth has plentiful water. The earth at that point was not in complete chaos, but the order was unsuitable or unsustainable for human habitation. We are told that "the Spirit of God moved upon the face of the waters" (Genesis 1:2, KJV). The primal earth was covered with water. God then spoke and there was light, illumination, wisdom, sapience. And where there is light there is heat—fire, the fourth of the four ancient elements, i.e. Earth (land), Water (sea), Fire (light), and Air (atmosphere). The first development towards God's supernatural order involved light and heat, which affected the water. Or if we understand this light as sapience, it brought distinction and discernment to human awareness.

The division of light and darkness in Genesis 1:4 is about time, measured by the oscillation between day and night observed from the perspective of the surface of the rotating earth. Time is a measure of motion, and the most basic motion is rotation. Was there an actual first day? Who knows, but logically there must be a first instance of any time-based series or mathematical set. However, the marking of that first day was never intended to suggest a time when the earth first began to exist or rotate. The time frame required to conceive of *that* is simply not available to human experience or imagination—or speculation. The biblical story was not intended to mark the first instance of a series, but rather to mark the beginning of an era, a smaller segment of a particular time-frame, the beginning of a story that would unfold over time, a particular series of events. It simply provides a reference point for the beginning of a story. Consequently, it is more literature than history—but this distinction in no way suggests that its essential meaning is untrue. Rather, this insight provides the ground or logical basis for historical truth conveyed through biblical literature, through story, the true story that accounts for all of the facts of the complex reality in which we dwell today.

The inclusion of the "firmament in the midst of the waters" (Gensis 1:7) suggested an expanse, space, separation, or division between waters below and waters above, which God called "heaven," a biblical word for *sky*, which is the primary definition of the Hebrew word used in the text (רָקִיעַ). Allow me to suggest a better, modern translation: *atmosphere*. The light (heat) coming to the water (sea) would produce heat and steam (mist), a variant form of water. The light/heat stirred the water. Originally there was very little gaseous water in the atmosphere, not enough to form clouds. Later in the story, clouds became a major contributor to the life of the world, creating seasons, when "the fountains of the great deep burst forth, and the windows of the heavens were opened" (Genesis 7:11) and additional subsoil water shot into the stratosphere. Prior to Noah's flood the earth was watered with dew, mist. During and following the flood, what we call the earth's weather and seasons were established, likely the result of earthquakes that broke the crust of the earth, brought about the beginning of the earth's continents, released water (steam) into the atmosphere, and caused the earth's rotation to wobble (or increased the existing wobble). Genesis tells us that the seasons were provided for the human measurement of time, specifically, years. Time is a necessary ingredient for stories.

The story of the first five days of creation is about the origin of the natural order of the world. Each earthly domain—sea, land, and air—were then populated with creatures—swimmers, crawlers, and flyers. There is an order to their existence, and that order is explained with language. There are norms or patterns of behavior and relationships that govern each creature, each kind. And each kind, each *species* in modern biological terminology, reproduce within the bounds of their own kind, their *species*. Like produces like, and while certain genetic variations provide normal adjustments for various climates, excessive variations do not survive. This genetic freedom within bounds preserves the integrity of the kinds (species) and promotes species health and longevity. Climatic adaptations within species survive because those adaptations also promote the health and longevity of the species. However, cross-species fertilization doesn't work, and that failure also promotes the longevity of the species. The stability of the various species seems to be linked somehow to the stability of the natural order. That stability provides what we call *sustainability*.[7]

TRINITY & DNA

The universe as we know and experience it has a kind of trinitarian DNA, understood analogously. There was an original order of the cosmos, an order of the natural world, and an order into which the human habitat would best fit. That order, in fact, plays a central role in the Bible. The point of the creation story was that the order of the human habitat was not created or established by human beings, though human beings could (and as the population grew, would) greatly effect the natural order through the use of language. The point of the Genesis story of creation is that the natural order of both the world and logic is a given, it had been created or established prior to and apart from any concern that human beings might impose upon it. How human beings fit into the natural order is a central theme of the Bible. And God's understanding and presentation of this order has always been opposed to the social and political order into which it has been delivered. God's order has always—since the Fall—been in opposition to the common, fallen, sinful order into which the world (human society) has been plunged. God's mission in the world is two-fold: first, He introduced language to humanity, and second, He intends to teach us the importance of truth, of the integrity of language and reality for the flourishing of humanity.

---

7   See Appendix, *Heaven And Earth*, p. 286.

Into this pre-fall, proto-natural order comes man (humanity) by the hand or breath of God to live as a species on the earth. I have suggested in other books[8] that we know and experience as human beings a kind of trinitarian DNA of the universe. Consider the similarities between the Trinity and DNA. God, who is Trinitarian, created a trinitarian universe for a trinitarian people in His Trinitarian image (Genesis 1:26). This idea is both simple and complex at the same time. There is an essential unity or commonality to its diversity. This analogy compares some aspects of biological DNA to the theological Trinity, and assumes some familiarity with the basic ideas of both.

Both DNA and the Trinity involve inheritance or information transfer from one generation or biological cell to another, and both involve some form of language that controls the inheritance. DNA inheritance involves a transfer of chemically coded information that maintains a level of strict biological pattern replication between generations, such that species integrity is maintained down to the level of family characteristic similarity. An analogous process functions in the Trinity through the concepts of Father, Son, and Holy Spirit through a kind of linguistic and/or spiritual information transfer or inheritance. A weakness of this analogy involves time because inheritance involves time. But the Persons of the Trinitarian Godhead are not subject to time, though with the birth of Jesus Christ we see that they can enter time. We can think of the Father and the Son as distinct Persons (and perhaps socially as different generations), and the Holy Spirit as the spiritual DNA that unites them. Don't hold to this analogy too tightly, for all analogies of the Trinity fail in one way or another. Nonetheless, it suggests some remarkably similar ideas that can help us understand the reality in which we live.

The point of this brief analogy is to indicate that the doctrine of the Trinity is not some arcane theological abstraction with no contemporary application, but is at the root of the very principle of life itself. Every living organism is engaged in the Trinity or a trinitarian-like genetic organization and replication. And in the case of humanity the human genome has been

---

8   *Colossians—Christos Singularis*, 2010 and *Peter's Vision of Christ's Purpose in First Peter*, 2011, Phillip A. Ross, Pilgrim Platform, Marietta, Ohio.

molded in the very likeness of the Trinitarian God. So, rather than being some dusty abstract idea lost in the stacks of an ancient theological library, the Trinity is a kind of picture of the very essence or seed of life itself.

The Trinity describes a complex unity, a one that is many, a being capable of reproduction (i.e., Father and Son, the ability to reproduce), such that a population or species is sustainable over time. Consider God's self-identification. God has identified Himself as "I am" (Exodus 3:14), or "I am who I am," or "I will be what I will be." There are three elements to this name: 1) a sense of personal subjectivity, 2) raw existence or being, and 3) a sense of future, of continuity over time. God has identified Himself as the historical continuity of personal subjective consciousness expressed through human language (*logos*) that is becoming the completed totality (*telos*), wholeness, fullness, of that consciousness. The idea of "mind"[9] may provide a better analogy than mere consciousness.

The "spark" of life given by God at the conception and/or birth of each individual life provides a specific amount or degree of consciousness or mind that matures over time, increasing both amplitude and complexity, through communication with others. And with the birth of additional individuals a kind of sum, vector, or composite of discrete consciousness grows as a unified whole or totality as the population grows and communication between people increases. That is, history accumulates over time making more and more information available to consciousness or mind(s) as populations grow.

An analogy to computers might also be helpful in that the growth or addition of computer nodes in an information network geometrically increases the complexity and computational power of the whole network, and of each individual node. The

---

9 "The mind is a set of cognitive faculties including consciousness, perception, thinking, judgment, and memory. It is usually defined as the faculty of an entity's thoughts and consciousness. It holds the power of imagination, recognition, and appreciation, and is responsible for processing feelings and emotions, resulting in attitudes and actions.

There is a lengthy tradition in philosophy, religion, psychology, and cognitive science about what constitutes a mind and what is its distinguishing properties." Source: https://en.wikipedia.org/wiki/Mind

wholeness of that consciousness or mind as a unity constitutes the approximation of human objectivity, where the unified whole can only be approached in a way that is analogous to using calculus to determine the area under a curve. Thus, God or God's perspective or God's Word as God intended it to be understood by each successive generation is as close to objectivity as human beings can understand, in as much as God can be conceived of as the sum of all consciousness over all time—and more. Thus, God can be identified with objective truth because genuine objective truth can best be defined as truth that issues from the Trinity, analogously from the unified complexity of a super dataset in a distributed network, grounded in the Bible.[10]

However, to suggest that God's consciousness is a kind of sum of all human consciousness fails to suggest that there is a definite structure involved. The idea of "sum" is not to be understood as if these discrete bits of consciousness or archetypes constitute something like a random pile of sand, but would be more like a sort of crystal, or even better: as a fractal or self-similar pattern. That is to say that the result is ordered.

> "In mathematics a fractal is an abstract object used to describe and simulate naturally occurring objects. Artificially created fractals commonly exhibit similar patterns at increasingly small scales. It is also known as expanding symmetry or evolving symmetry. If the replication is exactly the same at every scale, it is called a self-similar pattern. An example of this is the Menger Sponge. Fractals can also be nearly the same at different levels. This latter pattern is illustrated in small magnifications of the Mandelbrot set. Fractals also include the idea of a detailed pattern that repeats itself."[11]

---

10 This is not an argument that the Internet is God, but only that the Internet provides a useful analogy. Another analogy might be Carl Jung's idea of the collective unconscious, which refers to structures of the unconscious mind that are shared among beings of the same species or culture. According to Jung, the human collective unconscious is populated by instincts and by archetypes: universal symbols that are, for our purposes, better modeled on the covenanted archetypes of Adam, Abel, Cain, Noah, Abraham, Melchizedek, Moses, David, Christ, etc.

11 Source: https://en.wikipedia.org/wiki/Fractal

The self-similar pattern provides what the Bible calls *likeness*, found in biological "kinds" and in the human likeness to God. "Then God said, "Let us make man in our image" (Genesis 1:26). Notice that God referred to Himself as plural, suggesting the Trinity—plurality, community, relationship, and culture.

Yet, because God is Trinitarian, the repetition of the pattern is not merely static, but includes a dynamic element that provides a degree of uniqueness and originality for each manifestation of the repeating pattern, each appearing in a unique context of time and place. The human likeness to God is not the likeness of one individual to another, but is the common likeness of a related species because of the trinitarian quality of inheritance that produces over time a population of like entities. While each of the Persons of the Trinity (Father, Son, and Holy Spirit) are complete, whole, unique individual Persons, they are not merely independent or self-contained. Rather, each of the Persons of the Trinity are mutually reflective and dependent upon the others in every conceivable way—and at the same time each is completely whole, unique, and complete in themselves. This is the paradox of the Trinity: one, yet three; many, yet singular; diverse, yet equivalent; statically dynamic or dynamically static. Each part of the Trinity is also an infinite whole in and of itself.

The "secret sauce" of the Trinity, the ingredient that allows the Trinity to function as we understand, experience, and conceive it, is *time*.

> "Time has long been an important subject of study in religion, philosophy, and science, but defining it in a manner applicable to all fields without circularity has consistently eluded scholars. Nevertheless, diverse fields such as business, industry, sports, the sciences, and the performing arts all incorporate some notion of time into their respective measuring systems. Two contrasting viewpoints on time divide prominent philosophers. One view is that time is part of the fundamental structure of the universe—a dimension independent of events, in which events occur in sequence. Isaac Newton subscribed to this realist view, and hence it is sometimes referred to as Newtonian time. The opposing view is that time does not refer to any kind of 'container' that events and objects 'move through', nor to

any entity that 'flows', but that it is instead part of a fundamental intellectual structure (together with space and number) within which humans sequence and compare events. This second view, in the tradition of Gottfried Leibniz and Immanuel Kant, holds that time is neither an event nor a thing, and thus is not itself measurable nor can it be traveled."[12]

When we say that a thing is outside of time we mean it is outside of our comprehensible time flow. But between the beginning and end of our particular time frame there exists an infinite number of time frames that differ from ours by orders of magnitude, such that they are completely outside of our perception and/or awareness. We can imagine a time frame of a millionth of a second or millions of years, but we have absolutely no experience of such an idea as reality. We cannot know that the laws of physics as we understand them operate in the same way at infinitely different time frames.

The Trinity is both outside of time and simultaneously dependent upon or embedded in time. Time is necessarily involved in the Trinity because it involves succession or inheritance from one generation to another; and it is outside of time because the principle of succession or inheritance is necessarily and logically not contained within the generated series or order that manifests in time. These things contribute to the historic and current difficulties theologians have in trying to describe the Trinity. Nonetheless, we persevere in the effort because both the Bible and our experience witness to the reality of the Trinity, not just in our own personal lives, but in the objectivity of the world in which we find ourselves.

> "For those who believe, no proof is necessary. For those who don't believe, no proof is possible." –Stuart Chase

Trinity & Agency

In addition, consider another analogous way to understand the Trinity. In the beginning God acted in the world. Agency is defined as the capacity of an actor to act in a given environment.

---

12 Source: https://en.wikipedia.org/wiki/Time

> "...The capacity to act does not at first imply a specific moral dimension to the ability to make the choice to act, and moral agency is therefore a distinct concept. In sociology, an agent is an individual engaging with the social structure. Notably, though, the primacy of social structure vs. individual capacity with regard to persons' actions is debated within sociology. This debate concerns, at least partly, the level of reflexivity an agent may possess.
>
> Agency may either be classified as unconscious, involuntary behavior, or purposeful, goal directed activity (intentional action). An agent typically has some sort of immediate awareness of their physical activity and the goals that the activity is aimed at realizing. In 'goal directed action' an agent implements a kind of direct control or guidance over their own behavior."[13]

So, God acts as an agent, and in this world He is the first or original Agent, the prime Agent. Regarding God's agency, some action is engaged for some end purpose that unfolds over time. Think of it as God's will, which is being made manifest in history. The end or purpose to be accomplished is the result of the action, which precedes its accomplishment in the sequence of time. However, God makes His intended purpose precede the result He wants to accomplish. So, His purpose is the real cause that precedes every result, every effect for which there is a cause. This reverses the arrow of time in that the future achievement of the envisioned action becomes its cause in the present. The momentum of the action is not pushed into the present from the past, but is pulled into the present from the future by God's intended purpose of the action. Thus, God produces causes that exist in the future relative to the effects that result. This is nothing more than the operation of God's will, and is nothing more than what we call *planning*. However, this Copernican revolution regarding our understanding of the arrow of time is essential for a truly biblical understanding of God. God's will, God's agency, pulls events into the future—His intended future. Events are not simply pushed into the future by causes that have

---

13 Source: https://en.wikipedia.org/wiki/Agency_(philosophy)

existed in the past. God's future, the future that God intends for humanity, is the cause of human history. God is pulling or drawing history into His envisioned future. The drag on this system can be attributed to human resistance, which slows the process down, but is eventually overcome.

All agency involves purpose because it involves intentionality. But God is the only truly original and independent agent. Yet, all agents are representatives. Even God—and each of His Persons individually: Father, Son, Holy Spirit—each represents all of the other the members of the Trinity. All agents act on behalf of some purpose, some intended result, or on behalf of another agent or another person, but always for some intentional outcome. The acting agent is a representative of another, whether that other is a person, a directive, or a policy. This is why agency is a fruitful way to discuss and describe the Trinity. Any one Person of the Trinity always acts on behalf of the other Persons because all actions are unified in their purpose. Or we could say that any one Agent of the Trinity serves as a substitute for the other Agents of the Trinity because they have a unified will or common purpose. They all work for the same Agency, so to speak. Thus, the ideas of representation and substitution, essential to the doctrine of the Trinity, are also essential to the idea of agency.

The Trinity is composed of three Persons or three Agents, three Actors in an environment. In addition, each Person or Agent of the Trinity represents the others, and any one of which can substitute for any other because they all share the same end purpose. They exist and work in unity.

> "And God said, Let us make man in our image, after our likeness…" (Genesis 1:26).

ADAM & EVE

The Hebrew word translated *man,* which is the same word translated as *Adam* (אָדָם), literally means *human*. And the word translated *Eve* or *woman* (אִשָּׁה) means *life*. Together this first couple is named *Human Life*. God's story of humanity begins with the creation of Adam, who is the first *logos* fused human prototype, made, not from other creatures, but from the elements of the earth—dirt, humus. Adam is a new kind. There is something about Adam that is completely different from the previous kinds. This difference, identified as a new kind of *hominoid* and further identified as *sapien*—sapient. Consequently, the important element of the story is not actually about the creation of the first individual human being or *homo sapien*, it is about language being fused to humanity. Sapience issues out of language. "And God *said*..." (Genesis 1:3). Said to whom? Said to humanity. As John later testified, "In the beginning was the Word, and the Word was with God..." (John 1:1). The story is not about the origin of human flesh, it's about the origin of God giving Himself or His essential characteristic to human beings, "and the *Word* was *God*."

Language necessarily implies community, relationship, and culture. In fact, the story of creation is the story of the origin of sustainable culture or history, but not just any culture. It is about the culture and history of God, the Word, who exists eternally, outside of time, but who has come into our time, human time, earth time. We know this because the Bible says, "Let *us* make man in *our* image, after *our* likeness" (Genesis 1:26). This plural phrasing suggests an early reference to the Trinity, to the plural unity of God, which necessarily implies community, relationship, and culture. To simply use the word "our" implies community, relationship, and culture.

The story is not about the creation of a mere human individual because there is no such thing as a *mere* human individual, nor has there ever been. Obviously individuals exist, but not merely so, and never in isolation. Individuals always exist in community, in relationship, and in culture. This is a necessary result of procreation, the human birth process. While there is a logical necessity regarding the first member of a series or mathematical set (group, community, culture), in reality all we could ever do is speculate about an imagined first individual. So, God provided a story about our human beginning, the beginning of language, *logos*, that would satisfy both childish curiosity and would stand up to the deepest plumbing of our greatest wits.

And in this story, properly understood, we also find the elements of our human reality, the reality of our human trinitarian existence—individuals in corporate existence, individuals in communal existence. The biblical creation story is about God's Word made flesh, about language or *logos* inhabiting humanity. And because it is about language, it is about community, relationship, and culture. The Adamites would not have had the ability to speak in these terms, so God gave them a story that they could understand, and embedded in that story ideas that continue to reflect the mature truth of the human condition. Language develops complexity and articulation over time, much as information networks geometrically increase in complexity and computational power with each new distributed node in a computer network.

Of course, this level of description was simply not in the Adamites' linguistic or experiential wheel house, and still today this understanding of our origins will likely be beyond many people to fathom. However, this sort of understanding of ourselves will become increasingly common over time because it comports with our ongoing experience of the kind of life we live in the midst of technology and computers, etc. Here we find a worthy twenty-first century understanding of the biblical story of creation that honors faithfulness to Jesus Christ as depicted in the Bible.

Because Jesus Christ is the "second Adam," we must consider the similarities between Jesus Christ and Adam, not simply looking to Jesus as a kind of Adam, but also looking at Adam as a kind of Jesus. We do this with Augustine's adage in mind:

> "The New Testament is in the Old Testament concealed,
> the Old Testament is in the New Testament revealed."

The advantage of the New Testament is that it shines the light of Christ back into the Old Testament and reveals veiled truths that were always there but previously unknown, unrecognized. This relationship between Adam and Christ will be an ongoing concern in this study.

As Jesus represents a new type of Adam, so Adam may have represented a new type of *hominoid*, as different from what preceded it (earlier species of hominoids) as Jesus is different from Adam. Because Jesus manifested in flesh after a long period of anticipation, as seen in the Old Testament, so Adam may have had a similar kind of beginning that is lost to history because it preceded the development of language and writing.[14] The story of Adam and Eve suggests the creation or emergence of *homo sapiens*, of human discernment, the flowering of a new trait of judging wisely and objectively.

Thus this idea is not intended to either support or deny current evolution or creation theories, but it can stand along side such theories as an alternative or additional explanation regarding the origins of humanity as we know it. Just as Jesus Christ can be considered to be a kind of upgrade to Adam as a type of hominoid, so Adam may be considered to be an upgrade to any hominoids that may have preceded Adam. The idea here is not to undermine the unique element of Adam's creation, but to suggest that what was most unique about Adam's creation was the introduction of language, *logos*, to flesh, which previous hominoids, if there were any, seem to have lacked.

So, rather than understanding the creation of Adam literally from dirt, we might understand that God fused language capacities and skills to the physical elements of Adam's body, such that Adam became the first human being capable of language as we understand it. The symbolism of God creating Adam brings a defining element to humanity that does not rise from evolution, but precedes evolution in the sense that purpose or agency precedes that which causes a specific result. Spirit is fused to dirt. This idea fits well into either side of the creation/evolution debate and can serve as a commonality.

To be fully human today is not a simple biological matter, but requires the mastery of language, history, and culture. Our sense of identity and humanity is already fused with language and culture, and has been from the very beginning. And so the story goes that Adam communicated with God in the garden, because originally there was no one else to communicate with.

---

14 For a detailed justification of this idea see, *Concord Of Ages—The Individual And Organic Harmony Of God And Man*, Edward Beecher, 1860, 2013, Phillip A. Ross, editor.

The idea that language is fused to flesh again provides a commonality between the stories of creation and evolution.

TAKE TWO!

In Genesis 2 we see that God further identified two primary trees in the garden: the tree of life and the tree of the knowledge of good and evil (Genesis 2:9). God set up a dichotomy. Feeding on the tree of life was permitted, but feeding on the tree of the knowledge of good and evil was forbidden. Here we encounter the first instance of forbidance or law. God intervened to direct the action, behavior, and/or development of humanity by establishing a rule or guide, a kind of norm or law. God's intervention limited human freedom, and this has proven to be an enduring theme of the biblical story. Thus, this directive is of primary importance, but its significance is not available in the story at this point. This is the first instance of a rule or guide (law) given by God that Adam must apply to himself. Here, autonomy (self-rule) was married to theonomy (God-rule) in Adam (humanity).

Failure to comply, said God, would result in death, a kind of double death if we are to understand the literal reading of the text. I understand this double death to be the death, not of Adam the individual, but of the ensuing culture of Adam, his kind.[15] This stark juxtaposition of a cataclysmic consequence regarding the violation of God's rule, God's guide, provides tension, drama, and ultimate meaning to the story of the development of God's great love for humanity.

This idea of double death is tied to the biblical definition of the word *Eve* (חַוָּה). With the creation of Eve we have not merely an individual female of the species, but "the mother of all living" (Genesis 3:20), which is the literal meaning of the Hebrew word *Eve* and a reference to human population and culture. With Eve, or *through* Eve, God created human culture, a kind of wholeness or type of aggregated humanity in the trinitarian likeness of God—and also of Adam as a sub-type. Adam represents the individual, Eve represents humanity as a whole or

---

15 For more on this see: *Arsy Varsy—Reclaiming The Gospel in First Corinthians*, "Death," Phillip A. Ross, Pilgrim Platform, 2008, p. 355.

kind. This implication points to human culture itself as a creation of God, similar to God's creation of Adam as an individual.

In the person of Eve in relationship with Adam we have a complex unit from whom all of humanity will generate, a mating pair. Eve represents both one and many, the individual and the culture, at the same time, while Adam represents the new kind of hominoid with sapience (*homo sapien*). Here we find the idea that humanity is composed of various individuals who participate in a common society, a kind of corporate whole, unit or body. Humanity is composed of individual elements and a corporate, social element, sort of like two sides of a coin, bound together as one, but not the same, not identical. God's threat of death for eating the wrong fruit threatened the eradication of Adam's kind, of humanity in the likeness of Adam and Eve, the destruction of Adam's culture, the culture based on disobedience and sin.

WORK

Part of Adam's job involved naming the various creatures. God brought them to Adam one at a time, and Adam named them (Genesis 2:19). Here Adam functioned as a scientist, a taxonomist, what we call a biologist who specializes in the classification of organisms into groups on the basis of their structure, origin, and behavior. Naming did not mean the mere or random word assignment to correspond to various creatures, but had to do with using words to make an accurate description of the characteristics of the various creatures. The names had integrity. Language needed to accurately comport with reality. Adam created an inventory of available resources in the garden provided by God.

One of the things that Adam noticed as he worked on that job was that each species was composed of breeding mates for the purpose of replication. And as self-awareness began to arise in Adam he noticed that *he* had no such breeding mate among his catalog of garden resources. This was, no doubt, not a mere mental idea on Adam's part, but involved a kind of whole-body realization and emotional passion for the longevity of his own species. That awareness would develop into a longing that God would, in the later context of the story, call *love*. Adam (humanity) required love to survive, and the long story of that love is another central story of the Bible.

Love, as distinct from procreation, is a higher trinitarian expression in that it involves language—the sharing of information with sensitivity, reciprocity, and integrity. While words of love can be expressed between lovers, love also has a language of its own that is conveyed through various kinds of body language, including acts of kindness and commitment. And this bond or marriage between Adam and Eve then becomes the source of human generation.

Eve was created, not from the elements of the earth, but from the elements of Adam, from his side or rib, from Adam's own DNA, for the lack of a better way to describe this mysterious event. The story tells us that Adam had no such creation event from some previous creature. Adam was created from inanimate dirt, representing something completely new on earth. The biblical story is not about the technicalities of human creation, but is about the character of the created humanity. God alone knows what actually happened, but for the sake of the story there is no compelling reason not to grant these mysterious developments their given place in the story. Only then can we assess it accurately. Failure to do so hampers our understanding of the larger story line, the meta-narrative.[16]

With the creation of Eve came the human ability to reproduce, and in this sense Eve also represents the creation of human society, human culture, the institution of humanity as we know it. This is not an argument against Eve as an individual person, but is the recognition that through the miracle of reproduction God created more than two individuals. Eve facilitated the incubation of humanity. It is the acknowledgment that God created society, that society is a creature of God, similar to a species. While individuals have personality, cultures also have characteristics similar to personality. With the creation of Eve we acknowledge that God also created human society or human culture, which can also be considered to be a kind or type of hu-

---

16 See Appendix, "Metanarritive," p. 289.

man being (the verb not the noun), a particular way of being human. Human cultures are also creatures in that they can take on a life of their own, so to speak. This cultural creature, created by God, is another primary theme of the Bible, and plays a central role in the story of Original Sin.

SLITHERING TONGUE

The snake then brings into the story the corruption of language that involves deceit and/or misdirection, the failure of words to correctly convey the truth of what they actually represent, the failure of language to accurately represent what it is intended to represent. This failure is the very origin of sin, of missing the mark. Sin is at root deceit or the intentional occlusion of the whole truth, of the wholeness of truth, and of the truth of wholeness.[17] The expression of truth is a function of integrity, where integrity is undivided or unbroken completeness or totality of being, where integrity is the perfect identity of language with reality, where words perfectly describe what they are intended to represent.

The snake challenged the integrity of God's words, "Did God actually say?" (Genesis 3:1). Did God mean what He said? Or did He misspeak? Eve then added to God's words, "neither shall you touch it" (Genesis 3:3). God said nothing about touching. And the snake responded by flatly contradicting God, "You will not surely die" (Genesis 3:4). The temptation that led to the fall involved believing that individuals are able to know the difference between good and evil in and of themselves—without God. Eve did not consult Adam, nor God, but relied on her own innate sense.

> "When the woman saw that the tree produced fruit that was good for food, was attractive to the eye, and was desirable for making one wise, she took some of its fruit and ate it" (Genesis 3:6).

Individual perception and perspective are always limited, never complete, whole, or perfect. Eve was solely focused on herself,

---

17 Consider wholeness as a function of the Greek word τέλος: completion or end purpose.

on her own thoughts. She elevated her own thoughts and desires above or beyond God's instruction.

The Genesis story begins with God, not Adam. The story is primarily about God, which can be understood in this context to describe an advance of the Trinity in this world through Adam, in that language is an element of both trinitarian and DNA inheritance (divine and human). Language is the common vehicle of the inheritance of both biological and spiritual patterns, forms, and characteristics. This line of thinking suggests that the creation of Adam brought God's language to humanity. Looking ahead, we also see that the advent of Christ then brought the fullness or perfection of God's character to humanity, God's Word made flesh. What began in Adam is fulfilled in Christ.

This is not an evolutionary argument suggesting that people become gods or that humanity as a whole becomes God. There will always be an unbridgeable gulf between humanity and divinity, between what is proximate and what is ultimate, between what is finite and what is infinite—except in Christ alone, in the fullness of Trinity made flesh in Jesus Christ.

Christ plays the role of the mathematical set theory concept of the Aleph Null[18] in the set (or kind) known as humanity. However, there is a significant reality to the biblical idea of union with or in Christ. Indeed, if Christ does not effect people physically, and not just spiritually, then aspersions can be cast on the reality of the unity of Christ's divinity and humanity. Just as Christ came in the flesh as an actual human being, so our union with Christ must also share that same bond between divinity and humanity, between the spiritual and the mundane, between flesh and spirit.[19] There is a shared likeness (Genesis 1:16-27).

The story of Adam and Eve works to answer the ancient question about which came first, the chicken or the egg. The relationship between Adam and Eve is the prototype story of the chicken and the egg. Did the first chicken come from the first egg? Or did the first egg come from the first chicken? Questions about the first instance or prototype of a well-ordered mathe-

---

18 https://wiki2.org/en/Aleph_number
19 For more on this see: *Ephesians—Recovering The Vision Of A Sustainable Church In Christ*, Phillip A. Ross, Pilgrim Platform, 2014.

matical series or set cannot be determined without appealing to something outside of the series or set because the prototype is a model based on something beyond itself, beyond the bounded series describe in a mathematical set.

The biblical story posits God as the creator of the prototype, Adam, which God based on His/Their own Trinitarian likeness, which is God's most unique characteristic. So, the creation of the first man, the first instance of humanity, the story of Adam, tells us that Adam, the male, came first. The determination of whether this story is historically and/or biologically accurate is beyond the ability of human beings to determine. The meaning here is symbolical, not historical or biological. And the symbolism is not merely abstract, but reflects something significant about the reality of human being (the verb not the noun) and is integral to the meaning of God's words. It is an important element of the story.

Further speculation about origins is far more likely to be wrong than right. And since there is no compelling reason to doubt the veracity of this story at this point, for the sake of this larger unfinished biblical story, this particular element of the story should be considered to be true or axiomatic. Allow it to function in the role given to it by the Author for the sake of the unfolding story. Only then can it be properly evaluated.

God then breathed life or spirit (sapience) into Adam and placed him in a garden situated on the earth, a garden that God had been tending, a garden composed of sea, land, and air, filled with various fish and plants and creatures, all living within their various bounds or environments. And before God gave Adam a mate with which to breed, He gave Adam a job, a mandate: "Be fruitful and multiply and fill the earth" (Genesis 1:28) and supervise, till, and keep it. God also provided Adam with food, nourishment, in the garden. He could eat of any of the trees. Genesis 1 closes with the statement that God determined that everything that He had made was good, and He rested. There was no evil in the Genesis 1 story yet, so the determination between good and evil was not possible at this point.

Sin

Sin and corruption are intimately related. Corruption is defined as the process by which something, typically a word or expression, is changed from its original use or meaning to one that is regarded as erroneous or debased, from the perspective of the original. Sin entered the story through a talking snake, but if you understand the snake to be a literal talking snake you will sell yourself short of the richer, fuller meaning of the text. Yes, of course, that is exactly what the literal words mean, but the dictionary definition of the words does not convey the full meaning of the text. God is not an idiot, and neither were the ancient Hebrews. We all understand that language is symbolic, and literature even more so. God infused the creation story with much valuable symbolism, much of it is also encased in actual history.

Imagine a contemporary television cartoon that features a talking animal. If you reject the idea at the outset that animals cannot talk, and that it is grossly absurd to suggest that they can, and that therefore anything that such an animal might say is beyond the credibility of the audience, you will miss the meaning, joy, and fun of the cartoon. Such are the contemporary acolytes of scientism and the liberated fans of the academy who do this very thing with the snake in the biblical garden! Their foolish pride and supposed superior understanding blinds them to the literary meaning, symbolism, point, or lesson of the story. Such fools, failing to grant the premise of the story based on some faulty assumptions and prejudices about the Author, blind themselves to the meaning of the story—and they themselves become just like the talking snake in the story! They conflate the literal meaning of the words with the literary meaning of the story. Don't make this mistake.

Shining the light of the New Testament on this story, we remember that Jesus called the Pharisees *snakes*.

> "You serpents, you brood of vipers, how are you to escape being sentenced to hell?" (Matthew 23:33).

Snakes are mostly mouth, and many are poisonous. So the symbolism suggests a poison mouth, or poison words spoken by creatures capable of speech.

The story then tells us that a talking snake slithered into the garden and asked Eve,

> "Did God actually say, 'You shall not eat of any tree in the garden'?" (Genesis 3:1).

The snake, saying nothing blatantly untrue, challenged the veracity of God's word, and therein lies the very heart of sin, personified by the words of the snake. The snake brought corruption to human language. Sin involves the corruption or confusion of language. Eve's sin was believing the lie of the snake, his perspective that doubted the veracity of God's word, that God didn't mean what He said. Eve, relying on the word of the snake and her own thoughts, determined that what God had forbidden

> "was (actually) good for food, and that it was a delight to the eyes, and that the tree was to be desired to make one wise" (Genesis 3:6).

It was nutritious, beautiful, and beneficial.

So Eve (representing humanity, culture, society) ate of the fruit of the tree of the knowledge of good and evil. And that eating had absolutely nothing to do with a literal apple, but served as an analogy about trusting one's own ability to discern the ultimate differences between good and evil. Most people today still think that people are born with an innate sense of right and wrong, which shows that this issue is still very much alive and well in the contemporary world because that position is Eve's perspective. The idea that people have an innate sense of morality, a natural sense of right and wrong, comes from Eve, not from God. It is the heart or central characteristic of sin.

While the snake was in rebellion against God, evidenced by his challenge of the trustworthiness of God's word, Eve was not. Eve was only deceived. She believed the snake who had said that the forbidden tree would provide her with the very knowledge that made God wise. So Eve believed herself to be engaged in an exercise of divine wisdom and virtue. She participated in the snake's rebellion against God, but thought herself to be engaging directly in an exercise of Godly wisdom. She thought she was helping God. Her faith was genuine, but the object of her faith was the deception of the snake, not the Word of God. The person who has been taken in by a lie, while gullible, cannot be charged with deceit or rebellion. So,

> "she took of its fruit and ate, and she also gave some to her husband who was with her, and he ate" (Genesis 3:6).

Adam's sin was that he loved Eve more than he loved God, evidenced by the fact that he listened to and followed Eve rather than listening to and following God's rule. Adam should not have allowed Eve to come between him and God.

After waking up from his surgery (Genesis 2:21), he found the love of his life, his soulmate, and he was head-over-heels in love with his new bride. So when she brought him a luscious piece of apple pie and told him of her conversation with the snake, and how she planned to gain godly wisdom, Adam chose to believe Eve's understanding of God's rule, that God had not intended that they avoid the tree of the knowledge of good and evil, but only that it be engaged with special care and consideration because of its power to open their eyes and share with them God's ability to know good and evil for themselves.

Surely, they thought, *if God truly loves us and wants what was best for us, He would want us to know what He knows.* So they understood their eating of the fruit of the tree of the knowledge of good and evil to be an exercise of godliness, of growth and maturity, even sanctification. That's not how God saw it, but it is how they saw it after Eve's discussion with the snake.

This new-found knowledge soon revealed to them their weaknesses, especially when God asked them about what they had done (Genesis 3:8-9). Without the buffers of God's protection, God's wisdom, God's active counsel, the reality of their own ignorance was laid bare, and they were overwhelmed with a sense of personal vulnerability. When relying on one's own wits the first thing one notices are one's own weaknesses, one's own liabilities.

Then, when God called out to Adam, Adam hid. He tried to deceive God by hiding. Adam's essential sin was deception, willful blindness. Looking around, they then used what natural resources they could find (fig leaves) and worked to cover or strengthen themselves by making aprons (a kind of armor or protection) for themselves. Thus, their first self-initiated decisions were defensive. Their first creative thoughts and actions issued out of fear. When God called them to reestablish His relationship with them, they responded in fear. Adam said,

> "I was afraid, because I was naked, and I hid myself" (Genesis 3:10).

This will prove to be another persistent biblical theme.

The thought that Adam should have known better comes only after many thousands of years of growth and maturity on our part. While it is true that Adam acted on the basis of his own free will, his own agency, it is also true that his understanding of the choices he faced was severely limited at the time by his own innocence and naivete. He was a child in terms of human maturity. So, while Adam's choice was a matter of his own free will or agency, what he did was also inevitable, given his circumstances and immaturity. Adam's free will turned out to be illusory. God is not ignorant of the fallibility of human children or the value of human maturity. As the old adage goes: Learning how to live wisely comes from experience; and experience comes from making right choices; and learning how to make right choices comes from making wrong choices.

The consequence of their sin was expulsion from the garden. When doubt comes into a relationship, trust can only be restored through faithful experience over time. While trust can initially be given, once it's broken it can only be repaired by tested and proven faithfulness over time. Faith can survive betrayal, but only as it is continually proven and resolved through the ongoing trials and tribulations of further temptations, both great and small, that are resolved through fidelity and loyalty. The intimate, direct relationship between God and humanity, the likeness of Adam's kind to God, had been damaged by Adam's deceitfulness. Trust had been broken. They were cast out of the harmony of trust and fidelity in God's garden into a cursed world that was infected with sin as a result of that broken relationship. Because they believed the lie of the snake, they would need to follow the lie to its conclusion in order to be able to testify to the veracity of God's word, God's promise, God's wisdom. The consequences of the snake's seemingly harmless doubt about the veracity of God and His word blossomed into a world of cursed opportunities.

WHAT HAS HAPPENED?

So far, there are four characters in this story—God, the snake, Adam, and Eve. God, the One in charge, cursed all of the other characters who had been deceived by the lie. God's curse was a pledge of death and destruction. The consequence of sin would be death, the destruction of Adam as a kind (Genesis 2:17). What God meant about Adam's death was unclear at the time because Adam was not familiar with death yet. Adam and Eve did not die immediately, which seemed to confirm the idea that God didn't mean what He said. God meant the death of Adam as a type of humanity, the death of the culture of deceit and sin.

The curse upon the snake prevented him and his kind from enjoying eternal life. He would never become upright, and would feed on dust. The snake would not grow or mature or recover from the consequences of his doubt and rebellion. God also promised to break the relationship between the snake and the woman (Eve) and empower another seed, another human (national, ethnic, cultural) character that would one day destroy the snake so that humanity could live forever.

This allusion, which is an example of the light of Christ illuminating the Old Testament, points to Jesus Christ. But this revelation gets too far ahead of the unfolding story. It is important to acknowledge that we know more about the whole story than they did at the time. This will help us not to make the same mistakes that they made. God also

> "put enmity between you (the snake) and the woman, and between your offspring and her offspring; he shall bruise your head, and you shall bruise his heel" (Genesis 3:15).

Here is the primary theme that plays out in the Bible. The importance to the biblical story of the hatred and hostility between the lineage of the snake and the lineage of humanity cannot be overemphasized. The character of the snake issues from Satan, the father of lies (John 8:44).

The appearance of the serpent in the Garden is a curiosity, given that the world that God had made at that point was perfect. The Fall had not yet happened. Yet, the snake was already in the Garden. This suggests that there was more going on than we are told. Shining the light of Christ back on this story, I suspect that God's intention has always been the replacement of one kind of humanity or culture, Adam's type which was plagued with the corruption of deceit and sin, with a better kind of humanity or culture in the image and likeness of Jesus Christ. We might think of it as replacing the ancient religion of law and vengeance with the new religion of grace and mercy—forgiveness. This is, of course, an oversimplification, but it may prove useful.

The essential character of the snake is a poison mouth symbolizing deceit, or the lack of integrity between language and reality—corruption. Deceit is different than error, though they are related. Deceit involves intentionality, where error is accidental. Nonetheless, both result in error or a lack of integrity. The motive of the snake in the garden was to undermine the integrity of God's Word, to substitute the worldview of God with the worldview of Satan. The enmity between the children of Eve and the children of the serpent involves a conflict of worldviews. The deceit of the snake always involves a partial truth that obscures the whole truth (which is God's worldview). The essential conflict is between partiality and wholeness, between self-concern and love, between control and submission. The part cannot conceive of or represent the whole because the whole issues from a different order, a different level of conception, a different dimension or scale.[20]

---

[20] "New math shows how, contrary to conventional scientific wisdom, conscious beings and other macroscopic entities might have greater influence over the future than does the sum of their microscopic components."
Source: https://www.quantamagazine.org/a-theory-of-reality-as-more-

The curse of the woman multiplied her sorrow through natural conception and birth. More than the simple pain of childbirth, God's curse would bring sinful people to life through human reproduction, through Eve. Such people would be Eve's children, her family. Indeed, all those coming after Eve would be born in sin and would live out sinful, sorrowful lives as they wrestled with the ongoing cascade of deceit initiated by the snake through Adam and Eve. In addition, the woman, who would not be ruled by God, which she proved by ignoring Adam and eating the forbidden fruit, would now suffer under the rule of her sinful husband.

Adam's curse, the consequence of listening to and loving his wife more than God, turned what had been a labor of love (his work in the garden) into the toil of hard labor under harsh circumstances. Because Adam had turned his back on the abundant blessings of God in the Garden, Adam would now have to scratch out (farm) a paltry existence through hard labor in a world filled with thorns and thistles—and sinners. The abundance of God's blessings would not tolerate the sinfulness of Adam's choices. So, God withheld His blessing. Adam's curse would eventually result in Adam's death, the death of Adam as a species, as a kind, as a type of human *being* (the verb not the noun). Adam's culture, humanity in the likeness of Adam—or we could argue, in the likeness of the snake, will one day perish. We are still involved in this process.

Then God, out of great love and pity, knowing the ensuing struggles and difficulties awaiting Adam and Eve in their new world of sin, improved their clothing technology (a cultural process) by making them coats of animal skins, but only after sacrificing an animal for their benefit. Here death is introduced into the story as the first blood sacrifice was made by God for the preservation and protection of humanity during the journey of their accursedness. That journey would one day end in death as had been promised by God's curse, but it would be a death of God's choosing, a sacrificial death, a cultural death, that would also provide a new chapter in the long story of their preservation on earth. Again, in the light of Christ we remember that baptism

than-the-sum-of-its-parts-20170601/

CAIN & ABEL

The new seed that God promised was first fulfilled by the birth of Cain, followed soon after by the birth of Abel. Cain, like his father, Adam, was a farmer, but Abel, unlike either his father or his brother, was a herdsman, a keeper of sheep. So, Abel was involved in the new cultural technology that had been introduced by God when He made aprons to cover and protect the weakness of Adam and Eve.

Over time it was revealed that God preferred the sacrifices of Abel over those of Cain, the sacrifices that God Himself had initiated when He made aprons for Adam and Eve. God's preference offended Cain, and he got angry, hurt perhaps, surely offended that God did not value his gift (according to himself, which followed Eve's preference for her own judgments over God's). Cain then blamed his anger on God's preference for Abel's sacrifices, Abel's work. God made it known to Cain that He was not displeased with him or his work and offerings, and that Cain should continue his work and his offerings. God's preference did not amount to a rejection of Cain—not at all! But if Cain got so mad that he quit working and stopped his sacrifices, God said that trouble would ensue because Cain's central focus of working the ground—farming—to produce sacrifices would give way to some other desire of Cain's own making. Cain's temptation was, like his mother's, to mistake his own desires and preferences for those of God.

Cain then hatched a plan to kill Abel. So, he went with this plan into the fields to find Abel, "and slew him" in anger (Genesis 4:8). When God inquired about what he had done, he lied about knowing anything about Abel's whereabouts and replied, "am I my brother's keeper?" (Genesis 4:9). This question, of course, is not actually a question but a statement by Cain disavowing all responsibility for his brother. This issue of brotherly care will reverberate throughout the ages, and particularly in the pages of the Bible. What are our responsibilities for one another? Clearly, Cain, the first son of sin, rejected any responsibility for anyone else.

In consequence of Abel's murder, Cain was banished from the family to become a fugitive desert nomad, a hunter-gatherer. He ceased farming. A nomad cannot be a farmer. Also note that the biblical story says that farming had come first in human history for Adam's kind. But according to the Bible, humanity did not first emerge as hunter-gatherers, but as farmers in the Garden of Eden.

Cain feared for his life, thinking that anyone who found him, anyone who learned of his murderous act, would kill him. The implication here is that people already knew that the just punishment for murder was death. However, in a great act of grace and mercy God prevented Cain's death by marking him, identifying Cain as God's property, and promising that God would wreak sevenfold vengeance on anyone who murdered Cain. Cain was guilty, but God provided mercy for him.

Cain then went on to become the original founder of the city of Babel, whose kings would include the dreaded Lamech, who by twisting God's words about Cain declared,

> "If Cain's revenge is sevenfold, then Lamech's is seventy-sevenfold" (Gensis 4:24).

Where God's threat was actually a merciful promise to protect Cain, Lamech's threat was a vindictive promise to multiply his vengeance against anyone who got in his way. The seed of Adam's sin was growing.

The birth of Seth constituted the beginning of a people who would have a different history. Seth was a replacement for Abel, and God had preferred Abel's sacrifice. This meant that Abel had been engaged in work that was particularly pleasing to God, for which God had a purpose. So far in the story, Adam and Eve had fallen prey to the lies of the snake, and Cain had fallen prey to his own anger and killed his brother. So, prior to Seth there was no faithful person alive to continue the work of Abel's sacrifice.

By creating Seth, God resurrected the work that Abel had begun, the work that Cain brought to a close by killing Abel.

Seth was a kind of resurrection of Abel, a resurrection of the sacrificial work that Abel had been doing, the resurrection of God's purpose in human history. Thus, God called Seth to carry God's work forward. This call then began two separate spiritual or cultural lineages within Adamic humanity: those who followed or were like Cain, and those who followed or were like Seth. These lineages will continue to develop and play a significant role in the long story of the Bible. Because Seth was a replacement for Abel, he was also a replacement for Abel's sacrificial work with God's cultural technology, utilizing the various products of animal sacrifice. It is important to notice that animal sacrifice was God's idea, God's preference, God's means to God's end purpose.

While Genesis 4 ends with the birth of Seth, Genesis 5 opens with a listing of Adam's descendants, ending with Noah. The idea conveyed in chapter five is that much time had passed, giving time for the development of the human tribes that had begun with Cain and Abel to develop into significant populations.

Noah's Geyser

Noah's father was Lamech, from the genealogy of Seth, not Cain, not the Lamech previously cited above. Noah is the next significant figure in God's great plan for humanity, and Noah's story overlaps Adam's. Prior to the flood, people appear to have lived to be 600-1000 years old. The ages listed are clear and undeniable. Following the flood, the Bible reports a marked reduction of human longevity, concluding with Abraham (175 years old), Jacob (147 years old), and Joseph (110 years old). We could find that there is nothing important about this information and simply dismiss it because it makes no sense to us. Or we could find that the Author of the story intended to use this lifespan information to communicate something significant, so significant that it would remain meaningful throughout the ages.

In conjunction with Noah's flood, this information suggests that something important about the world in which we live has changed significantly. We surmise from the genealogy provided that prior to Noah's flood the environment of the earth was different from what it was after the flood. For one thing, if the lifespan of humans was much longer before the flood, as reported in the Bible, it is likely that the lifespan of other creatures was also longer. How can we understand this? There is a biological phenomenon called *indeterminate growth,* which means that the adult size of creatures depends largely on environmental conditions. Most fish, amphibians, lizards, and snakes are indeterminate growers. Such phenomenon may account for the huge size of what we now call *dinosaurs.* While this is only speculation, it comports with the biblical data.

Genesis 6 tells the story of the mixing of these two tribal clans that had begun with Cain and Abel. The "sons of God," Abelite men, found the "daughters of man" (Genesis 6:2), who were Cainite women, attractive and took them as wives. Why identify the "sons of God" with Abel? Because God had preferred the sacrifices of Abel, which would have put the Abelites in closer association with God; and because Cain had been excommunicated from God's culture. The Hebrew word translated *Nephilim,* describing some of the people who were on the earth in those days, could also be translated as *tyrants* (Cainites). Such a translation fits well with our understanding of the two tribes of the story, and is preferred to speculation about extraterrestrial visitations for its simplicity and believability.

The mixing of these two lineages produced wickedness in that "every intention of the thoughts of his (humanity's) heart was only evil continually" (Genesis 6:5). Violence and corruption (Genesis 6:11-12) became the norm for both lineages. Consequently, and in fulfillment of Adam's curse, Adam's death sentence (Genesis 2:17), God decided to

> "blot out man whom I have created from the face of the
> land, man and animals and creeping things and birds of the
> heavens" (Genesis 6:7).

God would not destroy all humanity, but would save a remnant. God's target for destruction was Adam's culture, including all of Adam's cultural supports, the animals and everything else they used as resources.

In preparation, Noah was instructed to build an ark, a boat large enough to hold sufficient provisions for all of the various species God had created. It took Noah a long time to complete this project, but he finally did. And

> "In the six hundredth year of Noah's life, in the second month, on the seventeenth day of the month, on that day all the fountains of the great deep burst forth, and the windows of the heavens were opened" (Genesis 7:11).

Note the specificity of the date and the order of events.

We are so used to hearing the Sunday School stories about Noah and the ark that we miss the actual chronology of the biblical story. The first thing that happened was not rain, but a great geyser eruption, probably many of them over forty days and nights. The actual size of the flood, while debatable, was sufficient for the purpose of the story. It produced the double death or extinction that God had warned Adam about (Genesis 2:17).

Rain followed the geyser eruptions in sufficient quantity to accomplish God's purpose of ending the story of Adam, so He could begin the story of Noah. How well the actual events of history fit God's story about Adam and Eve is a continuing debate. But within the confines of the biblical story itself we note the end of one era and the beginning of another. The consequence of Adam's sin manifested in a most significant way. God proved to be true to His word, His promises.

Noah's flood brought about the end of the period of human development we could call the *Adamic Era*, the culture of Adam, a time in which the environment of the earth was different than it is now, evidenced by the length of the lives lived at that time. Noah's flood ushered in the beginning of the *Noahic Era* in which the length of lives lived was significantly shortened. Noah's flood resulted in a set of very different environmental factors and circumstances. We know almost nothing about Adam's environment, and our faulty speculation about it, our speculation apart from the story of the Bible, will surely lead us away from God's story and into the errors of our faulty, sinful, limited, human imagination apart from God's Word, God's Christ.

NOAIC HUMANITY

The story of Adamic humanity is recorded in three episodes: creation, fall, and destruction. Yet, God redeemed humanity (the seed or genome) by saving Noah and his family. God is concerned about generations, about inheritance, the Father-Son thing, replication, reproduction, populations. Noah's salvation provided for the resurrection of God's ongoing work on the earth. It was a kind of restart in that Noah and his family were Adamites, but because God granted him grace or favor Noah represented a new beginning or resurrection of the lineage of Abel and Seth, those who provided God's preferred sacrifices, those involved in doing what God preferred. Noah's redemption from Adamic humanity was initiated and accomplished by God, yet Noah had a role to play in it. Noah was God's agent. And the first thing that Noah did following the flood was sacrifice to God (Genesis 8:20).

God identified Noah as righteous (Genesis 7:1), which is another way of saying that God granted him grace, proven by his survival in the ark. God saved Noah in order to move His plan for humanity forward. Noah's role was to build the ark according to God's instructions and timetable, which included the growth of a culture sufficient to build the ark. God's process of Noah's redemption reveals that the truth of redemption is greater than the truth of history, as do all of God's redemption stories. Redemption goes beyond history; redemption comes in spite of history; redemption overcomes history; redemption survives history. At the same time, history is important and must not be ignored or belittled because the veracity of the redemption is based on the veracity of the history, the veracity of His (God's) story. While the lesson of the story is more important than the factuality of the story, the factuality contributes to the veracity of the lesson. Real redemption cannot be built on false history or myths, as we currently understand the word *myth*. Fictional stories do not help real redemption.

Redemption always begins in, with, and through a remnant. This idea of the biblical remnant is introduced in Leviticus 2:1-3:

> When anyone brings a grain offering as an offering to the LORD, his offering shall be of fine flour. He shall pour oil on it and put frankincense on it and bring it to Aaron's sons the priests. And he shall take from it a handful of the fine flour and oil, with all of its frankincense, and the priest shall burn this as its memorial portion on the altar, a food offering with a pleasing aroma to the LORD. But the rest (יֶתֶר—*remnant*) of the grain offering shall be for Aaron and his sons; it is a most holy part of the LORD food offerings.

The remnant is that which is left over and dedicated to God. The offering was consumed by the fire, and what was left over was for the feeding of the faithful priests. When a plant grows it flowers, produces seed, and then dies. The remnant is the seed and its fruit, what is left over for the next season. In this analogy of sacred offering and plant life, what is left over is not useless scraps, but is that which sustains the species beyond the life of the individual plant—seed. In part, the purpose of the plant is to produce the seed, the remnant. The individual plant dies, the fruit rots and becomes food for the seed, which carries on. Such is the story of Noah and the next era or season of human history.

COVENANT CREATION

In the garden God had given Adam a command, a forbidance: don't eat of the fruit of the tree of the knowledge of good and evil. Some think of it as the first covenant. But God did not get Adam's agreement. At least no specific agreement on Adam's part was recorded in Genesis.

So, God seems to have made a correction in His process of command or covenant with Noah, first by favoring him, or as we say today, giving him grace, then giving him a much more specific covenant. In part, the giving of that covenant was an act of grace.

> "I will establish my covenant with you, and you shall come into the ark, you, your sons, your wife, and your sons' wives with you" (Genesis 6:18).

That grace then manifested in a response as Noah "did all that God commanded him" (Genesis 6:22). Noah expressed his agreement through his active response to God's grace, God's Covenant. He obeyed.

However, we find no formal, verbal agreement to God's covenant from Noah, nor any response on the part of Noah's family, though we assume that they had some level of agreement with Noah and had helped him build the ark, though Scripture does not specifically say so. God included them in the covenant, but we have no biblical evidence of them formally agreeing to it. It could be argued that their response of building and being on the ark similarly constituted a tacit agreement. But notice also that God's covenant was specifically with Noah as an individual, and part of Noah's responsibility was to bring his family with him in the ark. The language suggests that the covenant was between God and Noah, and his response to the covenant involved bringing his family along with him.

Again, the inclusion of Noah's family provides an allusion to culture, much like the creation of Eve provided an allusion to culture, to future population growth. This insight suggests that God was in the process of recreating or resurrecting human culture, but this time in the likeness of Noah. Noah's covenant or social agreement with God, like Adam's before him, created a particular type of culture for which Noah served as the archetype of righteousness, understood as having God's favor or grace. The prototype for this culture was Noah, whom God found righteous (Genesis 7:1). Part of that righteousness was the fact that Noah experienced God's judgment on humanity through the flood, which proved God's faithfulness to His Word, His curse of Adam and Eve. In contrast, Adam had no prior experience of or information about God's judgment, no way to know that God was true to His Word.

Of course, God's intention was to repopulate creation (the world, to carry forward the fusion of His Word to human being), so Noah's covenant could be considered to include and to apply to that new population as well. But there is no explicit response of Noah's family or their ensuing population of directly agreeing to God's covenant. As with Adam, who has been described as the federal head of humanity, the covenant with Noah was similarly representative. Noah was called and saved in order to become the new archetype, federal head, and chief elder of humanity during the new post-flood era, much as Adam had been before him.

The story tells us that the flood destroyed all animal and human life, except for what was preserved on the ark (Genesis 7:21). Following the geyser eruptions ("the fountains of the great deep" Genesis 7:11), it rained for forty days and the waters of the flood covered the earth for one hundred and fifty days. There is no debate about whether Noah's flood actually happened or not. The debate is about the extent of the flood. Did it actually cover the whole earth? Regardless of one's belief about the historicity of the extent or totality of the flood, the role of the flood in the biblical story was to completely exterminate Adamic humanity, the culture of Adam, as the punishment or consequence of Adam's sin, his Fall, which infected all of his progeny.

God had promised a double death (Genesis 2:17) if Adam consumed the fruit of the knowledge of good and evil. Eve believed the snake, and they both swallowed the snake's lie. So, God, demonstrating His faithfulness to His Word, did as He had promised by bringing the culture of Adam to an end with the flood. But as a further demonstration of His grace and mercy, God redeemed Noah and his family. A remnant or seed was preserved. God would resurrect His plan of redemption for humanity.

Noah's redemption began with God's covenant (Genesis 6:18), so after the flood waters receded, Noah built an altar and offered animal sacrifices to the Lord, indicating that he was continuing the worship practices of Abel, whom Cain had slain, identifying himself as an obedient covenant holder in the faith lineage of Abel and Seth.

According to the Talmud, God gave Noah a binding set of laws for him and his family to follow, and by implication, for all of humanity to follow because all of humanity would now trace its lineage to Noah and his family. Traditionally, Old Testament practice and custom came to be that any non-Jew who practiced these Noahide laws was regarded as righteous, as acceptable to God, was welcome in the Jewish community, and was assured of a place in the world to come. The seven Noahide laws as traditionally enumerated follow:

1. Do not deny God;
2. Do not blaspheme God;
3. Do not murder;
4. Do not engage in illicit sexual relations;
5. Do not steal;
6. Do not eat from a live animal; and
7. Establish courts and a legal system to ensure obedience to these laws.

Notice the similarity with the Ten Commandments of Moses. It is important to see that these laws provided for what we might call *Gentile salvation* in the Old Testament. All humanity issued from the same seed, be that seed Adam, or after the flood, Noah. Note also that both lines, the covenant keepers (Abel and Seth) and the covenant breakers (Adam and Cain) had a common origin in Adam. God had great hope for Noah, who would carry the faith lineage of covenant keepers forward. So, God promised never to repeat the extent of the destruction He brought upon humanity by the flood.

Many people find Noah to be a very flawed character, citing something that happened where Noah was found drunk and naked by his sons (Genesis 9:21-23). Sufficient details are not indicated to nail down exactly what happened, but we can imagine. The purpose of this episode was to reveal Noah's humanity, his ongoing flaws, his sin—even though God called him *righteous*. Noah was not a god, nor some sort of super saint, but was fully human, and humanly flawed. The implication is that Noah's character involved a historical, moral improvement over his predecessor, Adam, and that Noah followed the cultural worship practices of Abel, not Cain. That improvement involved Noah's experience of God's judgment by the flood, Noah's experience that demonstrated that God keeps His word. But Noah's improvement was not perfection. Again, Adam had no such experience.

Following Noah's drunken episode, the Bible tells us that Noah cursed Canaan, who would become the people of the progeny of Ham, who had seen Noah naked and did nothing to help him recover. God, acting through Noah, cursed the people of Canaan as a consequence of Ham's character, Ham's response to his drunken father. Noah also said,

> "Blessed be the LORD, the God of Shem; and let Canaan be his servant" (Genesis 9:26),

which expressed a blessing for his son, Shem, and his lineage, who were faithful to God. And for his third son, Japheth, Noah prayed,

> "May God enlarge Japheth, and let him dwell in the tents of Shem, and let Canaan be his servant" (Genesis 9:27).

So, of his three sons, Noah cursed one (Ham), blessed one (Shem), and prayed for the other (Japheth) to grow under the tutelage of Shem. And Noah died.

But Noahic humanity or culture continued to grow and their lineages are recorded in the Table of Nations (Genesis 10). Noah's three sons became the Semites, Hamites and Japhetites, and some of Noah's grandsons became the Elamites, Assyrians, Arameans, Cushites, and Canaanites. Other descendants included Eber who, according to tradition, is the father of the written Hebrew language, another was the hunter-king, Nimrod. Others became the Philistines, and the sons of Canaan, from whom came the Hittites, Jebusites and Amorites.

TOWER OF SIN

Early on, when all of these people spoke the same language they settled together in the plain of Shinar, where they conspired collectively.

> "Come, let us build ourselves a city and a tower with its
> top in the heavens, and let us make a name for ourselves,
> lest we be dispersed over the face of the whole earth"
> (Genesis 11:4).

Note that they wanted to make a name *for themselves*. These Cainites were the first builders of cities. God had mercifully spared Cain the death penalty for the murder of Abel by marking him and expelling him to wander the earth. God assigned him a nomadic existence, but Cain's son, Lamech, in denial of God's assignment, became a king of Babel, the greatest city of the time. Lamech refused God's grace, refused to be a wanderer. He did his own thing, he followed his own heart, his own dream. Such were the people who built the great Tower of Babel.

Why build such a tower? In order to "make a name" (Genesis 11:4) for themselves. For *themselves*! During the Noahic era humanity seems to have achieved what has been so illusive in our own age: they achieved some sort of human unity at Babel. And with that achievement "nothing that they propose to do will now be impossible for them" (Genesis 11:7), said God in the story.

God frowned upon this development and set out to stop it. But why? Why was this Babylonian unity problematic for God? Because the whole enterprise was an expression of Eve's sin of self-determination. The snake had convinced Eve that God had been mistaken about what He had said about the tree of the knowledge of good and evil, or that God did not mean what He had said, or that Adam had misunderstood what God said. So Eve determined *for herself* that the forbidden tree

> "was (actually) good for food, and that it was a delight to
> the eyes, and that the tree was to be desired to make one
> wise" (Genesis 3:6).

The integrity of God's word was doubted by the snake. That doubt was then taken up by Eve, and shared with Adam. Was God's Word true to the reality of the world? The flood should have answered that question, but sin has proven to be quite tenacious.

In the same way, the Cainites—people who had rebelled against God—decided to make a name for themselves, lest they be scattered over the face of the earth, lest they continue to be what God had made them as a consequence of his curse—wanderers, nomads. Their Babylonian unity was an agreement to disobey God's directive to wander, and to settle down instead. Thus, the founding of the city of Babel actively opposed God's order. Sodom had been a satellite city of Babel, in the image and culture of Babel. God so opposed it that He came down and confused their language so that they would no longer understand one another, and He then dispersed them all over the earth (Genesis 11:7-8).

This provides a simple explanation for the development of different languages and cultures throughout the world. God's goal in creation was the fusion of language to humanity, but when people refused to acknowledge and honor God's authority, God's Word, when Adam and Cain and their lineage refused to follow God's direction, the gift of language became dangerous because people could accomplish anything they set their hearts to accomplish. They could upset the delicate balance of nature that could trigger some cataclysmic result. The story tells us that their hearts were turned away from God, away from truth, away from the integrity of God and His Word. Human language would one day become the most powerful tool in the cosmos, and in the hands of irresponsible, immature, Godless people, would pose a catastrophic danger, as we witness today. So, God intervened by confusing their language, by making them unable to understand one another, which postponed the assemblage of the full power of human language, human unity, until a later date when all people would be more responsible, more mature, and would give serious ear to the Word or voice of God. We are still praying for that day to come! In the meantime God would demonstrate the problem of human immaturity, human faithlessness, in human history, in the pages of the Bible, by providing historical lessons of the wisdom of God and the foolishness of humanity, the foolishness of disobedience, the failure to consider the reality of God's Word. This is the story of the Old Testament.

The rest of Genesis 11 chronicles the further growth of humanity and the diminution of lifespans following a worldwide cataclysmic event to what has been more common since the great flood. These various peoples then scattered over the face of the world following the destruction of Babel, and took with them their different languages and broken elements of unity. The fall of Babel, which represented human unity apart from faithfulness to the God of the Bible, fractured the story of the biblical development of humanity by taking various pieces of that story through the development of various cultural traditions and different languages to different parts of the world.

This, then, according to the Bible was the real source of the various mythologies, world religions, and the various ideas and traditions about God that we find in mythology and various ancient religious traditions today. Again, all of these people were in the lineage of Cain, and represented faithlessness and the failure to keep God's covenant. They disregarded the God of the Bible and fashioned various gods for themselves, just as they had pledged to make a name for themselves. And in opposition to the various peoples and cultures that were scattered following the Babel incident, God called another individual to carry forward the language and traditions of Abel, Seth, and Noah—Abraham.

ABRAM

The Lord spoke to Abram and he listened. That's where the biblical tradition as we know it began. God speaks and people listen. People hear God. People seriously consider what God has to say. People respond to God with simple obedience. People honor God by following His advice, His commandments.

Again, the story of the creation of Adam is the story of God fusing language to humanity. Prior to the story of Adam, no human being spoke intelligently, effectively. (At least there is no such extant story.) God provided meaning to human utterance. As John said,

> "In the beginning was the Word, and the Word was with God, and the Word was God" (John 1:1).

The purpose for fusing language to human flesh was to give God the ability to accurately communicate with humanity, and humanity with God. Communication is always a two-way street.

We first meet Abram as an adult. God said to Abram,

> "Go from your country and your kindred and your father's house to the land that I will show you. And I will make of you a great nation, and I will bless you and make your name great, so that you will be a blessing. I will bless those who bless you, and him who dishonors you I will curse, and in you all the families of the earth shall be blessed" (Genesis 12:1-3).

The entire gospel in seed form is included in Abram's calling. He was to separate from his father, and the culture of his father, and live in obedience to God by being a blessing to all humanity.

His father, Terah or *Térach* (תֶּרַח, literally *ibex, wild goat,* or *wanderer*—a descendant of Cain), was a biblical figure in the Genesis story, the son of Nahor, son of Serug and father of Abraham, all of whom were descendants of Shem's son, Arpachshad. They were Shemites in the lineage of Adam and Cain, from the city of Babel, from the faithless side of the human family, wandering nomads. According to rabbinical tradition Terah was a priest, which meant that Terah's religion was the religion of Cain and Babel, a religion in opposition to the God of the Bible. Earlier God has sent Terah on a journey,

> "Terah took Abram his son, and Lot the son of Haran his son's son, and Sarai his daughter in law, his son Abram's wife; and they went forth with them from Ur of the Chaldees, to go into the land of Canaan" (Genesis 11:31).

Terah was on a missionary journey to bring the religion of Adam and Cain to Canaan, but Terah died on the way. He didn't make it to Canaan. So before or after Terah died (Scripture doesn't say), God told Abram to separate himself from his father, from Terah, or perhaps to leave the outpost where Terah had died, and continue on to Canaan. Again, Scripture doesn't say one way or the other. I suspect that Abram was not able to differentiate himself from his father, Terah, until Terah died.

Nonetheless, it is likely that Abram, at that time, thought that he had been called to take his father's religion to some other part of the world. There is no indication in Scripture that Abram opposed Terah at the time of God's call. So Abram, also a priest in the family religion, may have followed his father as a missionary at the time. Abram's eventual separation from Terah and the ancient religion of opposition to the God of the Bible, the wandering nomadic priest, plays a key role in the unfolding of the biblical story. Where Abram was to go, God didn't exactly say at that time.

In contrast to the scattered Babelites who wanted to make a name for themselves, God promised to "make of you (Abram) a great nation" (Genesis 12:2). Where the Babelites wanted to make a name *for themselves*, God now promised to make a great name for Abram. This is an important difference because one way excludes God and the other way depends on Him. And precisely because God will make Abram's name great, Abram will be a blessing to the world. The whole point of singling out Abram, of calling him away from his father, and away from the religion of his father, was to bless Abram and his seed, his sons, his children, and his ensuing culture. God blessed Abram by calling him, by speaking to him, by allowing him to hear the true Word of God, and by allowing Abram to speak true words of God. But there was a learning curve.

Abram will carry forward God's plan to fuse language to humanity. But more than simply providing mere language for humanity, God's intention is to provide language integrity for humanity, to provide language that is both true to God and true to reality in its expression. Unlike the language of the snake in the garden, who introduced doubt to language, who suggested that God may have said one thing but meant another, the language that God wanted for humanity was trustworthy language, words that were true to their meaning, language that provided an accurate and trustworthy correspondence to reality, language that could be a trusted channel of communication between God and humanity, between God and the reality in which humanity lived.

Unlike the language that Eve used when she justified her decision to eat of the fruit of the knowledge of good and evil, language that issued solely from herself, language that did not take God's word seriously, language that discarded God's communication about the tree, God's plan was to provide trustworthy language, language that would be an accurate reflection of His communication to humanity, and truth of reality. God's plan was for people to hear, speak, and act on language that could accurately and correctly discern the difference between good and evil, between truth and error, as defined by God, not by ourselves. God knows that our experience of reality is too short and insignificant to be trustworthy, that we—humanity, both individually and collectively—must trust and rely on God's discernment, not our own. Only God has a truly objective perspective.

So, God called Abram to reveal, not just the veracity of the biblical God to the world, but to reveal the reality of sin and the inability of human experience to accurately and correctly perceive, convey, or understand the whole truth of the amazing complexities of the world without God. Contemporary science has just begun to scratch the surface of the deep complexities of our world, and to reveal just how badly we have misunderstood the world in which we live. It's not that all of our previous insights and understandings are wrong—though many are, but that they are woefully inadequate to the reality in which we actually live. And this realization should open us to hear the words and stories of the Bible anew, with fresh ears, with an open mind, a mind that has not been prejudiced by our own flawed and erroneous history, our simple-minded biases and prejudices, both religious and secular.

ABRAHAMIC HUMANITY

This study provides an explication of God's covenant through many seasons or expressions. There is both a unity and a diversity to God's covenant(s), ranging from the primordial covenant with Adam to the contemporary covenant with Jesus Christ. The covenant with Abraham is foundational in many ways. The geological environment in which Abraham lived was much like the geological environment in which we live today, unlike the geological environment of either Adam or Noah. Where Adam's covenant was primordial, Noah's was transitional in that Noah survived a cataclysmic environmental change that resulted in what we experience as weather or climate. This event either introduced climate as we know it, or it significantly changed an existing climate into the form that we know today. The seasons that Adam knew were markedly different in significant ways than they are today, and the seasons that resulted from the great geyser flood were marked by probable changes in temperature, pressure, and precipitation. Of course, no one really knows for sure. It is possible, perhaps likely, that the tilt and wobble of the earth[1] were affected by Noah's flood.

God's covenant with Abraham involves several chapters or stages because it unfolds developmentally. It is difficult to nail down an original single incident or event. The story began with Abram's call (Genesis 12:1-3), which included the whole biblical

---

1 https://en.wikipedia.org/wiki/Milankovitch_cycles
https://answersingenesis.org/bible-questions/did-it-rain-before-the-flood/

gospel in seed form. And because it was in seed form, it needed to take root, grow, and develop. The fact that it came in seed form and grew over time reveals that God's covenant is a living thing, and that it is an expression of God's Trinity, God's DNA. God's covenant is living, which means that it is able to feed and reproduce—and the biblical story reveals that it does this. However, the lengths of the seasons of God's covenant are enormous. They encompass eons, thousands of years, or what we are calling *eras* of humanity. The Abrahamic era can be measured in three stages: calling, foundation, and cultural expression. We have already discussed Abram's calling in the previous chapter because there is also a sense in which the covenants overlap. The more we learn about the world in which we live, the more we realize its amazing complexity.

FOUNDATION

The story of the foundation of the Abrahamic covenant is not as simple as its plain statement, not as simple as our Sunday School lessons suggest. The gospel of God first needed to break free from the cult of Terah and the practice of vengeful, blood sacrifices that had been developed by the Cainites in Babel. Only then could it take root in Abram and the new cult that God was developing. So, God called and equipped Abram and his wife, servants, followers, and herds for the trek to Canaan. And Abram obediently obeyed and headed out to a land that he would never inhabit, carrying on the tradition of his father, Terah. The promise of land was not given to Abram personally, but was given to Abram's seed (Genesis 12:7). Nonetheless, in response to the promise of land Abram built an altar to the Lord at Bethel, acknowledging his gratitude to God as the source of the anticipated gift.

As he and his troupe continued their journey southward, they were driven into Egypt by a famine. In Egypt Sarai his wife caught the eye of Pharaoh, and Abram responded in fear by instructing Sarai to lie. They told Pharaoh that Sarai was his sister rather than his wife, fearing that Pharaoh might kill him in order to have Sarai. Note the similarity of Abram's response to Pharaoh to Adam's response to God in the garden. Both were afraid, and both lied, hoping that the lie would protect them. In this detail we see much of Abram's godless Cainite character and habits. Clearly, Abram was not chosen by God because he was different from others in Terah's clan. Abram was very much the son of his father.

Abram then accepted gifts from Pharaoh for Sarai, thinking that he would take her for his wife. But upon reception of Sarai into the household of Pharaoh, episodes of disease broke out. Perhaps the Egyptians were exposed to something from the wandering clan of Abram for which they had not developed immunity. It is easy to imagine such a scenario. Abram and Sarai may have felt some guilt for their deceit, and shortly Pharaoh discovered the deceit and chastised Abram and expelled him from Egypt. Abram took his wife, kept Pharaohs gifts, and departed into the Negev (Genesis 13:1).

Abram's retinue included his nephew, Lot, and between them they had collected much wealth, including livestock, silver, and gold while in Egypt, and, no doubt, the wealth brought more people into the caravan. Their caravan grew so large that they had trouble finding adequate water in the desert, and tension erupted among their clansmen. So, Abram and Lot agreed to divide the clan and separate. Abram gave Lot first choice about where to go, and Lot chose the fertile valley of Jordan. So Abram settled in the hills of Canaan (Genesis 13:12).

There were already cities in the Jordan valley, so Lot and his clan settled on the outskirts of Sodom and Gomorrah. Scripture notes that those in the Jordan valley were particularly wicked rebels against the Lord (Genesis 13:13)—children of Cain. On the other hand,

> "Abram moved his tents and went to live by the oaks of Mamre in Hebron, and he built an altar to the LORD there" (Genesis 13:18).

Lot moved in with the wicked heathen in Jordan, and Abram went into the hills to worship God. The two lineages of Cain and Seth (Abel) can clearly be seen taking different paths.

As might be expected, war broke out in the Jordan valley and Lot was caught up in it. In that war Chedorlaomer "defeated all the country of the Amakekites" (Genesis 14:8), and then conquered Sodom and Gomorrah, enslaving the people and taking "all their provisions" (Genesis 14:11). Lot, who had gone to Jordan with much wealth from Egypt, was also taken captive.

A refugee of the conflict in Jordan escaped to Marme and reported the events to Abram, who in support of his clan, his kin, mounted a successful rescue operation, freeing Lot and the captured booty. Following the operation, Abram met with the king of Sodom because much of the spoils had also belonged to him and the people of Sodom. They met under the leadership and auspices of Melchizedek, king of Salem, a city which would one day be known as Jerusalem. Melchizedek was both a king and a "priest of the Most High God" (Genesis 14:18). The name Melchizedek is composed of two elements meaning *king* and *righteous(ness)*. With the addition of the enclitic possessive pronoun, which means *my* king, the name literally translates to "my king is righteousness."

They worshiped together, and Abram tithed his winnings to Melchizedek, signifying his honor and respect of the priest of Salem. Abram then returned the rest of what he had captured to the king of Sodom, and

> "replied to the king of Sodom, 'I raise my hand to the LORD, the Most High God, Creator of heaven and earth, and vow that I will take nothing belonging to you, not even a thread or the strap of a sandal. That way you can never say, 'It is I who made Abram rich.' I will take nothing except compensation for what the young men have eaten. As for the share of the men who went with me—Aner, Eshcol, and Mamre—let them take their share" (Genesis 14:22-24).

Abram wanted no debts nor any tangled alliances that would cause trouble in the future. This attitude would become a model for God's people to emulate throughout Scripture, though they would repeatedly fail to do so. The kings then sealed their treaty and the return of the booty with a religious celebration of bread and wine administered by Melchizedek.

This encounter with Melchizedek will prove to be most auspicious in Paul's letter to the Hebrews, as Paul explains that Jesus

Christ was not a priest in the lineage and tradition of either Aaron or Levi (Temple priests), but was a priest in the order of Melchizedek (Hebrews 6:20) in fulfillment of Psalm 110:4. Paul also said that Melchizedek was

> "without father or mother or genealogy, having neither beginning of days nor end of life, but resembling the Son of God he continues a priest forever" (Hebrews 7:3).

This does not mean that Melchizedek had no parents, rather it means that his blood lineage was not recorded, it was not a matter of record. His priesthood was grounded outside of or apart from the Old Testament. What this means will be an ongoing element of discussion.

At the conclusion of the meeting between Abram, Melchizedek, and the king of Sodom, Abram had a vision in which God spoke to him.

> "Fear not, Abram! I am your shield and the one who will reward you in great abundance" (Genesis 15:1).

Abram led by honoring God in his political agreement with the king of Sodom, under the supervision of Melchizedek, priest of the God Most High. Then God promised Abram an heir, a son of his own, in spite of the fact that his wife, Sarai, was barren. And through that son would come Abram's descendants, as numerable as the stars in the sky. This was not just a promise that Abram would have a son, but was a promise that God would have a human culture of people like Abram, a people who would honor God above all else in all of their dealings. And because people need land in which to live, God also promised Abram sufficient land in which to prosper.

> "And he (Abram) believed the LORD, and he (God) counted it to him as righteousness" (Genesis 15:6).

Then, when Abram asked God how he could know that God would be true to His promises, God instructed him to cut several animals in half and lay out the halves such that there was a space between them. After doing so and at the end of the day Abram fell asleep and God gave him a vision of the future of his people. They would continue their journey toward Canaan, but would be afflicted for four hundred years. It was a vision of their captivity in Egypt, which would provide them with great possessions and power with which to capture and inhabit the land God had promised. Following the vision, "a smoking fire pot and a flaming torch passed between these pieces" (Genesis 15:17) of the sacrificed animals, and God finalized His promise by specifically naming the peoples that Abram's descendants would displace:

> "the Kenites, the Kenizzites, the Kadmonites, the Hittites, the Perizzites, the Rephaim, the Amorites, the Canaanites, the Girgashites and the Jebusites" (Genesis 15:19-21).

Abram could trust God's promises because God had laid them out with great specificity. So, as these things occurred the faith of Abram and his people would be strengthened. God's plan was to replace the culture of Satan, Adam's culture, Cain's culture, the culture of sin, with a culture of faithfulness, a culture of obedience to God's Word.

MISCALCULATION & SIN

But such a change would not be simple. It would take time, a lot of time because the change that was needed was extremely significant because sin was very deep-seated in humanity. Abraham is honored today because we think of him as the representative of simple faithfulness. God told him to go, and not knowing where he was to go, he went, trusting God. Then he honored God above his hard won wealth in his dealings with the king of Sodom. So, at this point in the story Abram has received the fullness of God's promise and has been given the greatest assurance possible that God will honor His promise. The stage is set for God to begin to fulfill the promise through the birth of a son to Abram and Sarai. But twenty-five years passed, and no son was born.

So, Sarai hatched a plan to give Abram her servant, Hagar, to serve as a surrogate mother, a common practice among barren couples. Perhaps she remembered that God had named Abram in the promise, that *he* would be the father of many, perhaps it was not about *her* child. Perhaps Abram was to father this multitude through a surrogate. It was not an unreasonable thought. So, Sarai convinced Abram and Abram impregnated Hagar.

During Hagar's pregnancy she began to look with contempt upon Sarai, likely because Sarai wanted to be the mother of Hagar's child, and Hagar was now feeling her own mothering instincts and emotional attachment to her child in utero. Abram intervened in order to bring peace to his household, and told Sarai to do as she pleased with Hagar. Sarai dealt harshly with her, and dismissed her. Hagar then fled into the desert in anger and angst.

In the desert Hagar reportedly encountered an angel of the Lord who told her to return to Sarai, promising Hagar that God would "surely multiply your offspring so that they cannot be numbered for multitude" (Genesis 16:10). This angel of the Lord said to Hagar:

> "Behold, you are pregnant and shall bear a son. You shall call his name Ishmael, because the LORD has listened to your affliction. He shall be a wild donkey of a man, his hand against everyone and everyone's hand against him, and he shall dwell over against all his kinsmen" (Genesis 16:11-12).

Here we have a covenant promise given by the angel of the Lord to Hagar that is oddly reminiscent of God's covenant promise previously given to Abram. It includes a promise of great fecundity attached to Ishmael, but rather than being a blessing to the world Ishmael would father a nation or culture of wild, untamable hostility toward everyone. Then Hagar named the God of her vision: *The God Who Sees*. It is noteworthy that Hagar named God because God would later name Himself (*I AM*). God is both particular and jealous of His name. The story concludes then with the birth of Ishmael (Genesis 16:15). Again, Hagar's vision and encounter with the angel of God is odd because it so closely mimics God's promise to Abram. And while it might appear to reinforce God's promise to Abram, it is in fact a different covenant, a different promise, from a god with a different name. It was a different prophecy and produced a different history regarding a different people.

God's covenant promise to Hagar qualifies as another fulfillment of God's curse of the serpent in the garden to create enmity between the seed of the serpent and the seed of the woman (Genesis 3:15). Ishmael would be in the lineage of the serpent and Isaac would be in the lineage of the woman, in the lineage of Abraham and Sarah, and of Seth. It is not insignificant that today Ishmael is recognized as an important prophet and patriarch of Islam. Muslims acknowledge that Ishmael was the firstborn of Abraham, born to him from his second wife, Hagar, and the rightful heir of Abraham according to the ancient tradition of Terah. Ishmael is recognized by Muslims as the ancestor of several prominent Arab tribes and as the forefather of Muhammad. But we have jumped ahead of the unfolding story.

Abram was eighty-six years old when Ishmael was born, and when he was ninety-nine God renewed His covenant promise.

> "Behold, my covenant is with you, and you shall be the father of a multitude of nations. No longer shall your name be called Abram, but your name shall be Abraham, for I have made you the father of a multitude of nations. I will make you exceedingly fruitful, and I will make you into nations, and kings shall come from you. And I will establish my covenant between me and you and your offspring after you throughout their generations for an everlasting covenant, to be God to you and to your offspring after you. And I will give to you and to your offspring after you the land of your sojournings, all the land of Canaan, for an everlasting possession, and I will be their God" (Genesis 17:4-8).

Only at this point did God change his name to *Abraham* because he would be the father of many nations. And only now did He institute circumcision as a sign or symbol of this covenant, the fulfillment of which would begin with the birth of Isaac. Every male in Abraham's household, and throughout the generations of Abraham's children, would be circumcised to remind them of God's covenant.

God also changed Sarai's name to *Sarah* and promised a son by her (Genesis 17:16), or reissued the original promise. Abraham was a hundred years old at the time, which caused him to doubt the viability of God's promise. Even after all that had happened, Abraham, in the midst of receiving a reissuance of God's covenant, doubted God's words, and prayed to refocus God on Ishmael, "Oh that Ishmael might live before you!" (Genesis 17:19). In response, God repeated the promise to give Sarah a child, and instructed them to name him Isaac.

Only at this point did Abraham perform circumcision on all of the males of his entourage, including Ishmael, his only son and heir at the time. Circumcision was a late addition to the Abrahamic covenant, and with circumcision we see the beginning of an emphasis on cultural identity through common cultural practice by the Abrahamites. With the institution of circumcision God intensified the practices of cultural identification, and with the change of name Abraham takes on a heightened role as the leader of his people. And yet, doubt clings to the story like barnacles to a ship.

The story of Isaac's birth and the destruction of Sodom are woven together. Three men wandered into Abraham's camp and prophesied the birth of Isaac. Again, Sarah laughed at the idea of giving birth in her nineties, and when asked about it she denied laughing because she was afraid. This story carries echoes of Adam and Eve in Eden regarding her deceit and fear. After that, the prophets departed for Sodom, a city of exceeding wickedness. God decided not to hide His judgment against Sodom from Abraham, who responded,

> "Will you indeed sweep away the righteous with the wicked?" (Genesis 18:23).

This is a serious question that has retained its importance since it was first asked. Abraham challenged God's judgment, God's character, by insinuating the injustice of destroying the good along with the evil. Abraham, wrestling with the idea of the tree of the knowledge of good and evil, then proposed a test.

If Abraham can find fifty righteous people in Sodom, would God spare it for their sake? How many righteous people would it take for God to spare Sodom? Fifty, forty-five, forty, etc. They finally agree on ten. If Abraham can find ten righteous men in Sodom, God will spare it. Abraham had an interest in Sodom because Lot was there, and Abraham believed that Lot was righteous. So Abraham accompanied the men into Sodom to find ten righteous men.

Feeling confident, Abraham took the prophets to Lot's house. However, they would rather spend the night in the town square, but Lot convinced them of the danger there, and they agreed. The story is odd. The men of Sodom then came to Lot's home and demanded that the visitors be sent out so that the Sodomites may know (יָדַע, *yada*) them. It's the same word used to describe Adam knowing Eve. The word has intimate, sexual overtones. Of course, it has other meanings and is used in other contexts of intimate knowledge, but the implication here has historically had sexual overtones regarding this Sodom story.

The sexual implications are furthered by Lot who recommended sending two of his daughters out to them so that they can *know* them—surprising behavior by a father to our contemporary ears. And Lot was one of the good guys! The daughters were not sent out, and conflict ensued as the men attempted to break into Lot's house. Lot unsuccessfully tried to stop them when they were suddenly smitten by blindness and could not find the door. The whole episode is as ugly as ugly gets. There are no good players, indeed, none are righteous, no, not one.

In the morning, the prophets, identified as angels, told Lot to take his wife and family and leave because they were going to destroy Sodom. Still, Lot lingered and did nothing. So Abraham seized him and took him and his family out of the city and told him to take refuge in the hills. But Lot was a city dweller, not a country boy. So he argued that he would die in the hills implying that he had lost all of his nomadic skills. Rather, Lot suggested that he go to a smaller city where there was not so much corruption. So, he and his family went to Zoar.

Lot lost his wife in the destruction of Sodom. They were told not to watch the destruction as sulfur and fire rained down on the city. But she looked back, and was turned into a pillar of salt. Lot escaped to Zoar with his daughters, but left Zoar and resided in the hills, in a cave. Lots daughters, not knowing other men, thought of Lot as righteous, probably the most righteous man in Sodom. But Lot had no son to carry on his lineage. So the daughters hatched a plan to get him drunk and have his children for the sake of extending the family line. So, they did. Two boys were born, Moab and Ben-ammi, who fathered the Moabites and Ammonites, who later became enemies of Israel.

The story of Abraham and Abimelech (Genesis 20) repeats a familiar theme. The result of the encounter with Pharaoh proved to be quite lucrative, and it seems that the same scenario played out with Abimelech, with a similar result.

> "Then Abimelech took sheep and oxen, and male servants and female servants, and gave them to Abraham, and returned Sarah his wife to him" (Genesis 20:14).

Again, there was a deceit that Sarah was available to the ruler. She was then taken into his household, and shortly thereafter it is revealed that she was actually Abraham's wife, with a reminder that God requires marriage purity. And she was returned with a gift. It almost sounds like a well-rehearsed scam they were using as they traveled.

Abraham was a hundred years old when Isaac was born.

> "And Sarah said, 'God has made laughter for me; everyone who hears will laugh over me' ... But Sarah saw the son of Hagar the Egyptian, whom she had borne to Abraham, laughing" (Genesis 21:6, 9).

There is the sense of laughing in derision in the Hebrew, which might account for Sarah's second dismissal of Hagar and Ishmael. Again, Hagar and Ishmael were dismissed and went into the wilderness of Beersheba, and encountered the angel of the Lord a second time. The Lord reiterated His promise to make Ishmael into a great nation. Then Hagar and Ishmael lived in the wilderness of Paran, and Hagar secured a wife for Ishmael from Egypt. And again, we see conflict and enmity in Abraham's family that will continue to play out in history down to our current day.

ISAAC

Following the establishment of a treaty with Abimelech, God tested Abraham by instructing him to take Isaac to the land of Moriah

> "and offer him there as a burnt offering on one of the mountains of which I shall tell you" (Genesis 22:3).

This situation revealed that Abraham had knowledge and experience with human sacrifice in high places, a theme that runs through the Old Testament. He knew what to do and what was required by God's command, and set out to fulfill it.

In order to develop another Old Testament theme, and to ween Abraham from his pagan roots in his father's religion, God introduced the idea of substitution in the story of the sacrifice of Isaac. God met Abraham where he was, in the midst of his idolatry in order to pull him into the light of God's truth. The lesson of the story is that Abraham was willing to sacrifice Isaac, but that God only wanted his willingness. So, God intervened by providing a ram, which was then sacrificed rather than Isaac.

> "So Abraham called the name of that place, 'The LORD will provide'; as it is said to this day, 'On the mount of the LORD it shall be provided'" (Genesis 22:14).

And following this event, God repeated His covenant promise to Abraham.

Abraham lived 175 years and died. Following his death Scripture provides two genealogical lists, one for the children of Abraham (Genesis 5:1-5), and one for the children of Ishmael (Genesis 5:12-16).

> "Abraham gave all he had to Isaac. But to the sons of his concubines Abraham gave gifts, and while he was still living he sent them away from his son Isaac, eastward to the east country" (Genesis 25:5-6).

Abraham distinguished three family lines: 1) Isaac inherited Abraham's wealth and continued the family line, 2) his other children had been sent away with gifts, in order to protect Isaac from their influence, and 3) Ishmael's children were listed separately. Clearly, Abraham's story is messy.

Jacob

Isaac's wife, Rebekah, was also barren, as Sarah had been. Isaac prayed for her and she became pregnant with twins. Again, the Lord brought a message to Rebekah that there were two different people who would become two different nations in her womb, and that the older would serve the younger, unlike the traditional custom favoring the oldest son. Esau was born first, and was the stronger twin. Esau became a skillful hunter. Jacob was likely smaller, and dwelt in tents—he didn't go out much. One day Jacob got Esau to sell him his birthright for a bowl of stew. It didn't seem very important to Esau at the time. It is also important to note that Isaac preferred Esau, while Rebekah preferred Jacob, suggesting that Isaac's preferences were still not in line with God's.

Isaac then had an encounter with king Abimelech that was very much like that of his father's encounter with Pharaoh. Isaac and Rebekah repeated the scenario of she and Isaac being brother and sister rather than husband and wife. They seem to have prospered for it, as had Abraham and Sarah. It appears that Isaac was very much like his father. Not much changed from generation to generation, suggesting the slow rate of cultural and personal change, and the inheritance of sin in those days.

As Isaac was dying, it came time for him to give his last blessing to his sons. Isaac was intent on giving the bulk of his blessing and wealth to Esau, and called for him. A long story of intrigue unfolded because Rebekah and Jacob had devised a plan to trick Isaac into blessing Jacob, while thinking he was blessing Esau. It is a story of deceit and cunning—and it worked! Isaac blessed Jacob with the family inheritance, again breaking with the tradition that the oldest son received the bulk of the inheritance, and caused animosity among the siblings—for generations.

The story focused on the consequences of Jacob's blessing. We learn that from the womb Jacob had struggled against his twin brother, Esau, from the very beginning. At birth Jacob held Esau by his heel, symbolizing Jacob attacking Esau's weakness.

The boys were quite different, even in the womb. Esau was strong, outgoing, and ruddy, while Jacob was a mamma's boy—a schemer, a thinker. Early on Jacob tricked Esau out of his birthright by trading it for a bowl of stew. Later, Esau married a Hittite woman, "and they made life bitter for Isaac and Rebekah" (Genesis 26:35).

The episode where Jacob stole Esau's blessing reveals a serious flaw in Jacob's character, as well as demonstrating God's ability to conform all events to His divine will. Jacob and his mother, Rebekah, successfully executed a complex plan to deceive Isaac in order to capture Isaac's blessing for Jacob rather than Esau. The story provides a great example of the growing complexity and need for God to intervene in human history in order to change the essential character of humanity (both individually and corporately, or culturally), to overcome our natural propensity for—even, love of—sin.

The sin that reared its head in the garden through the words of the snake and the eager gullibility of Eve to believe in the integrity of her own thinking proved to be a dominant element of human character. That sin involved, not only the inability of fledgling humanity to conceive the wholeness or totality of the reality in which they had been created, but the amplification of the passionate desire to believe that they could. The serpent had shown them how to justify their own thinking, to trust in themselves, to concoct explanations of things that had a kind of internal logic and cohesiveness that "made sense" to them. How could God expect them to be responsible for knowing things that they could not yet know? Sanity itself involves trusting one's own perspective.

It is incumbent to remember that God's ultimate goal is to establish integrity between human language and reality. God's goal is to teach us the truth about the reality in which we have been created, and this will always require that we learn how and when to trust God, God's Word, and how and when not to trust our own best thinking. The truth is that our own best thinking, both individually and culturally, will always be shy of the mark, short of the whole truth.

The story of Jacob and Rebekah stealing Esau's blessing shows us that God's purpose would prevail in its struggle with human sinfulness. God's intention was to bless Jacob by getting him to trust God, by teaching him how to trust God, even when Jacob was doing his best to ignore God and trust in his own ability to get what he wanted for himself. Jacob was a conniver, always looking out for his own best interests—and he was quite good at it.

The result of Jacob's conniving was that

> "Now Esau hated Jacob because of the blessing with which his father had blessed him, and Esau said to himself, The days of mourning for my father are approaching; then I will kill my brother Jacob'" (Genesis 27:41).

Esau was able to justify his hate for his brother because Jacob legitimately deserved it. Jacob's theft of the blessing was a lousy thing to do—even criminal. We also learn that God in His infinite wisdom was able to use Jacob's conniving to accomplish His divine purpose—even when Esau continued to manifest the character and spiritual lineage of Cain. And so hatred grew between the clans and continued to play out in the biblical story—and beyond, even into today.

In consequence, Jacob was sent to Laban, the son of Nachor, Abraham's older brother, for protection from Esau and in order to find a clan wife. Rebekah did not want Jacob to make the mistake that Esau made by marrying an unbeliever. Esau then, to Rebekah's dissatisfaction, married, in addition to his other wives, "Mahalath the daughter of Ishmael" (Genesis 28:9). Jacob, on his way to see Laban, had a dream. He saw a ladder that connected heaven and earth with angels traversing it. While the ladder symbolized communication between heaven and earth, the message of the dream involved God's promise of land.

> "'I am the LORD, the God of Abraham your father and the God of Isaac. The land on which you lie I will give to you and to your offspring. Your offspring shall be like the dust of the earth, and you shall spread abroad to the west and to the east and to the north and to the south, and in you and your offspring shall all the families of the earth be blessed.

Behold, I am with you and will keep you wherever you go, and will bring you back to this land. For I will not leave you until I have done what I have promised you.' Then Jacob awoke from his sleep and said, 'Surely the LORD is in this place, and I did not know it'" (Genesis 28:13-16).

In response Jacob made a vow at Bethel saying,

"If God will be with me and will keep me in this way that I go, and will give me bread to eat and clothing to wear, so that I come again to my father's house in peace, then the LORD shall be my God, and this stone, which I have set up for a pillar, shall be God's house. And of all that you give me I will give a full tenth to you" (Genesis 28:20-22).

Here we clearly see a definite response to God's covenant and gracious gift of land that was yet to be given. The content of Jacob's vow was very appropriate to his first journey to visit Laban. This vow becomes the central vow of the Old Testament in that the whole of the Old Testament becomes the story of this vow. If God would keep Jacob safe, provide food and clothing, and return him home safely, then Jacob would honor God by tithing to Him. It was a win/win scenario. At this point I find myself wondering: to whom would Jacob give the tithe? How would that work, covenanting and tithing to a dream?

In the next chapter Jacob met and fell in love with Rachael, Laban's daughter. Jacob then worked out a deal to work for Laban for seven years, after which he would receive Rachael as a wife. Jacob worked the time, but Laban substituted his older daughter, Leah, in the marriage ceremony. And Jacob didn't even notice until the next day! Laban excused his deceit by arguing that it was customary (necessary and legally justified) for the older daughter to be married before the younger. Jacob accepted the explanation and the marriage to Leah, but contracted for another seven years in order to also marry Rachael, his first love.

Jacob's children, named in Genesis (the numbers indicate birth order) are: by Leah: Reuben (1), Simeon (2), Levi (3), Judah (4), Issachar (9), Zebulun (10), Dinah (11); by Zipah, Leah's servant: Gad (7), Asher (8); by Bilah, Rachel's servant: Dan (5),

FOR THE WHOLE WORLD

Naphtali (6); by Rachel: Joseph (12), Benjamin (13). His only daughter mentioned in Genesis is Dinah. The twelve sons became the progenitors of the tribes of Israel.

Following the birth of Joseph, Jacob wanted to leave Laban and set out on his own. But Laban had profited greatly from Jacob's work. So, determining what belonged to Jacob and what belonged to Laban was difficult because Jacob had greatly increased Laban's stock. Did the increase belong to Laban or Jacob? Jacob's answer was to agree to cull the stock and separate the "spotted" from the "striped" animals. Jacob had devised a scheme to control the breeding of the stock such that the strong bred with the strong and the weak bred with the weak, and "the feebler would be Laban's, and the stronger Jacob's" (Genesis 30:42). The odd and complex biblical explanation of this breeding process demonstrated Jacob's flawed understanding of genetics, and the deeper realities in the world in which he lived. Nonetheless, God helped with the result, and the result was that Jacob's household and flocks increased greatly by the grace of God.

When Laban discovered what Jacob had done he believed that Jacob had cheated him. But Jacob, on the other hand, believed that Laban had cheated *him* all the years of his service, first by substituting Leah for Rachel, and then by not paying him the wages owed him. Jacob then had a dream where God reminded him of his vow and promised to care for him. So Jacob decided to leave Laban.

As Jacob separated his entourage from Laban, Rebekah stole Laban's household gods, pagan figurines, and took them with her. The symbolism of this act suggests that Rebekah still did not understand that the God whom Jacob served was other than the traditional gods dominant in the Middle East, the gods of Terah. When Laban discovered their departure and the missing idols he pursued them for seven days, after which God came to Laban in a dream and warned him to be careful in his relationship with Jacob. When Laban caught up with Jacob he upbraided Jacob for stealing away unannounced with Laban's daughters and grandchildren without a proper send off—and for stealing his household gods (figurines). Laban said he would have thrown a party and sent them off with his best wishes, had he known they were leaving. And while Laban had the power to punish Jacob for this indiscretion, Jacob's God had warned him not to. Finally Laban asked why Jacob had stolen his household gods.

Jacob answered that he left without notice because he was afraid that Laban would not allow his daughters to leave with him. Jacob did not know about the household gods at the time, and so promised that anyone found with said figurines would be killed. Rachel's guilt was not discovered because she hid the figurines by sitting on them and claiming to be in the midst of her menstrual cycle, which eliminated her person from being searched. The figurines were not found, so Jacob lambasted Laban for his lack of trust and appreciation of all that Jacob had done for him over the twenty years he had been in Laban's service.

Laban then recommended that they covenant together as a witness of their familial love and concern for one another. The terms of the covenant were that from that point forward Jacob would not harm Laban's daughters, and Laban would not harm Jacob or his family. Jacob's God was to be the arbitrator of the agreement. Then,

> "Jacob offered a sacrifice in the hill country and called his kinsmen to eat bread. They ate bread and spent the night in the hill country" (Genesis 31:54).

The use of bread in the administration of this covenant is reminiscent of Abraham's encounter with Melchizedek. It is not difficult to image that they also drank wine. Though not mentioned directly, the use of wine could be implied in that the Hebrew term for bread (לֶחֶם) can also be understood as food generally. Following this Jacob and Laban went their own ways.

As Jacob thought about returning home, he also thought about his brother, Esau, who, when he left some twenty years previously, had threatened to kill him. So, Jacob sent messengers ahead of the main caravan to tell Esau that he had profited from his stay with Laban, and was bringing gifts for Esau, hoping to appease his brother. In response, Esau rushed to meet Jacob, bringing four hundred men with him. When Jacob heard of

Esau's response he was afraid, thinking that Esau was coming to fulfill his previous threat. In response, Jacob then divided his caravan into two sections, so that if Esau attacked one, the other could escape. Jacob also prayed to God, asking for protection and promising fidelity.

As they were about to meet, Jacob began to put all of his gifts for Esau at the front of the caravan, hoping to show his sincerity and assuage Esau's anger. The night before they were to meet, Jacob had another dream—or was it a dream? Jacob and his caravan "crossed the ford of the Jabbok" (Genesis 32:22), a tributary to the Jordan River at night. Once on the other side,

> "Jacob was left alone. And a man wrestled with him until the breaking of the day. When the man saw that he did not prevail against Jacob, he touched his hip socket, and Jacob's hip was put out of joint as he wrestled with him. Then he said, 'Let me go, for the day has broken.' But Jacob said, 'I will not let you go unless you bless me.' And he said to him, 'What is your name?' And he said, 'Jacob.' Then he said, 'Your name shall no longer be called Jacob, but Israel, for you have striven with God and with men, and have prevailed.' Then Jacob asked him, 'Please tell me your name.' But he said, 'Why is it that you ask my name?' And there he blessed him. So Jacob called the name of the place Peniel, saying, 'For I have seen God face to face, and yet my life has been delivered.'" (Genesis 32:24-30)

That night Jacob became Israel, and the significance of this change represents something so momentous that it can only be described as a change commensurate to an order of magnitude. The change that began with Abraham turning away from the ancient gods and pagan culture of Terah, had finally reached a point of critical significance as Jacob received God's blessing, in spite of the fact that it had hobbled him. Jacob, unlike his father and grandfather, finally recognized God. He was finally able to clearly hear the voice of God, as distinct from the pagan gods of Terah. Unlike Abraham and Isaac, who had heard God only sporadically, Israel had awakened to more consistently hear/discern the voice of God. Jacob could hear and wrestle with God.

This event provided the model for the fulcrum of God's covenant in the Old Testament, symbolized by the change of Jacob's name and character (*supplanter*) to Israel (*wrestler with the God who prevails*). This change of name signified a change of character. Three significant things changed as a result of Jacob wrestling with this "man" or angel or dream or whatever: Jacob's heart changed, his mind changed, and his soul changed—his character changed. His change of name from Jacob to Israel represented the fruit of a change that had begun with Abraham, who also had his name changed.

God had called Abraham to separate from his father, Terah, and from Terah's pagan gods and culture, to set out on a different path that God would unveil as he went. But it involved a change so significant that Abraham was not able to embrace it fully. Abraham's failure to fully embrace the ways of the God who had called him was repeatedly demonstrated through the various stories about Abraham, and how he continued to manifest the character of various Babylonian gods, i.e., his deception of Pharaoh involving Sarah, and his near sacrifice of his son, Isaac.

The process of change then passed to his son, Isaac, who repeated many of Abraham's mistakes and worst qualities, but who was also able to make several personal advancements, though falling short of the critical mass that God intended. So, the process of change then passed to Isaac's son, Jacob. It took three generations for the change that God had intended for human character[2] to mature to the point that it would break forth in new life. That critical point had been reached the night that Jacob wrestled the angel of God to a tie, at which point God "touched his hip socket, and Jacob's hip was put out of joint" (Genesis 32:25), dislocated.

Let's think about this for a moment: a dislocated hip involves the pulling of the thigh bone out of the hip socket. Ouch! The pain would have been horrendous, resulting in a probable blackout. That kind of damage would require much time to heal, certainly not overnight, save in the case of divine intervention.

---

2   Forged in Israel, and ultimately perfected in Jesus.

The symbolism here is that Jacob's wrestling with God (or His angel, or whatever) produced maximum pain that resulted in a permanent limp as a reminder. But out of that pain new life was born, a new character was born in Jacob. Something new in the history of humanity was born, a fundamental change of character was born, with all of the expected pain, messiness, and struggle of ordinary childbirth, out of the stubborn carcass of human flesh. A new character stepped forward that day, and God named him *Israel.*

This momentous change in human character was akin to the creation of a new creature, a new kind or species—not merely genetically or physically, but both personally and culturally. This change, symbolized by the change of name, also represented the origin of a new human culture in that the individual, Israel, would become the nation, Israel. Just as future generations of people were present in the individual named Adam at creation, so future generations of people who would be known as Israel were present in the individual Jacob, who had become Israel by the stroke of God. God was birthing a new human culture.

Following the renaming of Jacob, Jacob asked for the name of the man or angel or whatever, who answered,

"Why is it that you ask my name?" (Genesis 32:29).

A better translation, based on nothing but the sense of the story, might be, "Do you really need to ask my name?" The implication was that Jacob was able to recognize his wrestling partner on his own, because that was the fruit of his new character. Israel was now able to recognize the God of Abraham on his own. He had new eyes, new insight, new interests and passions. He had been renewed in the likeness of the God of Abraham. The process, though not complete, was mature enough for him to be weaned from his dependence and addiction to the pagan gods and culture of Babylonia. Jacob, reborn into the realization of the God of Abraham, became Israel, the seed of God's nation that would change the world.

"So Jacob called the name of the place Peniel, saying, 'For I have seen God face to face, and yet my life has been delivered'" (Genesis 32:30).[3]

Jacob had been "delivered," "preserved," or "saved" that day. At this point, the story of Jacob becomes the root story, model, or archetype of what faithful Bible believers call salvation, new birth, and/or regeneration, which comes into fruition with Jesus Christ, and fully manifests in the life of Paul (Acts 9), and will mature into Christ's church.

RECONCILIATION

The first thing that happened following Jacob's regeneration or conversion unfolds in the story of his meeting Esau, the brother who had sworn to kill him. The brothers met, embraced, and wept together. Jacob explained that God had been good to him by increasing his wealth, and the gifts to Esau were simply an expression of his love. Esau responded, "I have enough, my brother; keep what you have for yourself (Genesis 33:9)." Jacob[4] then responded,

> "No, please, if I have found favor in your sight, then accept my present from my hand. For I have seen your face, which is like seeing the face of God, and you have accepted me. Please accept my blessing that is brought to you, because God has dealt graciously with me, and because I have enough (Genesis 33:10-11)."

Esau then accepted the gifts. So, the first act of Jacob following his rebirth or conversion was to reconcile with his brother, Esau. Following these formalities, Esau, who was a nomad without attachment to a particular place (reminiscent of Cain's punishment), invited Jacob to travel with him. Jacob refused, saying

---

3 Later, when Moses asked to see God's glory God replied, "I will make all my goodness pass before you and will proclaim before you my name 'The LORD.' And I will be gracious to whom I will be gracious, and will show mercy on whom I will show mercy. But, he said, you cannot see my face, for man shall not see me and live" (Genesis 33:19-20). See the section on Moses for more information, p. 86.

4 Though God had changed his name, Scripture still refers to him here as Jacob. Israel usually refers to the people he fathered, not to him as an individual.

that he had children and nursing flocks, which would only slow down Esau and his four hundred men. Esau then offered to leave some men behind to travel with Jacob, but Jacob refused the offer. So, Jacob would not travel with Esau, but promised to follow behind.

Jacob, functioning now as Israel, who recognized the voice of God and who would honor Abraham's call to separate from the pagan gods and culture of Babylon, could not simply follow Esau back into the culture and gods of Babylon. Israel needed to establish herself apart from the old traditional ways. Israel knew that Esau would not understand and would feel threatened by what he did not understand. So, Jacob promised to meet Esau at Seir, but went to Succoth, and from there to Shechem in Canaan, where he purchased a tract of land in fulfillment of God's promise to Abraham, and "erected an altar and called it El-Elohe-Israel" (Genesis 33:20).

Thus, Shechem became the first Israelite settlement in the land of Canaan. However, Israel's reconciliation with Esau was stillborn, in that no further contact between Jacob and Esau was recorded. Esau would understand this to be evidence of his brother's ongoing deceit and deception, in that Jacob failed to keep his promise to meet him in Seir. Esau had been willing to reconcile, but Israel could not simply return to a previous way of life without being absorbed in the larger culture of Babylon, to the detriment of God's plan. Israel needed time and space in which to develop the culture God had called him to develop. However, such development would prove to be more difficult than he first imagined.

Dinah

Genesis 34 opens with the defilement of Dinah, Leah's daughter, and the only daughter among the twelve sons of Jacob. Dinah had gone out to meet some of the women in the area, when

> "Shechem the son of Hamor the Hivite, the prince of the land, saw her, he seized her and lay with her and humiliated her" (Genesis 34:2).

The first violation of the new cultural mandate of Israel in their new homeland was sexual. The violation did not come from within Israel, but from the pagan culture in the land in which Israel had settled, from a prince of the land who had assumed his right to have the women of his choice. Most of the women of that culture would have been delighted to engage him and would have seen it as the opportunity of a lifetime. Prince Shechem had fallen in love with Dinah. Shechem asked Hamor, his father who was the leader of the clan, to secure Dinah to be his wife. Apparently, men had little concern for women's rights in those days. He had "seized" her and not tried to woo her. Nonetheless, Shechem wanted to "make things right."

When Israel's sons heard about it they were indignant. But Hamor told them of the prince's love for Dinah, that it was true love, and that it could be a model for further marriages of the two clans to live in peace and cooperation. Finally, Shechem said,

> "Let me find favor in your eyes, and whatever you say to me I will give. Ask me for as great a bride price and gift as you will, and I will give whatever you say to me. Only give me the young woman to be my wife" (Genesis 34:11-12).

He was seeking to make the best of a bad situation, a situation that he had created.

Israel and his sons responded deceitfully, saying

> "We cannot do this thing, to give our sister to one who is uncircumcised, for that would be a disgrace to us. Only on this condition will we agree with you—that you will become as we are by every male among you being circumcised. Then we will give our daughters to you, and we will take your daughters to ourselves, and we will dwell with you and become one people. But if you will not listen to us and be circumcised, then we will take our daughter, and we will be gone" (Genesis 34:14-17).

It seems that much of this negotiation has not been recorded, so the details are left to our imaginations. I imagine that much of Israel's story had been shared during the negotiations, telling them how Abraham had been called, and how that calling had passed to Isaac, and finally to Jacob. And how God had instituted circumcision as a sign of the covenant. So, if these Hivites wanted to share in Israel's blessing, they would need to accept the covenant, and the sign of the covenant—circumcision. They accepted the invitation to unite with Israel and with Israel's God, so they took this message back to their city to insure that the agreement would be widely accepted. They then took this message to their city gates, making it public:

> "These men are at peace with us; let them dwell in the land and trade in it, for behold, the land is large enough for them. Let us take their daughters as wives, and let us give them our daughters. Only on this condition will the men agree to dwell with us to become one people—when every male among us is circumcised as they are circumcised. Will not their livestock, their property and all their beasts be ours? Only let us agree with them, and they will dwell with us"(Genesis 34:21-23).

They all agreed and were circumcised. It's hard to imagine how that all happened.

Nonetheless, on the third day after the circumcision, while the Hivites were still sore, two of Israel's sons, Simeon and Levi, raided the Hivite camp, killed all of the Hivite males in retaliation for offending Dinah, and brought her home. Likely this means that they killed all the Hivite males who stood in the way of their taking Dinah back. The old habits of revenge were difficult to overcome. Under stress and difficulty the old habits of Babylonia reemerged as the rest of Israel's sons joined in by stripping the city of its wealth.

> "Then Jacob said to Simeon and Levi, 'You have brought trouble on me by making me stink to the inhabitants of the land, the Canaanites and the Perizzites. My numbers are few, and if they gather themselves against me and attack me, I shall be destroyed, both I and my household.' But they said, 'Should he treat our sister like a prostitute?'" (Genesis 34:30-31).

Immediately following, the biblical story shifts to God's response to this massacre. During this Hivite episode Scripture continually refers to Israel as Jacob, suggesting that the change of character God brought about was still tenuous, still in process. God told Jacob to return to Bethel and live there because he could not stay in Shechem without incurring more difficulties issuing from Hivite counter revenge. As part of that instruction Jacob told his family to

> "Put away the foreign gods that are among you and purify yourselves and change your garments. Then let us arise and go up to Bethel, so that I may make there an altar to the God who answers me in the day of my distress and has been with me wherever I have gone" (Genesis 35:2-3).

During their Hivite excursion they had taken on some of the pagan gods and culture of the Hivites, which God had forbidden them to do. So, Jacob collected the gods (figurines) and buried them. The story of the Shechem massacre spread through the land and caused other tribes to fear Israel. Then having safely arrived in Bethel, God renewed His covenant, saying,

> "'Your name is Jacob; no longer shall your name be called Jacob, but Israel shall be your name.' So he called his name Israel. And God said to him, 'I am God Almighty: be fruitful and multiply. A nation and a company of nations shall come from you, and kings shall come from your own body. The land that I gave to Abraham and Isaac I will give to you, and I will give the land to your offspring after you'" (Genesis 35:10-12).

Following this, Isaac and Rebekah died and were buried. The story then continues with an accounting of Esau's descendants, which were many.

THE WORD INTO THE WORLD

Joseph, Jacob's youngest son, was a lot like Jacob had been as a young boy. He was sensitive and smart. One day when Joseph was a teenager he was tending the flocks with his older brothers. He was much younger than they were, but he was his father's favorite, which caused some problems among the brothers. Scripture suggests that his brothers didn't treat him very well, as can be the case among brothers. That day "Joseph brought back a bad report about them to their father" (Genesis 37:2). He probably told his dad what was going on, that they were picking on him. It's a common scene.

To make things worse, Jacob made Joseph a special robe or coat. It was ornate and had many colors. Scripture does not say that it was a robe of authority, but that doesn't matter because it does say that Jacob favored Joseph, which meant that Joseph had Jacob's ear. Apparently, Jacob had not made similar coats for his other sons. Official or not, Joseph was in a position of authority, a position of privilege and blessing, suggested by his report to his father and his special robe. The fact that the youngest son had the highest privilege and authority did not set well with Joseph's brothers.

The scene is now set for God to act in the world, to make a splash in world history. God's action began with Joseph's dream.

> "He (Joseph) said to them, 'Hear this dream that I have
> dreamed: Behold, we were binding sheaves in the field,
> and behold, my sheaf arose and stood upright. And behold,
> your sheaves gathered around it and bowed down to my

sheaf.' His brothers said to him, 'Are you indeed to reign over us? Or are you indeed to rule over us?" So they hated him even more for his dreams and for his words. Then he dreamed another dream and told it to his brothers and said, 'Behold, I have dreamed another dream. Behold, the sun, the moon, and eleven stars were bowing down to me.' But when he told it to his father and to his brothers, his father rebuked him and said to him, 'What is this dream that you have dreamed? Shall I and your mother and your brothers indeed come to bow ourselves to the ground before you?' And his brothers were jealous of him, but his father kept the saying in mind" (Genesis 37:6-11).

God's action involved the playing out of this dream. Dreams are often symbolic so it should not surprise us to find symbolism used in the text. The first part of the dream is about work, labor, and Joseph's work played a position of prominence in the unfolding story. The second part of the dream brings additional clarity. The sun can represent Jacob or Jacob's authority among God's people (which only included Jacob's family at the time). The moon can represent his wife (or wives), in that the wife represents the lesser authority than the husband in the family. And the eleven stars can represent their sons, numbering twelve if we include Joseph. The grandiosity of the idea of sun, moon, and stars bowing to Joseph symbolizes God's involvement. The dream was not about Joseph's role in the family, but about God's role in the world. Regardless, the dream made the whole family uncomfortable. The brothers found more cause to dislike Joseph, but Jacob made an effort to remember Joseph's dream. He likely wrote it down.

One day when the brothers were pasturing the flock at Shechem, Jacob sent Joseph to see how they were doing. This means that Joseph was not working with them in the field, but had been with his father. It seems relatively harmless that Joseph would check up on his brothers, but when he did he found that the brothers were not at Shechem. They had gone to Dothan. Shechem, originally a Canaanite city, was in the territory of Manasseh, and would become the first capital of the nation of Israel. Dotham, which means "two wells," was about twelve miles north of Samaria. The existence of wells meant that it was a caravan stop because sufficient water was there.

The brothers saw or heard that Joseph was coming to check up on them, which seems to have been a regular feature of his family work, and the brothers were not happy about it. So, they conspired to kill him. Note this familiar murder theme, reminiscent of Cain, coming into play again. The plan was to kill Joseph and bury him in a pit, but retain his precious blood-stained robe as evidence that he had been mauled to death by some wild beast. If we are looking for an upgrade of moral character on the part of God's people, it's not here. The brothers appear to be as ruthless as any of the Cainites or any of the other Godless people in the world.

But Ruben stepped up to suggest that they not kill him, but throw him into a pit and let him die a natural death of dehydration. This way the brothers could claim to be guiltless of his death. Ruben also secretly harbored a plan to rescue Joseph and return him home, likely hoping for some reward. Ruben convinced the others of his plan, and they took his fancy coat and threw Joseph into a pit.

Shortly thereafter, a caravan of Ishmaelites stopped for water, and the brothers (without Ruben) hatched another idea. They would sell Joseph into slavery to the Ishmaelites who would take him to Egypt. And so they did. When Ruben returned he was brokenhearted to learn what they had done because it had spoiled his plan. Nonetheless, the brothers were proud that they had not only gotten rid of Joseph, but also had made a profit. They then slaughtered a goat, bloodied Joseph's robe, and went home to tell their father that Joseph had been killed by a wild animal. Jacob never recovered. He would mourn Joseph for the rest of his life.

Meanwhile, the Ishmaelites sold Joseph to Potiphar, a captain of the guard in Egypt. Joseph was smart and creative, so he worked himself into a good position in Egypt. He ended up working for Potiphar, who was an officer in Pharaoh's court. In fact, Potiphar

> "made him overseer of his house and put him in charge of all that he had. From the time that he made him overseer in his house and over all that he had, the LORD blessed the Egyptian's house for Joseph's sake; the blessing of the LORD was on all that he had, in house and field. So he left all that he had in Joseph's charge, and because of him he had no concern about anything but the food he ate" (Genesis 39:4-6).

Joseph had much freedom in Egypt because his duties required him to have access to many people and things. One day Potiphar's wife tried to seduce Joseph, but Joseph would have nothing to do with it. Potiphar's wife, feeling spurned, told Potiphar that Joseph had tried to seduce her, reversing the actual facts of the case. The accusation landed Joseph in prison.

> "But the LORD was with Joseph and showed him steadfast love and gave him favor in the sight of the keeper of the prison. And the keeper of the prison put Joseph in charge of all the prisoners who were in the prison. Whatever was done there, he was the one who did it. The keeper of the prison paid no attention to anything that was in Joseph's charge, because the LORD was with him. And whatever he did, the LORD made it succeed" (Genesis 39:21-23).

Note God's involvement, keeping Joseph safe and utilizing his organizational skills. The Lord was the key to Joseph's success. We can also note that Joseph appears to live a life of moral improvement, compared to previous Hebrew leaders. We see this exemplified in his behavior with Potiphar's wife, in his organizational abilities, and in his sense of responsibility. Scripture identified it as God's blessing. God's blessing had put him in a privileged position in Pharoh's court, even in prison.

Soon, two other prisoners from Pharaoh's kitchen staff were imprisoned, and at some point each had a troubling dream. The trouble was that they did not understand their dreams or what they meant. Joseph noticed their fallen countenance, and asked about their trouble. When they confided that the dreams had not been interpreted, Joseph reminded them that interpretation belongs to God. Joseph then asked about their dreams and interpreted them. Those particular dreams and their interpretation are not central to the story, so you can read them for yourself. They just set up Joseph as being a valuable dream interpreter in Pharaoh's court or orbit.

The story that Joseph could interpret dreams spread, so when Pharaoh had a dream that his priests could not interpret he called for Joseph. Pharaoh's dream was about a coming drought that would wreak havoc in Egypt and throughout the Middle East. The interpretation resulted in a plan to save enough food to weather the drought. It made sense, Pharaoh bought it, and put Joseph in charge of planning and executing the plan that would preserve Egypt through the drought.

> "Joseph was thirty years old when he entered the service of Pharaoh king of Egypt. And Joseph went out from the presence of Pharaoh and went through all the land of Egypt. During the seven plentiful years the earth produced abundantly, and he gathered up all the food of these seven years, which occurred in the land of Egypt, and put the food in the cities. He put in every city the food from the fields around it. And Joseph stored up grain in great abundance, like the sand of the sea, until he ceased to measure it, for it could not be measured" (Genesis 41:46-49).

Pharaoh was happy because Egypt prospered during the drought, even because of the drought—or actually because of Joseph's planning for the drought because Joseph's preparation increased Pharaoh's power and kingdom as various people turned to him for help during the drought.

In time the drought reached Israel, and Jacob and his family also had to come to Egypt for food. Joseph recognized them immediately, though they did not recognize Joseph, who then tricked them into coming to Egypt. At the height of the story Joseph's earlier dream was fulfilled as Jacob and his family prostrated themselves to an Egyptian authority that they did not recognize as being Joseph, their brother. The symbolic sun, moon, and eleven stars bowed to Joseph in fulfillment of the earlier dream.

Joseph then revealed his identity to them, and arranged for all of Israel's children and grandchildren to live in Egypt, where they prospered greatly under Joseph's care for many, many years.

Jacob eventually died in Egypt, fully satisfied and greatly blessed by what God had done for him and his family. He could claim that God had been faithful to His promise to Abraham to make him the father of many.

After Joseph died, a different Pharaoh arose who had not known him. And because Israel (Jacob's people) had instituted cultural practices that differentiated Israelites from their neighbors, following the traditions of Abraham, the new Pharaoh became concerned that the Israelites were outnumbering the Egyptians in Egypt. So he put the Israelites to work building Egyptian fortresses, cities. Soon, he became frightened by what he imagined they could do if they all turned against him. So he hatched a plan to reduce their population by killing Hebrew babies as a way of reducing their power in Egypt. He ordered Hebrew midwives to kill the male babies.

> "But the midwives feared God and did not do as the king of Egypt commanded them, but let the male children live" (Exodus 1:17).

One of those male children was named Moses.

Moses

> "Now a man from the house of Levi went and took as his wife a Levite woman. The woman conceived and bore a son, and when she saw that he was a fine child, she hid him three months. When she could hide him no longer, she took for him a basket made of bulrushes and daubed it with bitumen and pitch. She put the child in it and placed it among the reeds by the river bank. And his sister stood at a distance to know what would be done to him. Now the daughter of Pharaoh came down to bathe at the river, while her young women walked beside the river. She saw the basket among the reeds and sent her servant woman, and she took it. When she opened it, she saw the child, and behold, the baby was crying. She took pity on him and said, 'This is one of the Hebrews' children.' Then his sister said to Pharaoh's daughter, 'Shall I go and call you a nurse from the Hebrew women to nurse the child for you?' And Pharaoh's daughter said to her, 'Go.' So the girl went and called the child's mother. And Pharaoh's daughter said to

her, 'Take this child away and nurse him for me, and I will give you your wages.' So the woman took the child and nursed him. When the child grew older, she brought him to Pharaoh's daughter, and he became her son. She named him Moses, 'Because,' she said, 'I drew him out of the water'" (Exodus 2:1-10).

Moses grew up in Pharaoh's court which provided him with a royal education. He was a man of great privilege, but was also made aware of his Hebrew lineage. He was raised as Pharaoh's grandson by Pharaoh's daughter. Nothing is known of Moses' younger years.

What we do know is that one day he witnessed an Egyptian beating a Hebrew. And perceiving it as an injustice, he killed the Egyptian in the process of stopping it, thinking that no one saw him do it. He was wrong, and rumors of his homicide spread through the community, finally reaching Pharaoh, his grandfather. Pharaoh could not let it stand and condemned Moses to death. So Moses fled to Midian.

Again, Moses took the role of protector of Hebrews acting with chivalry toward some Midian women at a well. They were daughters of a Midianite priest who offered Moses work and shelter, thinking that Moses, an apparent Egyptian, was a good man, having done what he did for his daughters. Soon after, Jethro, the Midianite priest, offered his daughter Zipporah to Moses. So, Moses married her and remained with Jethro.

While Moses was in Midian God heard the cry of oppression from His people in Egypt. Moses was likely aware of it as well, having been close to Pharaoh's court, and now an Egyptian fugitive. One day Moses had an epiphany.

> "Now Moses was keeping the flock of his father-in-law, Jethro, the priest of Midian, and he led his flock to the west side of the wilderness and came to Horeb, the mountain of God. And the angel of the LORD appeared to him in a flame of fire out of the midst of a bush. He looked, and behold, the bush was burning, yet it was not consumed. And Moses said, 'I will turn aside to see this great sight, why the bush is not burned.' When the LORD saw that he turned aside to see, God called to him out of the bush, 'Moses,

Moses!' And he said, 'Here I am.' Then he said, 'Do not come near; take your sandals off your feet, for the place on which you are standing is holy ground.' And he said, 'I am the God of your father, the God of Abraham, the God of Isaac, and the God of Jacob.' And Moses hid his face, for he was afraid to look at God" (Exodus 3:21-6).

There is a similarity in this story to the vision that Abraham had as God was covenanting with him.

"When the sun had gone down and it was dark, behold, a smoking fire pot and a flaming torch passed between these pieces" (Genesis 15:17).

Both stories revealed God's local presence in the immediate experience of Abraham and Moses. Both involved fire, and both facilitated God's covenant. Both involved language that is both concrete and symbolic, suggesting an analogous meaning. While both descriptions can be understood in a literal sense, the unusualness of the images suggest that the writer had difficulty conveying his intended meaning or experience, as if the message was fuller and richer than human language can capture. The language suggests the commingling of transcendence and immediacy, infinitude and finitude.

The story tells us that God engaged Moses in an extended dialog about the affliction of His people in Egypt. God said that He had come to deliver His people out of their captivity and slavery in Egypt, and that He was calling Moses to lead the charge. Moses balked, "Who am I that I should go to Pharaoh and bring the children of Israel out of Egypt?" (Exodus 3:12). God answered:

"But I will be with you, and this shall be the sign for you, that I have sent you: when you have brought the people out of Egypt, you shall serve God on this mountain" (Genesis 3:12).

There are several important things to notice about this. First, none of this was Moses' idea. Moses tried to dodge getting drafted into doing God's work. Second, God's response encapsulated the gospel of Jesus Christ, though nothing was known of

Christ at this point in the story. God said to Moses from the burning bush, "I will be with you." God, who had provided humanity with language, would be with Moses for a particular purpose: so that the people of God could worship God in truth and in spirit. The two elements of this gospel message are: God's presence with His people, and His people's presence with God in worship. God's long range goal and purpose is to bring or establish language integrity in human culture. Language is the most powerful gift that God has given humanity, but its power depends on its integrity, its ability to accurately represent reality.

Moses then inquired about God's identity. Who will he represent when he speaks to Pharaoh?

> "God said to Moses, 'I AM WHO I AM.' And he said, 'Say this to the people of Israel, 'I AM has sent me to you'" (Genesis 3:14).

The Hebrew word translated I AM (הָיָה) literally means: 1. to exist; 2. to be or become; 3. to come into being, i.e. to happen, to occur. God identifies Himself as existence itself, or a personification of existence itself, except that where the idea of personification suggests an abstraction, here God identifies Himself as immediate and imminent rather than abstract.

> "God also said to Moses, 'Say this to the people of Israel, "The LORD, the God of your fathers, the God of Abraham, the God of Isaac, and the God of Jacob, has sent me to you." This is my name forever, and thus I am to be remembered throughout all generations'" (Exodus 3:15).

Here God also identified Himself as having historic integrity with previous generations, beginning with Abraham, with whom God established a special covenant of grace. The message that Moses was to bring to Pharaoh and the Hebrews was that God was aware of the slavery of His people, and was about to deliver them out of slavery in Egypt to a land of promise and wealth. This deliverance would not be immediate but would involve a protracted journey through "the land of the Canaanites, and the Hittites, and the Amorites, and the Perizzites, and the Hivites, and the Jebusites" (Genesis 3:17).

That journey would begin with a three day trip into the wilderness in order to sacrifice to or worship God. The immediate concern was worship apart from Egypt.

In addition, God knew that the separation of His enslaved people from Egypt would not come easily, but would only happen if Pharaoh was "compelled by a mighty hand" (Genesis 3:19). So, God would cause great challenge, trouble, difficulty, violence, and suffering to Egypt that would result in the ejection of the Hebrews from Egypt. The result would be the plunder of Egypt by the Hebrews, who would leave Egypt laden with Egyptian gold, silver, and clothing.

However, Moses was not yet convinced to take the job. He was to tell Pharaoh everything that God had told him, but Moses complained,

"Oh, my Lord, I am not eloquent, either in the past or since you have spoken to your servant, but I am slow of speech and of tongue. ... Oh, my Lord, please send someone else" (Exodus 4:10-13).

Moses' faithless response angered the Lord, so the Lord recruited Moses' brother, Aaron, to be the spokesman, and the two of them would represent God together. Note that Moses knew himself to lack linguistic integrity, but was nonetheless chosen to bring God's law, the Ten Commandments, to Israel. The problems in the Torah then, are not God's fault, but Moses' fault.

God's anger also had to do with Moses' commitment to His people, culminating in the odd story of Zipporah's circumcision of Moses' son. The text of this story is unclear about exactly who was circumcised, but the more important point was that Moses had not either been circumcised himself, or he had failed to circumcise his son, thus dropping the ball regarding the Abrahamic tradition of covenantal circumcision. The consequence of that story produced Moses full identification with the people of Israel.[1]

---

1 See Appendix: *The Circumcision Performed By Zipporah*, p. 286.

So, God brought ten plagues upon Egypt that resulted in the willing ejection of the Hebrews, who left laden with treasure. The plagues were given as a witness to God's power. That power did not simply free Israel, but also caused the Egyptians to willingly eject them from their servitude. The miracle was not simply freeing Israel from Egypt, but involved *making* the Egyptians *willingly* accomplish God's purpose. The story is long, complex, and famous. It is certainly worth your time to read. The lesson was that God used unbelievers to accomplish His will, thus establishing God's sovereignty. The story of Moses' leadership out of Egypt is messy. Time and again both Moses and Israel complain about one another. Both were reluctant to follow God's plan. But God was always faithful to His Word. He did what He said He would do.

PASSOVER

The final plague in Egypt involved the death of the first born sons of every family. The Jews were instructed to prepare themselves to leave Egypt the morning after the night the plague hit. They were to eat a special meal, and remain dressed all night, ready to leave at a moment's notice. They were also instructed to put the blood of the lamb they would eat for dinner that night on the doorposts of their homes. The spirit of death would see that blood and pass over that house, sparring the first-born sons of the Jews who followed these instructions.

So the Jews prepared themselves and the night of plague came. The spirit of death passed over the homes of the Jews. And they left Egypt the next morning in the midst of Egyptian calamity and mourning. And from that day forward Israel celebrated Passover.

> "This day shall be for you a memorial day, and you shall keep it as a feast to the LORD; throughout your generations, as a statute forever, you shall keep it as a feast. Seven days you shall eat unleavened bread. On the first day you shall remove leaven out of your houses, for if anyone eats what is leavened, from the first day until the seventh day, that person shall be cut off from Israel. On the first day you shall hold a holy assembly, and on the seventh day a holy assembly. No work shall be done on those days. But what

everyone needs to eat, that alone may be prepared by you. And you shall observe the Feast of Unleavened Bread, for on this very day I brought your hosts out of the land of Egypt. Therefore you shall observe this day, throughout your generations, as a statute forever" (Exodus 12:14-17).

As Israel traveled through the desert, she was guided by a pillar of fire at night and a pillar of cloud by day. Whatever these pillars were—possibly volcanoes, but we don't know for sure—they were seen by all and provided guidance. The fire provided light in the night, and the cloud provided direction during the day. Whatever these pillars were, they were immediate, available, direct, experiential, and helpful. Calvin provided an insightful comment in support of the idea that God's purpose was the institution of language integrity:

> "although the words of Moses seem in some measure to include the Lord in the cloud, we must observe the sacramental mode of speaking, wherein God transfers His name to visible figures; not to affix to them His essence, or to circumscribe His infinity, but only to show that He does not deceitfully expose the signs of His presence to men's eyes, but that the exhibition of the thing signified is at the same time truly conjoined with them" (*Calvin's Commentaries*, Exodus 13:21).

There needs to be integrity of correspondence between language (the sign) and reality (the thing signified) in order for language to be useful. If this is not the case, the meaning and/or usefulness of language is in doubt. Without this integrity language cannot be trusted to provide accurate information about reality. Science, technology, and morality (social cohesion) depend upon the veracity of language and communication.

Desert Wandering

Following the miraculous crossing of the Red Sea where Moses parted the water allowing Israel to cross, and drowning the Egyptian chariots that were chasing them, Israel immediately landed in the wilderness of Sin.[2] And the people grumbled against Moses because they missed the good food they had in

---

2 See Appendix, *Sin*, p. 289.

Egypt. So the Lord sent Manna, a fine, flake like edible growth that came with the morning dew and frost. It had a short shelf life of one day, except on Saturdays, when its shelf life was doubled. It provided sufficient sustenance for the Israelites in the desert, but was bland of taste.

> "Now the house of Israel called its name manna. It was like coriander seed, white, and the taste of it was like wafers made with honey" (Exodus 16:31).

In the very next chapter of Exodus we find the people complaining about the lack of water to drink.

> "So Moses cried to the LORD, "What shall I do with this people? They are almost ready to stone me" (Exodus 17:4).

God instructed Moses on how to get water for his people. The story revealed a flaw in Moses' character that kept him and that generation of desert wanderers from entering the Promised Land.[3] That particular generation, having grown up in Egypt, were so poisoned by their Egyptian experience that they were not able to overcome it. And God could not allow them to bring that poisonous attitude into Canaan, where His work with the development of His people would enter its next phase.

The Amalekites were aware of Egypt's defeat at the Red Sea and decided to pile on to that defeat by invading Egypt themselves. But between them and Egypt were the Israelites, laden with Egyptian loot. At this point Israel was completely unorganized and an easy target. Deuteronomy 25:17-19 fills out the story:

> "Remember what Amalek did to you on the way as you came out of Egypt, how he attacked you on the way when you were faint and weary, and cut off your tail, those who were lagging behind you, and he did not fear God. Therefore when the LORD your God has given you rest from all your enemies around you, in the land that the LORD your God is giving you for an inheritance to possess, you shall

---

3 See "Divergence," *Galatians—Backstory/Christory*, Phillip A. Ross, Pilgrim Platform Books, Marietta, Ohio, 2015, p. 132.

blot out the memory of Amalek from under heaven; you shall not forget."

The Amalekites attacked the weakest of the Israelites, stragglers who could hardly keep up with the main caravan. They acted like beasts, lions or wolves that go after the weak, the young and old stragglers. They separate them from the herd and pounce on them. In this way, the Amakekites functioned as beasts, as the lowest bestial aspects of humanity. Thus, they represent what God intends to eliminate from humanity. God intends to exterminate human bestiality and to inculcate human sapience.

> "Then the LORD said to Moses, 'Write this as a memorial in a book and recite it in the ears of Joshua, that I will utterly blot out the memory of Amalek from under heaven.' And Moses built an altar and called the name of it, The LORD Is My Banner, saying, 'A hand upon the throne of the LORD! The LORD will have war with Amalek from generation to generation'" (Exodus 17:14-16).

A better translation of verse 16 comes from the KJV: "For he said, Because the LORD hath sworn [that] the LORD [will have] war with Amalek from generation to generation." Here we have the literal words *having a hand on the throne of God* conveying a derived or symbolic meaning related to swearing an oath. The words about swearing an oath are not literally present in the Hebrew, but the meaning is central. The meaning here reinforces the seriousness of the idea of war against Amalek, because God has sworn to make it happen.

The command to completely exterminate *the memory* of Amalek[4] suggests something important, something that must not be overlooked or understated. This idea or phenomenon of what may look like genocide has caused many people to abandon the Bible because they think that this sentiment on God's part does not do justice to the idea that God's chief characteristic is love. However, the guiding presupposition in this study of God's great plan for humanity is that the Bible is veracious, defined as the quality of being correct, true, or as close to the truth as possible.

---

4   See Appendix: Amalekites, p. 290.

Even the errors of Scripture provide valuable lessons about God and His truth. The claim that there are no factual errors in the Bible is nonsense, and simply reveals a paucity of serious study on the part of the claimant.

The only way to understand this comment (Exodus 17:14-16) and maintain the veracity of the Bible is to assume that God's perspective and judgment against the memory of Amalek is right and just, that God's judgment in this matter is righteous. Any other position undermines the righteousness of God.

Our contemporary difficulty with this matter is that we know very little about Amalek, and tend to assume that the Amalekites are not much different than people today. However, we have no basis upon which to make such an assumption, other than our tendency to think that all people of all times, ages, and cultures are more similar than different.

We make such contemporary assumptions within the context of a modern, multicultural, global mindset that has never existed prior to the modern era. We, like people in any culture, are not aware of how our own culture has effected us, how it has changed our beliefs, habits, ways of life, and worldview. So, it is difficult for us to understand previous cultures, peoples, mindsets, etc. People always read their own cultural assumptions into the evaluations they make. No one is ever completely objective. Our best efforts to be objective are always tainted with a whole slew of assumptions that come from our own personal and cultural experience.

The only way for us today to properly evaluate Exodus 17:14-16 is to read it very carefully and do so against the backdrop of the whole of the Bible, Old Testament and New. We cannot be other than we are—postmodern people in the twenty-first century. Of course, we need to try to understand these verses from the perspective of those who first heard or read them. But we must not try to force our own understanding into their ancient categories. Rather, it is incumbent on us to realize that the Bible speaks afresh to every generation, bringing new light and understanding to the extant people of God. What God intended for them was for *them*, and what God intends for us in these verses may be different from what He intended for them. It is not that God has changed, but people have changed in the light of Christ. If people have not changed, then the whole Christian enterprise has been for naught. In addition, the different meanings acquired through different generations does not necessarily violate the veracity of Scripture any more than the different stages of growth from acorn to oak violate the truth of the character of the tree. God is alive, and life is dynamic not static.

God has defined Amalek as His chief rival or enemy. The spirit and culture of Amalek is absolutely and completely opposed to God—the God of the Bible, to what He stands for, and to His mission in the world. It is important to understand that the seed of Amalek is Esau, whom God hates (Malachi 1:3; Romans 9:13).

However, we must now make a distinction that the early Hebrews were unable to make. We must separate the humanity of the Amalekites from their culture. We know from our familiarity with the rest of the Bible and the continuity of its long story that God does not oppose the humanity of any people, but He does oppose human cultures that are not established on truth, the truth only He is able to provide through Scripture. God opposes cultures that do not engage in and honor linguistic integrity regarding the true character of reality. God is not interested in the death of His enemies, but He is interested in their conversion, their growth regarding linguistic integrity in the light of His truth. Thus, God's call for the blotting out of the memory of the Amalekites is not a call for the death of Amalekite people, but is a call for the elimination of Amalekite culture, or the elimination of those aspects of their culture that are not in line with the linguistic integrity of His Word, those aspects that are not true. God was not opposed to the Amalekites, but to the spirit and culture of Amalek, the memory and culture of Amalek.

We may come to an understanding of this by comparing it to a current issue in our contemporary world. ISIS[5] came into existence in 2014 when a group of fundamentalist Islamists declared the existence of an Islamic Caliphate, a governing body

---

5   See Appendix, ISIS, p. 292.

that has not existed since the Persian Empire prior to World War I. Interestingly, ISIS shares similarities with the worldview of ancient, biblical Amalekites, not just philosophically and theologically, but historically.

There is convincing argumentation that Islam is a seventh century resurrection of a very ancient religion that fits with what we know about the Amalekites.[6] Regardless, God's war with Amalek can be illustrated by the current situation we have with ISIS. ISIS will not abandon its jihad against the West, or America, or all cultures that are not governed by ISIS. ISIS is absolutely committed to the dominance of the world by ISIS, and will not share sovereignty with any other nation or culture. This illustrates God's problem with Amalek and the Amalekites. The problem is that no one can coexist with someone who is wholly committed to the destruction of the other. However, the important distinction to be made here is based on the whole of the Bible, which teaches God's love and concern for humanity, and differentiates between the culture and the people. Paul described it this way:

> "For we do not wrestle against flesh and blood, but against the rulers, against the authorities, against the cosmic powers over this present darkness, against the spiritual forces of evil in the heavenly places" (Ephesians 6:12).

So, as we read Paul's teaching back into the Old Testament, we discover that this was God's message all along. A more careful reading of the Old Testament text from Paul's perspective reveals this. But the sinfulness of Israel at that time blinded the ancient Israelites to the subtlety of God's words. And yet their historic blindness now serves to further illustrate the importance of hearing God's Word accurately and fully. Their blindness gave rise to Paul's clarification, which further emphasized the point. Herein lies the importance of understanding the whole biblical story, of reading each verse, each story, in the context of the whole story.

---

6   *Moon-O-Theism—Religion of A War and Moon God Prophet* (2-vols.), Yoel Natan, Lulu.com, 2006.

The other thing to note about this verse is that God said that *He* would blot out the *memory* of Amalek. It is not a command for Israel to take such action, but is a simple statement that God would do it Himself. Nor does it mean the death of persons; it means an adjustment in thinking or memory—history. Of course, this does not mean that God would do it apart from Israel's involvement. And this is illustrated by the battle scene that precedes this section.

> "Then Amalek came and fought with Israel at Rephidim. So Moses said to Joshua, 'Choose for us men, and go out and fight with Amalek. Tomorrow I will stand on the top of the hill with the staff of God in my hand.' So Joshua did as Moses told him, and fought with Amalek, while Moses, Aaron, and Hur went up to the top of the hill. Whenever Moses held up his hand, Israel prevailed, and whenever he lowered his hand, Amalek prevailed. But Moses' hands grew weary, so they took a stone and put it under him, and he sat on it, while Aaron and Hur held up his hands, one on one side, and the other on the other side. So his hands were steady until the going down of the sun. And Joshua overwhelmed Amalek and his people with the sword" (Exodus 17:8-13).

Clearly, Israel thought that the Amalekites were the enemy. They did not differentiate between culture and people. But having been exposed to Paul's teaching *we* cannot go back to the ancient Israelite understanding about the Amalekites. Rather, we must factor Paul's teaching into our understanding of God's Word.

At that time Israel thought that their power came from Moses's elevation of God's staff. Their perspective was magical, so God worked with them as they were. And the staff remained elevated and Israel won the battle. Had God not worked with them in this regard Israel may have been wiped out by the Amalekites. But God could not allow that to happen without abandoning his long-term mission. He had promised to work with Israel, and He had to keep His promise in order to demonstrate the integrity of His language, His Word.

According to Exodus 17:8 Amalek attacked Israel, Israel was not the aggressor. So Moses engaged the beliefs of Israel at that time to provide courage and leadership by holding up his staff in their sight. They believed that this act by Moses would grant them victory, and they were encouraged and strengthened by that belief. The objectivity of that belief was immaterial because the subjective power of visualization gave the Israelites the edge that won the battle.

Visualization is often used in modern sports and other performance-based activities to improve performance execution. We understand today that belief and/or confidence can have very powerful effects personally and socially. Did Moses engage in such visualization tactics that day on the battlefield? Of course he did. Visualization of the truth of God's Word is the definition of faith. Regardless, we understand today that there were no magic spells associated with Moses holding up his staff. But neither do we deny God's presence and active involvement.

JETHRO

Exodus 18 begins long into Moses' stay with his father-in-law, Jethro, a Midianite priest. Jethro was *not* an Israelite, and yet he said:

> "'Now I know that the LORD is greater than all gods, because in this affair they dealt arrogantly with the people.' And Jethro, Moses' father-in-law, brought a burnt offering and sacrifices to God; and Aaron came with all the elders of Israel to eat bread with Moses' father-in-law before God" (Exodus 18: 11-12).

Jethro was a convert. And because he was a convert he was able to bring an outsider's view to Moses' style of leadership. Moses had been adjudicating all of the cases that people brought before him—and there were many. Too many, according to Jethro, who asked:

> "What is this that you are doing for the people? Why do you sit alone, and all the people stand around you from morning till evening?" (Exodus 18:15).

Jethro correctly observed that Moses would not be able to keep up with the demands on him, and recommended that he appoint "able men from all the people, men who fear God, who are trustworthy and hate a bribe" (Exodus 18:23) to share the work load of adjudication. Moses agreed and took his advice. Herein lies the origin of the ancient Israelite court system.

On the heels of the establishment of ancient Israelite courts, God led Israel to Mount Sinai, where God said to Moses:

> "'Thus you shall say to the house of Jacob, and tell the people of Israel: You yourselves have seen what I did to the Egyptians, and how I bore you on eagles' wings and brought you to myself. Now therefore, if you will indeed obey my voice and keep my covenant, you shall be my treasured possession among all peoples, for all the earth is mine; and you shall be to me a kingdom of priests and a holy nation. These are the words that you shall speak to the people of Israel. So Moses came and called the elders of the people and set before them all these words that the LORD had commanded him. All the people answered together and said, 'All that the LORD has spoken we will do.' And Moses reported the words of the people to the LORD. And the LORD said to Moses, 'Behold, I am coming to you in a thick cloud, that the people may hear when I speak with you, and may also believe you forever'" (Exodus 19: 3-9).

Here for the first time we find Israel in full acknowledgment of God's covenant and their complete agreement to live in obedience to it, even though at this time they did not know what it entailed. *Following* their agreement God gave Moses the Ten Commandments.

In all likelihood, the journey in the desert to Mount Sinai occurred in the midst of volcanic activity to supply the pillar of fire by night and cloud by day. Could God use geological activity for His own purposes? Of course. Regardless, what led Israel was a pillar of cloud by day and a pillar of fire by night, and the natural explanation fits very well with volcanic activity. So, having arrived at the foot of Mount Sinai, we can speculate that following their covenant agreement with God, there was an increase of volcanic activity on Mount Sinai that produced a cloud, which served to symbolize the idea that the source of the covenant was God, not Moses.

> "When Moses told the words of the people to the LORD, the LORD said to Moses, 'Go to the people and consecrate them today and tomorrow, and let them wash their garments and be ready for the third day. For on the third day the LORD will come down on Mount Sinai in the sight of all the people. And you shall set limits for the people all around, saying, "Take care not to go up into the mountain or touch the edge of it. Whoever touches the mountain shall be put to death. No hand shall touch him, but he shall be stoned or shot; whether beast or man, he shall not live." When the trumpet sounds a long blast, they shall come up to the mountain'" (Exodus 19:10-13).

Imagine that Mount Sinai was an active volcano at the time. It is easy to comport the verses above with the reality of a volcano, with some lava flowing down, and instructions not to get near it. Again, this natural explanation does not remove or effect God's presence or role in this event. It just serves to make it more real for us today. Why would Moses think that a volcano was God? Because he witnessed the burning bush, another fire related event. God spoke to him from the fire, both times.

TEN COMMANDMENTS

Exodus 20 delivers the Ten Commandments. God began by stating His authorization to give law.

> "I am the LORD your God, who brought you out of the land of Egypt, out of the house of slavery" (Exodus 20:2).

He is God, we are not. He brought Israel out of Egyptian slavery. Because God brought Israel out of slavery we might think that He brought them into freedom. And He did! But it is a limited freedom, a freedom within certain boundaries. So, He began to set out freedom's boundaries.

> "You shall have no other gods before me" (Exodus 20:3)

First rule: no other gods before Me, beside Me, except Me. The acceptance of this rule insures that the responsibility for obedience to all of God's rules falls squarely upon those who have covenanted with God, both individually and collectively. No one else can make countervailing rules. God can break or change His laws, but no one else can. This also means that the Ten Commandments are perpetual, ever binding throughout history.

> "You shall not make for yourself a carved image, or any likeness of anything that is in heaven above, or that is in the earth beneath, or that is in the water under the earth. You shall not bow down to them or serve them, for I the LORD your God am a jealous God, visiting the iniquity of the fathers on the children to the third and the fourth generation of those who hate me, but showing steadfast love to thousands of those who love me and keep my commandments" (Exodus 20:4-5).

Literally: no carved idols. At the time figurines and statutes were widely used to represent the gods that God would not allow. He also disallowed any and all worship of (bowing down to) idols, and all service or work done for idols. Obviously, this would include making such figurines or statues. God forbade all activity associated with idolatry, which suggests that He was involved in changing their religion from the ancient religion of Ur that had been brought by Terah, which dominated the Middle East. Abraham had begun this process of change by instituting circumcision, which served to identify Israel as a unique people. This Second Commandment served to further sever Israel from her pagan roots in and experience of Ur so that God could begin afresh, or as fresh as possible.

A curse was added to help insure compliance. God threatened to visit

> "the iniquity of the fathers on the children to the third and the fourth generation of those who hate me" (Exodus 20:5).

God's threat involved inheritance or the social momentum of history. God would not only punish any offenders of His law, but would continue to punish the children, grandchildren, and great grandchildren of the offenders. What is being said here is not that God is vindictive, but that the nature of this sin is such that it is easily inherited by one's children, grandchildren, and great grandchildren because sin is not simply personal, but always has a cultural element that can be shared with others.

However, this curse is followed up by the promise of blessing related to obedience that is far greater than the curse. While the curse can last four generations, the blessings of obedience can last thousands of generations. The idea of multiple generations suggests the superior cultural nature of God's law.

> "You shall not take the name of the LORD your God in vain" (Exodus 20:7).

This rule is not simply about swearing in general, though that's an important issue. Rather, it is about swearing an oath to God. Such oaths must be taken very seriously, so seriously that the swearing of an oath to God must include a significant change in the person who makes the oath. To take something in vain means to make nothing of it. Nothing comes of something taken in vain.

The *thing* taken in this case is the name of the Lord. The name of a thing was a representation of the thing, of the essential character of the thing. The name symbolized and represented the character of the thing. And in this case, to take the name of the Lord meant to take on the character of the Lord personally. When Jesus' followers were first called Christians in Antioch, it was a name of derision. Unbelievers saw Jesus as a great failure, and called His followers "little Christs," or little failures. The idea was that a little failure was even worse than a great failure. But Paul reinterpreted the idea to mean that Christians were to "put on Christ" (Galatians 3:27), or to adopt the characteristics of Jesus. He even named some of them:

> "love, joy, peace, patience, kindness, goodness, faithfulness, gentleness, self-control" (Galatians 5:22-23).

To take the Lord's name in vain is to fail to engage the change of character that God has been working to bring to humanity, to make nothing of it, or allow it to come to nothing. Whether you are a believer or not, the story of the Bible is that God sent Jesus to provide a moral upgrade from the ancient religion of vengeance to the new religion of forgiveness, from the morality of selfishness to the morality of service, kindness.[7] To take the Lord's name in vain is to ignore or to make nothing of this story, this reality. To fail in this regard is to be guilty of squandering an extraordinary opportunity.

> "Remember the Sabbath day, to keep it holy. Six days you shall labor, and do all your work, but the seventh day is a Sabbath to the LORD your God. On it you shall not do any work, you, or your son, or your daughter, your male servant, or your female servant, or your livestock, or the sojourner who is within your gates. For in six days the LORD made heaven and earth, the sea, and all that is in them, and rested on the seventh day. Therefore the LORD blessed the Sabbath day and made it holy" (Exodus 20:8-11).

The world in which we live is a world of patterns and cycles—day and night, Spring, Summer, Fall, Winter, hot and cold, consume and defecate, work and rest, etc. We are creatures of habit who live in habitats, places where habits are engaged. This commandment points to the story of God's creation of the world, identifying God as the creator of our earthly and human habitat and the cycles and patterns of life. The various cycles maintain our existence and provide health and meaning for our lives. Ignorance and neglect of these cycles in which we live destroys our health and happiness—physical, mental, and spiritual. So, God has ordered our work/life cycle to reflect the order of His creation.

Because we are like God, created in His image, our ideal cycles are similar to His. He created the world in six days and rested on the seventh; so we also should work six days and rest on the seventh. However, the rest of our sabbath is not mere sleep, but involves the restoration of our relationship with God, a relationship that fills us to overflowing with meaning and purpose.

---

7 The root meaning of kind (מִין) is a group of people or things having similar characteristics. In the beginning God created various kinds, and the kinds treat one another kindly, as belonging to the same familial group.

Furthermore, the Eighth Day sabbath[8] of Christ has brought the foundation for the restoration of human fulfillment, of true holiness and happiness, of vital health and wholeness. Christ is God's *shalom* enfleshed, and we are called to share in it. It's a simple pattern, easy to engage, and full of blessings. We are to grow in the kindness (as previously defined) of God.

> "Honor your father and your mother, that your days may be long in the land that the LORD your God is giving you" (Exodus 20:12).

The command to honor our own mothers and fathers is a command to respect and appreciate tradition and history. But because God is involved in a world-wide religious change, moving from practices of vengeance to practices of forgiveness, all traditions are not in view here. We are called to abandon the traditions of vengeance and to embrace the new traditions of forgiveness. We are to take our natural affection for our own children, our desire to raise them right, and apply that affection to others, not neglecting the special status of our own children but abandoning our fear that others will take vengeance on us. It is through the practice of embracing the sentiments of love and forgiveness that our addiction to fear and vengeance can be overcome.

> "You shall not murder" (Exodus 20:13).

The Hebrew word (רָצַח) also covers causing human death through carelessness or negligence.

> "You shall not commit adultery" (Exodus 20:14).

All forms of sexual engagement with anyone other than one's own spouse are forbidden. Sexual orgasm produces highly addictive endorphins in the human body, making orgasm one of

---

8 Christians worship on the Eighth Day for a variety of reasons, central to which is the fact that Christ fulfilled the Sabbath and that fulfillment inaugurated God's eternal Sabbath, which stands outside of time yet applies to time. See: Exodus 22:30; Leviticus 9:1; 12:3; 14:10,23; 15:14,29; 22:27; 23:36,39; Numbers 6:10; 7:54; 29:35; 1 Kings 8:66; 12:32,33; 2 Chronicles 7:9; 29:17; Nehemiah 8:18; Ezekiel 43:27; Luke 1:59; Acts 7:8; Philippians 3:5.

the most—if not the most—addictive experiences possible. God has chosen to bind that particular, universal addiction to Himself by channeling sexuality through the marriage covenant, which mirrors our covenant with God. We see in the First Commandment that God requires our absolute fidelity to Him as God. God is jealous for this one-to-one relationship with Him; and this jealousy is reflected in the marriage covenant. God has chosen to use the power of sexual experience to strengthen the integrity of our love for Him by insisting that we honor our marriage covenant, and thereby honor all of our covenanted social responsibilities, i.e., honesty, integrity, faithfulness, loyalty, etc.

> "You shall not steal" (Exodus 20:15).

The commandment against theft includes all forms of fraud, confiscation, and usury. We are not to take advantage of others. Rather, we are to serve one another willingly and lovingly.

> "You shall not bear false witness against your neighbor" (Exodus 20:16).

False witness includes deceit and lying for the purpose of personal gain or the personal gain of others. Personal gain includes more than money and wealth. It includes the whole array of psychological gain that provides us with some advantage that we can exercise over others, i.e., power, prestige, and pride.

> "You shall not covet your neighbor's house; you shall not covet your neighbor's wife, or his male servant, or his female servant, or his ox, or his donkey, or anything that is your neighbor's" (Exodus 20:17).

To covet (חָמַד) is to delight in or desire. We are commanded to take control of our own desires, to not live in subjection to our preferences, attractions, fascinations, addictions, etc. We are not to allow our desires to control our behavior, but subject our behavior to God's law, God's desires. The strongest of these desires is the sexual desire, which God aptly lists here, but this commandment is not limited to sexual desire. What we know as the advertising business is built on the exploitation of human covetousness. So, our ability to obey this command means disconnecting from the constant barrage of advertisements. This may include disengagement from electronic devices, or training one's self to disregard advertising messages.

Of course, the idea of coveting includes much more than advertising, but for contemporary people it is extremely difficult to get beyond personal subjugation to advertising. The constant barrage of advertising is one of the most dangerous and spiritually debilitating experiences ever devised, and few people today ever escape it.

In response to God's gift to Moses the people responded:

> "Now when all the people saw the thunder and the flashes of lightning and the sound of the trumpet and the mountain smoking, the people were afraid and trembled, and they stood far off and said to Moses, 'You speak to us, and we will listen; but do not let God speak to us, lest we die.' Moses said to the people, 'Do not fear, for God has come to test you, that the fear of him may be before you, that you may not sin.' The people stood far off, while Moses drew near to the thick darkness where God was" (Exodus 20:18-21).

Again, note the allusions to volcanic activity. Also note that the people showed no interest in hearing God themselves. They were gripped by fear that hearing God would bring them death. This issue of *hearing* God is very important to the long story of the Bible, and the significance of the people's fear and unwillingness to hear God directly must not be overlooked. Moses assured them that God's intention was not to kill them but to test them, to test their faithfulness. God's strategy was to keep them in fear in order to control their temptation to sin. So the people backed off while Moses "drew near to the thick darkness where God was" (Exodus 20:21).

Looking at this verse with the light of Christ (knowledge of the whole biblical story) we see something odd that Moses' contemporaries did not see: that God was dwelling in thick darkness. The many verses that associate God with light suggest that this scene is, at best, odd. In the light of Christ it suggests that the Ten Commandments are to be associated with darkness, not only light. This is not to say that the Commandments are bad or not useful, but only that something about them is related to darkness. Something was being occluded. The people were not willing to hear God directly, but only through Moses.

We might make sense of this by noticing that the Ten Commandments came to people who did not know God personally, and who had no desire to know Him. Their only connection to God was fear. Isaiah had prophesied about this as he looked forward to a day when the Messiah would come:

> "The people who walked in darkness have seen a great
> light; those who dwelt in a land of deep darkness, on them
> has light shone" (Isaiah 9:2).

Matthew recalled Isaiah's prophecy and applied it to Jesus Christ as its fulfillment (Matthew 4:14-16). Both Isaiah and Matthew understood these Old Testament Jews, who were still living, to be veiled in darkness. God had caused them to dwell in darkness. But why would God do this? To His own people? We know from the theology of the Reformation that the purpose of the law is three-fold: 1) as a curb to keep sin in check, 2) as a mirror to show us our guilt, 3) as a guide to reveal the path forward. If people are to see the reality of God, they must first see their own reality. And God's law shows us the reality of our own sinfulness. We can only see our sinfulness by looking at ourselves from God's perspective, from the perspective of God's law, which sets the minimum acceptable behavior regarding sin. Thus, the first thing that people see when genuinely confronted by the reality of God's law is their own sinfulness, their own lack of conformity to God's law.

Life on earth provides such a strong contrast regarding obedience to God's law, that the best descriptor of our historic reality is "darkness." Moses alluded to this reality by shrouding God in thick darkness on the mountain of revelation. Indeed, the history of God's people in the Old Testament is a history of thick darkness that culminated in the destruction of Jerusalem and the Temple in A.D. 70. For those who have eyes to see, who understand the whole story of the Bible, the story of the Old Testament leads to the conclusive destruction that finally manifested in A.D. 70.

Back to our story, Moses came down from Mount Sinai with the Ten Commandments in hand. He did not come down with the array of laws found in Exodus 21-31, ten chapters of detailed applications of the Ten Commandments and various punishments for disobedience. These chapters were added later as Moses and the elders that Jethro recommended worked out some of the details. But that's another story.

The unfolding story of God's revelation picks up in Exodus 32 where we learn that the people became frustrated when Moses' return from the mountaintop was delayed. So they asked Aaron, Moses' brother who was charged with being the priest who communicated with the people, to make them idols of gold. Aaron complied and

> "received the gold from their hand and fashioned it with a graving tool and made a golden calf. And they said, 'These are your gods, O Israel, who brought you up out of the land of Egypt!'" (Exodus 32:4).

At this point Aaron and the people were comfortable with the familiarity of their old religious paganism. Moses was the leader of a new religion that God was bringing to them, and Aaron was to be the spokesperson. But Aaron had not spoken with God, nor had he read the Ten Commandments yet. Moses had been gone for some time, and Aaron's actions simply established his existing paganism, and that of the people. Note also that Aaron did not identify the golden calf to be the god of Israel, the people did! Without godly leadership people tend to default to idolatry. Granted that at this point Moses had not returned with the Ten Commandments so no one knew the details of the covenant they had agreed to, so they did not know the content of God's law.

The recitation of this incident was not intended to affix blame on Aaron, nor on the people. It was simply a report of what happened, and the report reveals the propensity of humanity for idolatry. This point is obscured by the placement of the ten intervening chapters of Exodus (21-31), which makes it easy to lose this storyline. Nonetheless, Aaron did his priestly duties by building an altar for the golden calf and declaring a feast in its honor.

> "And they rose up early the next day and offered burnt offerings and brought peace offerings. And the people sat down to eat and drink and rose up to play" (Exodus 32:6).

Before Moses returned, God informed him that his people were already in default of their covenant promises. We might chide God for accusing the people of faithlessness when at that point they did not know what He expected because His law had not yet been shown to them. But at that time they did not know that they were being called to something new, and that they had reverted to their old ways. They did not know God or what God wanted of them. They did not know how to be faithful, so they just did the same old religious things they always had done.

Interestingly, Moses and God then negotiated for the lives of the people. Here we see Moses wrestling with God as Jacob had done. God's wrath burned hot against them because of their idolatry, and He wanted to destroy them and make a great nation of Moses, as He had promised Abraham. But Moses intervened, reminding God about what He had already promised to Abraham—and these were the children of Abraham! Did God want to break His promise by killing them and starting over? And what would people think of Him if He were to do that? So,

> "the LORD relented from the disaster that he had spoken of bringing on his people" (Exodus 32:14).

When Moses finally returned with the tablets to the people he found them dancing before the golden calf. And

> "Moses' anger burned hot, and he threw the tablets out of his hands and broke them at the foot of the mountain (Exodus 32:19).

Moses, flush with anger, melted the golden calf, ground the gold into power and made the people drink it. Moses' genius was that he was able to successfully negotiate with God, but his weakness, shown in this episode, was his fiery temper and independent creativity. First, he broke the tablets in a fit of anger. Second, did

God tell him to make the people drink powered gold? No! He did that of his own accord, which revealed his most serious flaw.

Moses took Aaron aside to hear his report. When Moses got back to the people, they were running wild, completely out of control, causing "derision of their enemies" (Exodus 32:25). Their enemies—Moses' enemies, God's enemies—felt completely justified as they laughed and made fun of those who wanted to follow God or Moses. Moses was incensed and God's honor was shamed. So, Moses issued a challenge: "Who is on the LORD's side? Come to me" (Exodus 32:26). Apparently, only the sons of Levi responded. And Moses said to them:

> "Thus says the LORD God of Israel, 'Put your sword on your side each of you, and go to and fro from gate to gate throughout the camp, and each of you kill his brother and his companion and his neighbor'" (Exodus 32:27).

God responded out of thick darkness to kill all who would not come to the Lord's side, and about three thousand people died that day at the hand of the Levites. Moses then consoled the Levites who had killed their own families and neighbors:

> "Today you have been ordained for the service of the LORD, each one at the cost of his son and of his brother, so that he might bestow a blessing upon you this day" (Exodus 32:29).

The difficulty in trying to justify any of this is that it cannot be done. There is nothing justifiable about this episode—not Moses, not Aaron, not the people, nor the bloodshed. It all issues from the thick darkness of sin. Again, God brought sin upon Israel as a consequence of Adam's sin. Here we see that the consequences of Adam's sin survived the great flood and the promises to Abraham. The long story is that the consequences of Adam's sin persist until Jesus puts an end to them.

The immediate story continues when the next day Moses went back up the mountain to the Lord, hoping to make atonement for the sin of his people and get another copy of God's law. Moses brought some conditions to God: forgive their sin or blot me out of your book right now; forgive them or I quit! And the Lord agreed:

> "Whoever has sinned against me, I will blot out of my book" (Exodus 32:33).

In the meantime, Moses was to lead the people, and God would send an angel to lead Moses. Nevertheless, said God,

> "in the day when I visit, I will visit their sin upon them" (Exodus 32:34).

Moses' leadership would not absolve them of their sin. Who was God talking about? The Levites had already killed those who would not commit to God's side, so He must have meant the Levites, who had added to their sin by violating the Sixth Commandment against murder. So, the Lord sent a plague upon them "because they made the calf" (Exodus 32:35).

When it was time to leave Mount Sinai God again commanded Moses:

> "Depart; go up from here, you and the people whom you have brought up out of the land of Egypt, to the land of which I swore to Abraham, Isaac, and Jacob, saying, 'To your offspring I will give it.' I will send an angel before you, and I will drive out the Canaanites, the Amorites, the Hittites, the Perizzites, the Hivites, and the Jebusites. Go up to a land flowing with milk and honey; but I will not go up among you, lest I consume you on the way, for you are a stiff-necked people" (Exodus 33:1-3).

This message was not good news to the Israelites, who called it a "disastrous word" (Exodus 33:4) and removed their ornaments as they mourned for themselves. Neither did God refer to them as *His* people, but as the people that Moses had brought from Egypt. God did not go with them, but sent an angel to guide them, for they would be destroyed if they approached God full of sin. He called them stiff-necked, or stubborn. Note also that God omitted the Amalekites from the list of people that He would drive out of Canaan. Previously He said that the Amalekites would be an ongoing problem.

For The Whole World

Moses continued to negotiate on behalf of his people by acknowledging that he had brought this people out of Egypt, but Moses complained that God had not provided sufficient leadership. Moses implored God to consider these Israelites to be His people because Moses had favor in God's sight. Moses wondered how the people would gain God's favor if God did not go with them. And if God would go with them, they would be unique among the nations *because* God went with them. God finally agreed.

> "This very thing that you have spoken I will do, for you have found favor in my sight, and I know you by name" (Exodus 33:17).

God's agreement gave Moses confidence. So, Moses asked to see God's glory (כָּבוֹד), which literally means *weight*, and figuratively suggests His splendor or abundance. But Moses could not bear God's glory, so God showed him his *goodness*, saying:

> "I will make all my goodness pass before you and will proclaim before you my name 'The LORD.' And I will be gracious to whom I will be gracious, and will show mercy on whom I will show mercy" (Exodus 33:19).

God would demonstrate His character by dispensing grace and mercy, but not to everyone. Even Moses was forbidden to see God's face, to know God fully, intimately, because Moses would not be able to deal with the full weight of his burden as the Israelite leader. Moses was only allowed a glimpse of God's "back parts," not His face (Exodus 33:22-23). While Moses wanted to see God's full glory, he was in no position to make sense of God, in part because God's story was yet to be unfolded in human history. Knowledge of God is not abstract or theoretical, but is intimate and personal, but also social and comprehensive. The full knowledge of God, His glory, would have to wait for its full revelation in human history.

REWRITE

Exodus 34 is about the rewriting of the Ten Commandments after Moses broke them in anger when he came down the mountain the first time. A careful reading of the story as it is presented provides some oddities. God promised that He would rewrite the Ten Commandments (Exodus 34:1) if Moses would provide new tablets. Back up on the mountain God "proclaimed the name of the Lord." That is, He spoke of His own character:

> "The LORD, the LORD, a God merciful and gracious, slow to anger, and abounding in steadfast love and faithfulness, keeping steadfast love for thousands, forgiving iniquity and transgression and sin, but who will by no means clear the guilty, visiting the iniquity of the fathers on the children and the children's children, to the third and the fourth generation" (Exodus 34:6-7).

This is quite a change from Exodus 32:10, where God first reacted to the sin of Israel's folly of dancing before the golden calf that Aaron had made.

> "Then the LORD said to Moses: 'I have seen this people. Look what a stiff-necked people they are! So now, leave me alone so that my anger can burn against them and I can destroy them, and I will make from you a great nation'" (Exodus 32:10).

Here God's anger and wrath dominate His reaction, where in Exodus 34 His grace and mercy dominate. Moses' previous response was also quite different. The first time Moses said:

> "Alas, this people has sinned a great sin. They have made for themselves gods of gold. But now, if you will forgive their sin—but if not, please blot me out of your book that you have written" (Exodus 32:31-32).

This second time he said:

> "If now I have found favor in your sight, O Lord, please let the Lord go in the midst of us, for it is a stiff-necked people, and pardon our iniquity and our sin, and take us for your inheritance" (Exodus 34:9).

Here Moses leaned on the idea that God *had* found favor with Moses, and because of this Moses asked God to extend that favor to Israel. God agreed, and reminded Moses of His covenant and its uniqueness and its wonder, and cautioned that

> "it is a fearful thing that I am doing with you. Obey what I am commanding you this day. I am going to drive out before you the Amorite, the Canaanite, the Hittite, the Perizzite, the Hivite, and the Jebusite. Be careful not to make a covenant with the inhabitants of the land where you are going, lest it become a snare among you." (Exodus 32:10-12).

Again, as God directs Israel to maintain her Mosaic culture by avoiding covenants with non-Israelites, we see that the Amalekites are excluded from the list of people God would drive out of Canaan. Then God reiterated the Ten Commandments to Moses, but this list of commandments is different than the first list in Exodus 20. Compare the commandments of Exodus 34:17-26 with those of Exodus 20, note that these latter appear to be the ones that Moses (not God)

> "wrote on the tablets the words of the covenant, the Ten Commandments" (Exodus 34:28).

When Moses brought these new tablets down "the skin of his face shone" (Exodus 34:29), but he was not aware of it. As he spoke to the people, they became afraid because "the brightness of the heavenly glory appeared in the face of Moses."[9] And when he finished speaking he put a veil over his face.

> "Whenever Moses went in before the LORD to speak with him, he would remove the veil, until he came out. And when he came out and told the people of Israel what he was commanded, the people of Israel would see the face of Moses, that the skin of Moses' face was shining. And Moses would put the veil over his face again, until he went in to speak with him" (Exodus 34:34-35).

Paul addressed issue:

> "Since we have such a hope, we are very bold, not like Moses, who would put a veil over his face so that the Israelites might not gaze at the outcome of what was being brought to an end. But their minds were hardened. For to this day, when they read the old covenant, that same veil

---

9   *Calvin's Commentaries*, Exodus 34:29, public domain.

remains unlifted, because only through Christ is it taken away. Yes, to this day whenever Moses is read a veil lies over their hearts. But when one turns to the Lord, the veil is removed. Now the Lord is the Spirit, and where the Spirit of the Lord is, there is freedom. And we all, with unveiled face, beholding the glory of the Lord, are being transformed into the same image from one degree of glory to another. For this comes from the Lord who is the Spirit" (2 Corinthians 3:12-18).

Paul said here that the whole of Moses' teaching and cultural practices operated under a veil, a shield, a filter. The purpose of a veil is to obscure or hide something. Neither Moses nor the early Israelites could see the fullness of God. Something was hidden from them, something they could not bear, something they were unable to see, something that was brought to light by Jesus Christ. Shielding or protecting is the benefit of a veil.

The role or doctrine of the veil in the Old Testament is important because, according to Paul (above), Christ removes the veil from the true teaching of the Bible. Christ removes the veil from our eyes so that we can see or understand the biblical story more clearly. But for now in the biblical story the veil was placed on Israel. What is the veil? The law served as blinkers or blinders for Israel, an analogy to a piece of horse tack that prevent horses seeing to the rear and, in some cases, to the side. They serve to keep the horse on the path by restricting their vision, their distractions.

Tabernacle

The first worship center Israel built was the Tabernacle, a portable earthly dwelling place for God, a place for sacrifices. It was a place, a mobile tent built to precise specifications, where God would dwell with His people. God specified to Moses every element of the Tabernacle and of the sacrifices to be made there. In the Tabernacle was the Ark of the Covenant, a gold covered wooden box to contain the tablets of the Ten Commandments. Other sacred items would also be added: Aaron's rod and some manna.[1] The Tabernacle was also furnished with various items used for worship and sacrifices—a table for bread, lampstands, an altar for incense and sacrifices, a bronze basin, curtains, and vestments for the priests.

The remainder of Exodus provides instructions for the building and use of the Tabernacle and its accouterments. Upon completion, the Tabernacle served as a signal beacon to guide Israel through the wilderness.

While we need to take the language of the cloud by day and fire by night literally, we must not be content with a literal reading because there is also much symbolism to be harvested. And yet, much of the symbolism is unclear at this point in the story. Indeed, it is veiled, shrouded in mystery yet begging for interpretation. It's mere presence sets up the desire and conditions for clarity or revelation, for the coming of someone or something that will provide clarity or reveal what was concealed or veiled.

---

[1] Curious that manna was included because it would only last one day, except of Saturdays.

The purpose of the Tabernacle was to escort Israel through the wilderness, to prepare them for arrival in Canaan, the land that God was going to give them.

> "Then the cloud covered the tent of meeting, and the glory of the LORD filled the tabernacle. And Moses was not able to enter the tent of meeting because the cloud settled on it, and the glory of the LORD filled the tabernacle. Throughout all their journeys, whenever the cloud was taken up from over the tabernacle, the people of Israel would set out. But if the cloud was not taken up, then they did not set out till the day that it was taken up. For the cloud of the LORD was on the tabernacle by day, and fire was in it by night, in the sight of all the house of Israel throughout all their journeys" (Exodus 40:34-38).

Moses could not enter the Tabernacle when the glory cloud was present because God had said,

> "you cannot see my face, for man shall not see me and live" (Exodus 33:20).

Moses wanted to see God's glory, but he was not able. It's not simply that God hid it, but that Moses was unable. Think of it like asking to see the whole universe, but there is too much of it. We do not have the capacity, either in time or intelligence to be able to take it all in. So it is with God's glory. God protected Moses' sanity because God knew that the fullness of His glory would cause Moses to blow a gasket, so to speak. But we now know that Christ changed everything! In Christ we can see God fully, as much as we need.

> "And the Word became flesh, and dwelt among us, and we saw His glory, glory as of the only begotten from the Father, full of grace and truth" (John 1:14).

In Christ, God's glory is manifest in such a way that we are able to see and understand as much of God as is humanly possible. The full revelation of God in Christ is an ongoing historical process that is still becoming increasingly clear over time. There is an historical accumulation of data and experience that contribute to God's revelation in Christ, and it takes time and effort for us to collect and assimilate that data in ways that contribute to the brightness of the revelation of Christ. However, God's revelation in Christ is the central mission of God in this world, and it has been unfolding for millennia.

Leviticus, Numbers, and Deuteronomy are about the development of the laws and traditions of ancient Israel, and their forty-year journey through the wilderness. Why did that journey take so long? The text provides example after example of them failing to believe, trust, and obey God—including Moses. The people whined about the difficulty of the journey in comparison to the pleasantries of Egypt, and about the harshness and unfairness of Moses' leadership. The bottom line was that that generation had too much Egypt in them, and God did not want them to mix Egyptian culture into the new culture He was creating for them.

Leviticus applies the Ten Commandments to the culture of ancient Israel, providing additional explication, clarity, extension, and consequences. Remember that Moses could not keep up with the people who came to him for clarification and adjudication of the new law. So, he followed Jethro's advice and appointed other elders to assist him. Leviticus is the conclusion of that process in conjunction with the elders in written form.

> "These are the commandments that the LORD commanded Moses for the people of Israel on Mount Sinai" (Leviticus 27:34).

However, Leviticus was given for the establishment of the culture of the Tabernacle, which itself was a temporary measure in the unfolding story of Israel. There is much to learn from Leviticus, including its place in history, and its application to the contemporary world in the light of Christ.

The first ten chapters of Numbers are about Israel's application of Moses' law and the orderly organization of the new culture and its religion. The people were divided into various groups and units with varying responsibilities. Emphasis is placed on military preparedness and worship procedures for the Tabernacle. Israel was in the initial process of becoming a complex society.

> "In the second year, in the second month, on the twentieth day of the month, the cloud lifted from over the tabernacle of the testimony, and the people of Israel set out by stages from the wilderness of Sinai. And the cloud settled down in the wilderness of Paran. They set out for the first time at the command of the LORD by Moses" (Numbers 10:11-13).

It was a huge undertaking to disassemble the Tabernacle in an orderly fashion so that it could be reassembled correctly when they arrived at their destination. Much description is given to the details of this process. Many things could cause disorder and bring confusion into the camp that would cause problems in the reassembling process. Any encounter with other people during the journey would likely bring confusion. So, contact was avoided and military protection for orderly travel was paramount.

> "So they set out from the mount of the LORD three days' journey. And the ark of the covenant of the LORD went before them three days' journey, to seek out a resting place for them. And the cloud of the LORD was over them by day, whenever they set out from the camp. And whenever the ark set out, Moses said, 'Arise, O LORD, and let your enemies be scattered, and let those who hate you flee before you.' And when it rested, he said, 'Return, O LORD, to the ten thousand thousands of Israel'" (Numbers 10:33-36).

They set out as a military unit in order to protect their fledgling culture and the Tabernacle, knowing that the other people in the region were dominated by the ancient religion of Ur and its variants, a religion and culture of sin and vengeance. That was simply the reality of the situation for ancient Israel. So, God provided protection through military organization, which became the source of Israel's military might.

The "ten thousands of Israel" (Numbers 10:36) is simply a different way of saying *hosts*. God is first called the "LORD of hosts" in 1 Samuel 1:3, a name which occurs many times in the Old Testament. The word *LORD*, capitalized, refers to Yahweh, the self-existent, redemptive God. And the word *hosts* (צָבָא) is a translation of the Hebrew word, literally meaning "a mass of people," often understood to be a reference to armies. Indeed, large armies won battles.

But in the light of Christ we understand God's army and references to God's war to be, not primarily a function of military might, but of social and church organization. For today we know well that it takes much more than front line soldiers to win wars. Wars are ultimately cultural conflicts where the winner imposes its culture on the loser. And God's ultimate purpose involves the reordering of human culture, moving it from cultures devoted to sin and vengeance to cultures devoted to mercy and forgiveness.

JOSHUA

Moses did not enter the Promised Land, nor did the generation of people he led through the wilderness. Getting the people out of Egypt was one thing, getting Egypt out of the people was quite another. Those who left Egypt with Moses had been so influenced by Egyptian culture that they would always be significantly affected by various elements of that culture. And God did not want to bring Egyptian culture into Israel. Israel needed a fresh start, so God allowed the generation who had grown up in Egypt to perish before permanently establishing Israel. Just before Moses died, he appointed Joshua to be his successor.

Joshua had been one of the twelve spies of Israel sent by Moses to explore the land of Canaan. Of the twelve, only Joshua and Caleb had the faith to see what God wanted them to see, and the courage to plan to defeat the Canaanites. The others succumbed to faithlessness, fear, and hopelessness.

Joshua then sent spies into Jericho who came upon Rahab, the prostitute. Rahab recognized that God was truly with the spies and protected them from discovery by the Jericho authorities. In exchange the spies agreed to save Rahab from death when they invaded Jericho.

In preparation for battle Joshua "circumcise(d) the sons of Israel a second time" (Joshua 5:2). The faithless generation who wandered in the wilderness failed to circumcise their children born in the wilderness. After that, Joshua was visited by an angel of God, and asked Him, "Are you for us, or for our adversaries?" (Joshua 5:13).[2] He answered that He was on neither side, but that He was the commander of army of the Lord. The point was that God was on neither side. At the battle of Jericho God lead Joshua's forces in a most unusual way. Joshua's army was commanded to march around Jericho seven times, and the last time around the priests were to blow their trumpets. When they did, the walls of Jericho fell and Joshua won the battle. The battle and the win belonged to the Lord.

The battle for Ai ended in Israel's defeat. God had commanded Israel to exterminate the culture of Canaan. But Achan disobeyed and did not destroy the "devoted things" (Joshua 7:1), objects of religious use. Then the battle for Ai was lost, and Joshua turned to God (after the fact!) for advice. God told Joshua of Achan's sin, that Achan, and by implication all Israel, had preserved religious relics from Jericho. Joshua had Achan stoned to death as punishment, and planned a second attack of Ai. The second attack secured Ai for the Israelites because

> "Israel struck them down, until there was left none that survived or escaped. But the king of Ai they took alive, and brought him near to Joshua" (Joshua 8:22-23).

The Israelites killed all of the people of Ai.

> "Only the livestock and the spoil of that city Israel took as their plunder, according to the word of the LORD that he commanded Joshua" (Joshua 8:27).

However, God did not tell them to preserve the livestock and spoil, but to destroy everything. Joshua believed that he had obeyed God's command by burning Ai to the ground. Yet, some things were preserved. Joshua thought that Israel was in obedience to the Lord, but that was not so. And later we find that many people were spared and continued to dwell in Canaan. Is-

---

2 This mysterious figure appears and is identified as the commander of the Lord's army (host). Hearkening back to Moses and the Burning Bush, this mysterious figure said to Joshua, "'Take off your sandals from your feet, for the place where you are standing is holy.' And Joshua did so" (Joshua 5:15).

rael thought that their "obedience" to the Lord was good enough, but it wasn't.

The battle for Jericho went well because Israel allowed God's commander (the angel) to direct the fight. But at Ai, Joshua took control and failed to accede to the letter of God's instructions. And rest of the history of the Old Testament is about Israel's struggles with the false religions that God instructed them to completely destroy.

The chief moral issue in the book of Joshua comes in the form of God's command to destroy every creature living in Jericho (Joshua 6:17, 21). The command is repeated and modulated some in Joshua 8:2,

> "And you shall do to Ai and its king as you did to Jericho and its king. Only its spoil and its livestock you shall take as plunder for yourselves. Lay an ambush against the city, behind it."

The morality of the total destruction of a people falls hard on our contemporary ears, but it is in the Bible. So, we must figure out a way to deal with it without minimizing or avoiding the ethical concerns.

God's concern regarding Jericho, Ai, and Canaan generally is the same concern He had for the people Moses brought out of Egypt: He could not allow them to contaminate the new culture He was building with Israel. He was also using Israel to punish them for their idolatry. God found it necessary to allow those individuals who had been rescued from Egyptian slavery to die in the Wilderness, and not enter the Promised Land. Just as they would have infected God's new culture with leftover Egyptian ideas and practices, the Canaanites would also have infected Israel with other pagan ideas and practices. God intended to start with a clean sheet. He did not want any of the ancient religion of sin and vengeance to infect His new culture of mercy and forgiveness. That was God's ideal plan, though He knew that it would not happen for quite some time, and had already put His plan to bring Jesus Christ into motion. Of course, Israel had no idea of this at the time.

Thus, God commanded Joshua to make a clean sweep, to destroy every aspect and fragment of Canaanite culture right away. Part of God's strategy here was to convince the Canaanites that the plan was to wipe them out, hoping that those who did not fight would flee—which would also provide the clean slate that God required for the Promised Land. Sure enough, Joshua was able to keep to God's plan for a while. Jericho and Ai were quickly destroyed, and rumors of Israel's might spread. The conquest continued, but as it succeeded it slowed down. After several years of fighting, the conquest was still not complete (Joshua 13:1).

Much of Israel's conquest of Canaan came as God's judgment against Canaan, which was a continuation of His judgment against all those who continued the ancient religion and culture of Adam and Cain. The clear story of the Old Testament is that the whole world was caught up in the cultural momentum of violence and revenge. The violent only responded to violence, and any successful effort to end the violence (which would need to employ violence) only further encouraged the spirit of wrath and vengeance. The overall story clearly demonstrates that all of God's best representatives were themselves very much caught up in this prevailing, pagan, cultural momentum, though God was in the process of extricating them from it.

Joshua 24:15 is a familiar verse that is pasted into all sorts of placards and art with the common impression that Joshua was asking people to choose between two sides or forces, between good and evil. But what is seldom seen is that Joshua laid before the people three options, not two.

> "Now therefore fear the LORD and serve him in sincerity and in faithfulness. Put away the gods that your fathers served beyond the River and in Egypt, and serve the LORD. And if it is evil in your eyes to serve the LORD, choose this day whom you will serve, whether the gods your fathers served in the region beyond the River, or the gods of the Amorites in whose land you dwell. But as for me and my house, we will serve the LORD" (Joshua 24:15-15).

Joshua was saying, *If you think it is wrong to serve the Lord, then choose either the pagan gods of Egypt, whom our fathers (Moses) could not escape in the wilderness, or the pagan gods of the Amorites. But as for me and my family, we will serve the Lord.* God is not among the two choices, but provides an alternative to both. This is the same issue that was brought by the angelic commander of the Lord's army earlier. Joshua was saying that Israel needed to move or grow beyond its captivity to the forms of Mosaic culture that had been created for their wilderness wandering, that something in the culture of their wilderness wandering would keep them from the new life that God had in store for them. The culture of the wilderness would be inadequate for their settlement in the Promised Land. He was not suggesting the wholesale abandonment of Mosaic Law, but was suggesting that there needed to be some adjustments if they were to get beyond the blindness that God had used to keep Moses from the promised land, to protect the promised land from the pagan gods of Egypt that they had been unable to shake.

JUDGES

The book of Judges begins with the continued conquest of Canaan, but Israel fell short of the mark.

> "Manasseh did not drive out the inhabitants of Beth-shean and its villages, or Taanach and its villages, or the inhabitants of Dor and its villages, or the inhabitants of Ibleam and its villages, or the inhabitants of Megiddo and its villages, for the Canaanites persisted in dwelling in that land. When Israel grew strong, they put the Canaanites to forced labor, but did not drive them out completely. And Ephraim did not drive out the Canaanites who lived in Gezer, so the Canaanites lived in Gezer among them. Zebulun did not drive out the inhabitants of Kitron, or the inhabitants of Nahalol, so the Canaanites lived among them, but became subject to forced labor. Asher did not drive out the inhabitants of Acco, or the inhabitants of Sidon or of Ahlab or of Achzib or of Helbah or of Aphik or of Rehob, so the Asherites lived among the Canaanites, the inhabitants of the land, for they did not drive them out.

> Naphtali did not drive out the inhabitants of Beth-shemesh, or the inhabitants of Beth-anath, so they lived among the Canaanites, the inhabitants of the land. Nevertheless, the inhabitants of Beth-shemesh and of Beth-anath became subject to forced labor for them. The Amorites pressed the people of Dan back into the hill country, for they did not allow them to come down to the plain. The Amorites persisted in dwelling in Mount Heres, in Aijalon, and in Shaalbim, but the hand of the house of Joseph rested heavily on them, and they became subject to forced labor" (Judges 1:27-35).

Israel occupied the Promised Land, but did not do so as God had commanded them. They did not utterly destroy the Canaanites, but allowed the pagan, Canaanite religion and culture to continue. We can carp about the morality of God's command to completely eliminate the Canaanite people and culture, that God has no right to commit genocide.

However, our considerations must include the idea that God's concern was the elimination of the Canaanite religion and culture, not necessarily the Canaanite people (Ephesians 6:12). God's willingness to spare converts is documented in the story of Jonah and the Ninevites, and in the story of Rahab, the Canaanite prostitute who was spared and is included in Jesus' lineage. God's war is not against flesh and blood—people, but is against powers and principalities—cultures and institutions. In addition, we must include the rest of the biblical history, which for the most part is the story of the continuing conflict between the religion and culture of Israel and the religion and culture of the other religions and cultures, a conflict in which much, much blood has been—and continues to be—spilled.

> "Now the angel of the LORD went up from Gilgal to Bochim. And he said, 'I brought you up from Egypt and brought you into the land that I swore to give to your fathers. I said, "I will never break my covenant with you, and you shall make no covenant with the inhabitants of this land; you shall break down their altars." But you have not obeyed my voice. What is this you have done? So now I say, I will not drive them out before you, but they shall become thorns in your sides, and their gods shall be a snare to

you.' As soon as the angel of the LORD spoke these words to all the people of Israel, the people lifted up their voices and wept" (Judges 2:1-4).

Israel's conquest of the Promised Land proved to be a failure in God's eyes because the continuing presence of Canaanite religion and culture would corrupt His effort to establish Israel as the kind of people He envisioned them to be. It was not that God's vision for Israel had been wrong, nor that God was inadequate to accomplish it. Rather, the fault lay with the Israelites themselves. They did not believe or obey God's command.

Did their disobedience surprise God? Of course not! But it did surprise Israel because she thought she was being faithful. They did conquer Canaan, and they did establish their own religious and cultural practices in opposition to those of the Canaanites. They had obeyed God, but their obedience was not as careful as God required. And the consequences of that failure on their part would be illustrated to them by their own history throughout the pages of the Bible, for those with eyes to see.

And Joshua died and was buried.

> "And there arose another generation after them who did not know the LORD or the work that he had done for Israel" (Judges 2:10).

Their failure of careful obedience in not eliminating Canaanite religion and cultural practices in their new homeland produced the failure to fully inculcate God's new religion and cultural practices among their own children. They failed to pass their religion and culture on to their own children. But before we judge them too harshly, we should consider our own situation in the twenty-first century, because for the most part, we Christians have done the same thing. We are still in this boat, this conflict between the ancient religion of sin and vengeance and God's new religion of mercy and forgiveness. God's story is not yet finished.

But we are again getting ahead of the story.

> "And the people of Israel did what was evil in the sight of the LORD and served the Baals. And they abandoned the LORD, the God of their fathers, who had brought them out

of the land of Egypt. They went after other gods, from among the gods of the peoples who were around them, and bowed down to them. And they provoked the LORD to anger. They abandoned the LORD and served the Baals and the Ashtaroth. So the anger of the LORD was kindled against Israel, and he gave them over to plunderers, who plundered them. And he sold them into the hand of their surrounding enemies, so that they could no longer withstand their enemies. Whenever they marched out, the hand of the LORD was against them for harm, as the LORD had warned, and as the LORD had sworn to them. And they were in terrible distress" (Judges 2:11-15).

In their distress the Lord raised up "judges," charismatic leaders, military leaders who were able to organize Israel and "saved them out of the hand of those who plundered them" (Judges 2:16). Yet, once Israel prevailed militarily and the crisis passed, the people returned to their faithless ways, whoring after other gods and worshiping them.

"But whenever the judge died, they turned back and were more corrupt than their fathers, going after other gods, serving them and bowing down to them. They did not drop any of their practices or their stubborn ways" (Judges 2:19).

This went on for some 350 years, far longer than the history of the United States of America. The pattern repeated itself again and again, generation after generation. God would raise up a military savior, only to have Israel return to her faithless ways once the crisis was over. The book of Judges records the stories of Israel's faithlessness in the light of God's faithfulness in providing guidance and salvation.

The stories of the Judges are classic and deserve attention. It is unlikely that the book of Judges provides a complete history of everything that happened during this time. But the stories that are preserved sufficiently reveal a pattern of God's faithfulness and Israel's unfaithfulness. The stories center around various judges: Othniel, Ehud, Shamgar, Deborah, Gideon, Abimelech, Tola, Jair, Jephthah, Ibzan, Elon, Abdon, and Samson. We'll briefly look at the story of Samson because it is representative and quite instructive.

SAMSON

Israel had fallen to the dominance of the Philistines for forty years when Samson was born. Samson's mother had been barren, like many other mothers of biblical heroes. And, similarly, an angel appeared to her and said,

> "Behold, you are barren and have not borne children, but you shall conceive and bear a son. Therefore be careful and drink no wine or strong drink, and eat nothing unclean, for behold, you shall conceive and bear a son. No razor shall come upon his head, for the child shall be a Nazarite to God from the womb, and he shall begin to save Israel from the hand of the Philistines" (Judges 13:3-5).

The interaction between Samson's parents and the angel is detailed and significant. At first they didn't recognize the angel, thinking that it was just a man. But by the end of the scene they fall on their faces, prostrate to the Lord in worship. The bottom line was that Samson was born, and dedicated to the Lord as a Nazarite.[3] And the spirit of the Lord began to stir in him.

When he reached the age for marriage, Samson told his parents that he wanted to marry a beautiful Philistine woman that he had seen. They tried to dissuade him, and point him toward a good, Jewish girl.

> "But Samson said to his father, "Get her for me, for she is right in my eyes" (Judges 14:3).

Samson's choice of words is significant. Had we read the stories of each of the preceding judges, we would have found this to be a common theme that had begun with Eve in the Garden—doing what was right *in one's own eyes*. This theme also echoes through Proverbs:

---

[3] One who voluntarily took a vow described in Numbers 6:1–21. "Nazarite" (נזיר) means consecrated or separated. This vow required the person to: 1) abstain from wine, wine vinegar, grapes, raisins, intoxicating liquors; 2) refrain from cutting the hair on one's head; and 3) not to become ritually impure by contact with corpses or graves.

> "There is a way that seems right to a man, but its end is the way to death" (Proverbs 14:12).

We see that Samson was caught up in the spirit of the day when he justified his choice for a wife. At the same time, the biblical writer is quick to tell us that Samson's decision was also guided by the Lord.

> "His father and mother did not know that it was from the LORD, for he was seeking an opportunity against the Philistines. At that time the Philistines ruled over Israel" (Judges 14:4).

It was not that Samson was being strategic in his choice of a wife by choosing someone whom he could use in his struggle against the Philistines. Rather, the biblical writer was telling us that it was *God* who was using Samson's weakness for the accomplishment of God's next move in His long range plan.

On the way to visit the prospective bride, Samson was attacked by a young lion. But Samson prevailed and tore the lion in pieces. Somehow his parents were not aware of this event, nor did he tell them of it. After talking with the prospective bride, Samson repeated his decision, indeed "she was right in Samson's eyes" (Judges 14:7).

On another visit to the woman, Samson came upon the carcass of the lion he had killed, and found that it was occupied by bees. So, he scooped out a handful of honey and ate it. But again, did not tell anyone where the honey came from.

At the wedding party thirty young companions were brought to entertain Samson, and as part of the festivities Samson put a riddle to them. The giving of riddles in social situations was a Philistine cultural practice intended to celebrated wisdom and intelligence. In this case it would establish the character of Samson in the Philistine culture. A wager was raised: if they could figure it out Sampson would give each of them a new set of clothes. But if they couldn't, they would give Samson thirty sets of clothes. Samson needed an edge, an advantage. So, instead of a fair riddle that could be solved with deduction, Samson's riddle was based on his private experience of killing the young lion and later finding bees and honey in its corpse. It was a story which he had told no one. Thus, Samson's riddle was a trick, a kind of joke for the wedding party that would demonstrate Sampson's superiority. Samson put it to them:

> "Out of the eater came something to eat; out of the strong came something sweet" (Judges 14:14).

After three days they were stumped. They could not figure it out. So, on the fourth day they went to Samson's new Philistine wife and threatened to burn her and her father's home if she would not tell them the answer. So, she pleaded with Sampson to tell her the answer, weeping and turning on all her feminine charms in the process. On the seventh day Samson succumbed to her feminine wiles and told her. And she then told the men, who answered the riddle with another riddle, demonstrating that they knew the secret to Samon's riddle.

> "What is sweeter than honey? What is stronger than a lion?" (Judges 14:18).

Samson determined that his wife had told them the answer, which meant that *they* had cheated.

> "And the Spirit of the LORD rushed upon him, and he went down to Ashkelon and struck down thirty men of the town and took their spoil and gave the garments to those who had told the riddle" (Judges 14:19).

Angry, Samson returned home, and in his absence his wife-to-be was given to the best man at his wedding because they thought Samson had abandoned her. Such were the relationships between Israel and the Philistines. Samson left in a fit of anger.

After his temper cooled, Samson returned to visit his proposed wife to consummate the wedding, but her father would not allow it. When Samson learned that she had been given to another, his anger flared again. He caught three hundred foxes and tied them in pairs by their tails, and set their tails on fire. He then turned them loose in the fields of the Philistines, burning their crops and orchards.

When the Philistine elders learned that Samson had done this, they "burned (Samson's wife-to-be) and her father with fire"

(Judges 15:6), assuring that Samson would not have her. When Samson learned of the death of his wife-to-be, he beat the Philistine elders in retaliation. So the Philistines then raided Judah in retaliation, saying,

> "We have come up to bind Samson, to do to him as he did to us" (Judges 15:10).

Note the pattern of vengeance for vengeance as an expression of justice on the part of both Samson and the Philistines. This is just a particular instance of this long standing pattern identified as the ancient religion of vengeance. This story demonstrates that Samson, who is God's man, God's judge, is still very much caught up in the old, pagan religion.

The men of Judah then confronted Samson,

> "'Do you not know that the Philistines are rulers over us? What then is this that you have done to us?' And he said to them, 'As they did to me, so have I done to them.' And they said to him, 'We have come down to bind you, that we may give you into the hands of the Philistines'" (Judges 15:11-12).

Samson was bound and delivered to the Philistines as an act of justice and appeasement. As the Philistines were collecting him, he broke his bonds, found the jawbone of an ass (donkey), and slew a thousand Philistines with it. Clearly, this story has acquired a mythical element of exaggeration, not uncommon in Middle Eastern cultures. But the mythical element does not make the story untrue. Rather, the myth was intended to emphasize the truth of something that otherwise might be overlooked. Here, the story teaches that vengeance multiplies vengeance by inflaming personal anger and offense. The story illustrates the uncontrollability of vengeance. Samson's anger was so hot that he felt as if he could slay a thousand Philistines with nothing but the jawbone of an ass. And perhaps he did! No doubt he slew all who came at him. To doubt the literal interpretation of the story is to miss the larger lesson or point that it teaches.

After this, Samson had managed to escape his captors and was now alone in the desert long enough to become quite thirsty. So, he called out to the Lord.

> "You have granted this great salvation by the hand of your servant, and shall I now die of thirst and fall into the hands of the uncircumcised?" (Judges 15:18).

In typical Jewish style, Sampson accused God with a question. So God showed him where to find water. Samson's experience with the Philistines established him as a judge in Israel, where he served for twenty years after these escapades. Was Samson a faithful leader? Not really. He was a seriously flawed man that God used to accomplish His purposes.

SAMSON & DELILAH

Samson's weakness regarding women was well established before he met Delilah, as was his reputation as a hot-headed strongman. Judges 16 opens by reasserting both of these facts about Sampson. In addition, Delilah was a woman that Samson loved, but did not marry, which made his relationship with her immoral according to the Bible.

One of the first things that we are told about her is that she agreed to betray Sampson for money, "1,100 pieces of silver" (Judges 16:5). The Philistine lords wanted to know the source of his amazing strength so that they could overpower him. When Delilah asked him about it he lied to her three times, suspecting her potential betrayal. Each time he told her a lie about what would bind him, the Philistines tried it, and it failed. So Delilah played the love card.

> "How can you say, 'I love you,' when your heart is not with me? You have mocked me these three times, and you have not told me where your great strength lies" (Judges 16:15).

She pressed him day after day about it, and finally he confessed that he was a Nazarite, and his great strength was attributed to his long hair. If it was cut, he would be like other men. She rocked him to sleep one day and called the Philistines to cut his hair. Then *she* said, "The Philistines are upon you,

Samson!" (Judges 16:20). He awoke and tried to defend himself, but his strength had left him because the Lord had abandoned him.

> "And the Philistines seized him and gouged out his eyes and brought him down to Gaza and bound him with bronze shackles. And he ground at the mill in the prison" (Judges 16:21).

Then the Philistines gathered to sacrifice to their god, Dagan, because they saw Samson's capture as a great victory. So they all gathered at Dagan's temple, and called for Sampson so that they could publicly ridicule him. They put him between two pillars of the temple so everyone could see him. Once there, Sampson called upon the Lord.

> "O Lord GOD, please remember me and please strengthen me only this once, O God, that I may be avenged on the Philistines for my two eyes" (Judges 16:28).

Note that Samson's motivation was vengeance, suggesting that he was still governed by the ancient religion that God opposed. Nonetheless, the Lord provided Samson strength enough to pull down the temple, killing all who were there, including himself. Thus ended Samson's reign as judge of Israel.

Though Samson was a very flawed man, evidencing very little faithfulness to the ways of God, God still used him. God exhibited His faithfulness in the face of Samson's unfaithfulness, which was a common theme among Israel's judges.

GIBEAH

The battle at Gibeah, a hill in the territory of Benjamin, was triggered by an incident in which the concubine of a Levite was raped by a group of Benjamites, and later died. Nearly identical to a story about Lot,[4] the Levite was accosted by men who sought to have homosexual sex with him. He agreed to send out his concubine to satisfy them. In the morning he found the concubine unresponsive on his doorstep. He later cut her body into twelve pieces, and sent the pieces throughout all the territories of

---

4   Genesis 19:1-ff, treated on p. 64, above.

the Israelite tribes as a declaration of war and a call to united revenge against the perpetrators of her sexual violation and death.

The outraged tribes of Israel gathered an army and sought justice from the tribe of Benjamin, asking for the miscreants to be delivered for judgment. The Benjamites refused to hand them over, so the gathered army then sought vengeance, and in the subsequent war, the people of Benjamin (Israelites) were systematically slaughtered, including women and children. When Benjamin was nearly extinguished, it was decided that the tribe should be allowed to survive, and all the men from another town, Jabesh Gilead, who had refused to take part in the slaughter of the tribe of Benjamin, were also killed, so that their daughters could be wed to the surviving men of Benjamin. The Benjamites are portrayed here as the absolute worst of the Israelites.

The whole episode drips with astonishing cruelty and immorality on everyone's part, from the raping of the concubine to the consequent slaughter of the Benjamites and others. No one in this episode was even remotely moral, and the story was told in order to establish the character of the Israelite people who had conquered the Promised Land in fulfillment of Abraham's mission. Indeed, God's mission had reached a new low point.

The point of this story will grow in its meaning with the calling of Saul, a Benjamite, to be king of Israel. So, we turn to that chapter in Israel's history to apply the lessons of the Gibeah incident, which sets up the calling and kingship of Saul.

SAMUEL

Samuel is a pivotal character in the story of ancient Israel. He was called by God before he was born. His mother, Hannah, had been barren, and went to the Tabernacle seeking God's help to have a child. She

> "vowed a vow and said, 'O LORD of hosts, if you will indeed look on the affliction of your servant and remember me and not forget your servant, but will give to your servant a son, then I will give him to the LORD all the days of his life, and no razor shall touch his head'" (1 Samuel 1:11).

In due time she conceived and named her son, Samuel. She also wrote a poem dedicating him to service to the Lord (1 Samuel 2:1-10). Samuel began his service to the Lord at the Tabernacle when he was quite young, and he also became a Nazarite.

But the Tabernacle was suffering from serious decline. As if the story of Sampson isn't enough, we learn from the story of Eli, the High Priest, and his worthless sons who served as priests in the Tabernacle. That story concludes with the Lord's rejection of Eli and his household, including his sons, which led to Eli's death. This story of spiritual apathy and corruption then sets up the story for Samuel to become an instrument of reform for ancient Israel.

Samuel began to hear the Lord when he was quite young. Note that Samuel was able to hear the Lord speaking. At first he thought that Eli had been calling him in the night. So he went to Eli, but Eli denied calling him. Finally, Eli told him to ask God to speak to him, and He did. God said to Samuel:

> "Behold, I am about to do a thing in Israel at which the two ears of everyone who hears it will tingle. On that day I will fulfill against Eli all that I have spoken concerning his house, from beginning to end. And I declare to him that I am about to punish his house forever, for the iniquity that he knew, because his sons were blaspheming God, and he did not restrain them. Therefore I swear to the house of Eli that the iniquity of Eli's house shall not be atoned for by sacrifice or offering forever" (1 Samuel 3:11-14).

Samuel was afraid to tell Eli what the Lord had said to him. And when he finally did, Eli responded,

> "It is the LORD. Let him do what seems good to him" (1 Samuel 3:18).

As Samuel's reputation began to grow, Israel became enmeshed in a conflict with the Philistines, and Israel lost the first skirmish. So, "the people," under the authority of the sons of Eli, brought the ark of the covenant from the Tabernacle to the military encampment, where it should not have been but was met by Israel's army with shouts of courage and hope that God would now defeat the Philistines. But the Philistines prevailed.

"And the ark of God was captured, and the two sons of Eli, Hophni and Phinehas, died" (1 Samuel 4:11).

When Eli heard the news, he fell in a feint and died, crying

"The glory has departed from Israel, for the ark of God has been captured" (1 Samuel 4:22).

The Philistines then took the ark to their temple in Ashdod, thinking that it was a great prize. But the morning after they brought the ark to their temple, their God, Dagon, was found prostrate, face down before the ark. Thinking it was an anomaly, they set Dagon back up. The next morning Dagon was again prostrate before the ark, but this time Dagon's head and hands had been cut off and were lying on the threshold.

"The hand of the LORD was heavy against the people of Ashdod, and he terrified and afflicted them with tumors, both Ashdod and its territory" (1 Samuel 5:6).

They then decided to move the ark to Gath.

"But after they had brought it around, the hand of the LORD was against the city, causing a very great panic, and he afflicted the men of the city, both young and old, so that tumors broke out on them" (1 Samuel 5:9).

So they sent the ark to Ekron.

"But as soon as the ark of God came to Ekron, the people of Ekron cried out, 'They have brought around to us the ark of the God of Israel to kill us and our people.' They sent therefore and gathered together all the lords of the Philistines and said, 'Send away the ark of the God of Israel, and let it return to its own place, that it may not kill us and our people.' For there was a deathly panic throughout the whole city. The hand of God was very heavy there (1 Samuel 5:10-11).

They then decided to return the ark to Israel, and after much consultation sent it laden with offerings of gold. Samuel then used the returned ark as an impetus for Israel to purge herself of foreign gods. So they did, "and they served the LORD only" (1 Samuel 7:4). Samuel's prayers and sacrifices were then instrumental in subduing the Philistines, and cementing Samuel's leadership position.

The Tabernacle was in a state of decline and disarray when Eli died. So, it is not surprising that Samuel's leadership position is a bit unclear to us today. The stories suggest that he was in line to become a judge or even the succeeding High Priest, but never quite say so. He also functioned as a prophet, outside of the Tabernacle order. He was a charismatic[5] leader whom God called to stand in the gap, between the rotting Tabernacle and the yet-to-be-envisioned Temple of David.

The Tabernacle was built to be a movable worship center, to hold Israel together during her wilderness journey. Movement of Israel and the Tabernacle was a difficult, complex, and time consuming process. And the larger Israel grew, the more difficult moving the whole company became.

During the conquest of Canaan, the main Israelite camp was at Gilgal, (Joshua 4:19; 5:8-10). After the conquest and division of the land among the tribes, the Tabernacle was moved to Shiloh in Ephraimite territory (Joshua's tribe) to avoid disputes among the other tribes (Joshua 18:1; 19:51; 22:9; Psalm 78:60). It remained there during the disastrous 300-year period of the biblical judges.

Samuel entered the picture at the end of the period of judges, and facilitated Israel's turn to imitate a pagan monarchy.

> "And Samuel said to all the house of Israel, 'If you are returning to the LORD with all your heart, then put away the foreign gods and the Ashtaroth from among you and direct your heart to the LORD and serve him only, and he will deliver you out of the hand of the Philistines.' So the people of Israel put away the Baals and the Ashtaroth, and they served the LORD only. ... Samuel judged Israel all the days of his life. And he went on a circuit year by year to Bethel, Gilgal, and Mizpah. And he judged Israel in all these places. Then he would return to Ramah, for his home was there,

---

5   The idea here is not that charismatic leaders spoke in "tongues" or foreign (non-Hebrew) languages, but that charismatic leaders are able to "hear" God because they have "ears to hear" (Mark 4:9, 23; Matthew 11:15). They hear God, who speaks every tongue or language, in their own native language. See Acts 2:6.

and there also he judged Israel. And he built there an altar
to the LORD" (1 Samuel 7:3-4, 15-17).

Samuel, like Eli before him, made his sons judges over Israel. All of the various temple and social functions in ancient Israel were family affairs, as sons were trained in their father's occupation. And like Eli's son, Samuel's sons

"did not walk in his ways but turned aside after gain. They took bribes and perverted justice" (1 Samuel 8:3).

So the elders gathered and said to Samuel,

"Behold, you are old and your sons do not walk in your ways. Now appoint for us a king to judge us like all the nations" (1 Samuel 8:5).

It was *not* God who called for a king, it was Israel, the people. Nor did they ask God to define the role of the king, but wanted a king like the pagan nations had. Their request displeased Samuel, who took their request to the Lord, who answered:

"Obey the voice of the people in all that they say to you, for they have not rejected you, but *they have rejected me from being king over them*. According to all the deeds that they have done, from the day I brought them up out of Egypt even to this day, forsaking me and serving other gods, so they are also doing to you. Now then, obey their voice; only you shall solemnly warn them and show them the ways of the king who shall reign over them" (1 Samuel 8:7-9, italics added).

Samuel warned them that the king would take from their own families to build an army. He would take their sons, their daughters, their harvests, their treasure, and their fields in order to build a culture to support the army. He concluded,

"you shall be his slaves. And in that day you will cry out because of your king, whom you have chosen for yourselves, but the LORD will not answer you in that day" (1 Samuel 8:17-18).

This is a pivotal event in the long history of Israel that is often overlooked. However, the remainder of Israel's history must be understood in the light of this key event. Kingship in Israel was not God's idea, and God told them that it would not end well. But they didn't care. They didn't listen to God or His representative, and demanded a king anyway. So God gave them what they desired in order to teach them a lesson about desiring the right things. God gives people what they want, even when they want things that will harm them (Romans 1:24-27). The gospel of Jesus Christ is not simply a matter of choosing Jesus, but of learning how to want what God wants for us.

The people did not care about Samuel's warning.

> "No! But there shall be a king over us, that we also may be like all the nations, and that our king may judge us and go out before us and fight our battles" (1 Samuel 8:19-20).

So, the Lord instructed Samuel to find a king that would satisfy Israel's pagan demand, and pointed Samuel to Benjamin. *Benjamin!* The Lord directed Samuel to Benjamin to find a king to satisfy the people's demand. Recall the story of Benjamin a few pages previously, and let the significance of this event sink into your soul and enlighten your eyes.

> "There was a man of Benjamin whose name was Kish, the son of Abiel, son of Zeror, son of Becorath, son of Aphiah, a Benjaminite, a man of wealth. And he had a son whose name was Saul, a handsome young man. There was not a man among the people of Israel more handsome than he. From his shoulders upward he was taller than any of the people" (1 Samuel 9:1-2).

The story of Saul begins with lost donkeys, a detail pregnant with irony for enlightened eyes. The donkeys belonged to Saul's father, Kish, who had sent his sons, including Saul, to find them. They looked and looked but could not find them. When Saul suggested that they return without the donkeys, his servant told him of a seer who may be able to help them. The seer turned out to be Samuel. So they brought a gift, a bribe, to Samuel asking for his help in finding the lost donkeys.

The text is careful to note that the Lord had previously told Samuel that He would send a man from Benjamin to be anointed king over Israel. When they met, Samuel treated Saul with respect and deference, which surprised Saul, who understood that the Benjamites were "the least of the tribes in Israel" and his clan as "the humblest of all the clans of the tribe of "Benjamin" (1 Samuel 9:21).

Here we have what is known in biblical literature as a *double entendre*, a word or phrase open to two interpretations, one of which is usually risqué or indecent. The two interpretations pertain to the Lord choosing people from positions of low standing. God doesn't choose the qualified, He qualifies the chosen. And while this is true and valuable because Jesus Christ Himself was a man of low regard, it is also true that the sins of Benjamin had been particularly horrifying and worthy of genuine disgust. Nonetheless, Samuel agreed to help Saul find the donkeys.

But first Samuel anointed Saul with oil saying,

> "Has not the LORD anointed you to be prince over his people Israel? And you shall reign over the people of the LORD and you will save them from the hand of their surrounding enemies. And this shall be the sign to you that the LORD has anointed you to be prince over his heritage'" (1 Samuel 10:1).

Samuel then told Saul that he would encounter a group of prophets on the way home and out of that meeting

> "the Spirit of the LORD will rush upon you, and you will prophesy with them and be turned into another man" (1 Samuel 10:6).

Saul would experience something like regeneration. But

> "When he turned his back to leave Samuel, God gave him *another* heart. And all these signs came to pass that day" (1 Samuel 10:9, italics added).

Another heart, not a *new* heart. The choice of words is significant. The Hebrew (אַחֵר) literally means to hinder, and is from a root word meaning procrastinate. Saul would become a conflicted and troubled man.

When Saul met the prophets, he prophesied among them. A popular movement had arisen to establish a centralized monarchy so Israel could be like other nations. Samuel assembled the people at Mizpah in Benjamin to appoint a king. Saul met the prophets and prophesied himself on his way home to Gibeah, along with a number of followers (1 Samuel 10:17-24).

The Ammonites,[6] led by Nahash, brought siege to Jabesh-Gilead. Under the terms of surrender, the Benjamites of Jabesh-Gilead were to be forced into slavery and have their right eyes removed. So, they sent word of this to Saul and the gathered tribes of Israel. The tribes west of the Jordan then assembled an army under Saul.

> "He took a yoke of oxen and cut them in pieces and sent them throughout all the territory of Israel by the hand of the messengers, saying, 'Whoever does not come out after Saul and Samuel, so shall it be done to his oxen!' Then the dread of the LORD fell upon the people, and they came out as one man" (1 Samuel 11:7).

Saul then led the army to victory over the Ammonites, and the people congregated at Gilgal, the last location of the Tabernacle, where they crowned Saul as king (1 Samuel 11).

> "Then the people said to Samuel, 'Who is it that said, "Shall Saul reign over us?" Bring the men, that we may put them to death.' But Saul said, 'Not a man shall be put to death this day, for today the LORD has worked salvation in Israel.' Then Samuel said to the people, 'Come, let us go to Gilgal and there renew the kingdom.' So all the people went to Gilgal, and there they made Saul king before the LORD in Gilgal. There they sacrificed peace offerings before the LORD, and there Saul and all the men of Israel rejoiced greatly" (1 Samuel 11:12-15).

And as Samuel's reign as the last judge came to an end he said to the people:

> "Do not be afraid; you have done all this evil. Yet do not turn aside from following the LORD, but serve the LORD with all your heart. And do not turn aside after empty things that cannot profit or deliver, for they are empty. For the LORD will not forsake his people, for his great name's

---

6   Descendants of the people whom God told Joshua to completely destroy, but who had not been destroyed.

> sake, because it has pleased the LORD to make you a people for himself. Moreover, as for me, far be it from me that I should sin against the LORD by ceasing to pray for you, and I will instruct you in the good and the right way. Only fear the LORD and serve him faithfully with all your heart. For consider what great things he has done for you. But if you still do wickedly, you shall be swept away, both you and your king" (1 Samuel 12:20-25).

God would not forsake them, in spite of their faithlessness. Though their kingdom was not God's idea, He would help them establish it, but not so that it would be a blessing for them. Rather, He would help them build their kingdom in order to teach them the consequences of not wanting what God wanted for them. God would continue to be faithful in spite of their rejection of Him, but their rejection of Him would not be without consequence, which Samuel reminded them of with his last words.

The rest of the Old Testament is the story of the playing out of the consequences of Israel's decision to have a kingdom like the other pagan kingdoms of the world, until it concluded in 70 A.D. with the destruction of the Temple and the loss of their land.

King And Temple

Saul

One of the first things to note about Saul is that he had no training or expectation to serve as Israel's king. Saul was a Benjamite warrior, from the tribe that had perpetrated the Gibeah incident that had caused the other tribes to nearly eliminate the tribe of Benjamin. From the time of the incident the Benjamites were considered to be the lowest of the low, the tribe that was morally bankrupt. Saul, who was a head taller than most Israelites, and strikingly handsome, was the people's choice. And God ratified the choice, knowing how it would turn out. He ratified it because He knew that it would reveal the folly of refusing God's direction and leadership.

In the third year of Saul's reign he went to war with the Philistines, whom he routed and proudly announced his win throughout the land. There was also a shadow message that accompanied Saul's announcement: "Israel had become a stench to the Philistines" (1 Samuel 13:4). Saul thought that he had defeated the Philistines, but the Philistines understood the defeat to be a single battle, and they mustered a much larger army to respond.

> "When the men of Israel saw that they were in trouble (for the people were hard pressed), the people hid themselves in caves and in holes and in rocks and in tombs and in cisterns, and some Hebrews crossed the fords of the Jordan to the land of Gad and Gilead. Saul was still at Gilgal, and all the people followed him trembling" (1 Samuel 13:6-7).

Saul was at Gilgal, where the Tabernacle had been set up. He was there so that sacrifices could be offered to solicit God's help with the impending fight with the Philistines. Samuel, who functioned as Judge or High Priest was to come and preside over the sacrifices. Samuel was to be there in seven days, but he was late. Rather than wait, Saul ordered the sacrifices to begin without Samuel. "And he (Saul) offered the burnt offering" (1 Samuel 13:9).

By doing this, Saul had usurped Samuel's priestly position or role in the liturgy of the sacrifices. Saul, the king that God didn't want but ratified anyway, brazenly took a position in the Tabernacle establishment that had never been authorized by God.

> "As soon as he had finished offering the burnt offering, behold, Samuel came" (1 Samuel 13:10).

Samuel asked, "What have you done?" (1 Samuel 13:11). Saul explained that the people, his army, had grown antsy, and in order to hold them together and to seek the favor of the Lord for the impending fight, he (Saul) "forced myself (himself), and offered the burnt offering" (1 Samuel 13:12). Saul had taken unauthorized liberty with the Lord by not keeping God's commands, by violating the Tabernacle establishment structures that God had given. Saul was not a priest, and was not authorized to act as one. Samuel's response was instantaneous.

> "You have done foolishly. You have not kept the command of the LORD your God, with which he commanded you. For then the LORD would have established your kingdom over Israel forever. But now your kingdom shall not continue. The LORD has sought out a man after his own heart, and the LORD has commanded him to be prince over his people, because you have not kept what the LORD commanded you" (1 Samuel 13:13-14).

Samuel left, and Saul went to Gibeah, where he "numbered" (1 Samuel 13:15) the people. Saul took a census to determine the strength of his army, rather than depending on God to fight for him. Jonathan, Saul's son, then took it upon himself to defeat the Philistines. He devised a good plan and it worked. Israel defeated the Philistines again. But note that just as Saul had ignored God's order, Jonathan ignored Saul's orders by not telling his father until it was over.

Saul then made a vow of vengeance, that no one should eat until after the next battle, anyone who did would be cursed. Saul hoped that his vow would cause the Lord to bless them in battle. There were at least two things wrong with Saul's vow. First, it was a vow of vengeance, which ran counter to God's long range plan for humanity. In addition, Saul sealed it with a curse rather than a blessing. And lastly, it had no authorization from God. It was more like a superstition than a prayer.

Jonathan had not heard about Saul's vow, so when he came upon some honey in the comb he ate it. When the people told Jonathan about his father's vow, Jonathan denounced Saul, calling him foolish because soldiers needed sustenance and nutrition to strengthen them, not silly vows. Israel defeated the Philistines, and because they had not eaten, they were famished.

> "The people pounced on the spoil and took sheep and oxen and calves and slaughtered them on the ground. And the people ate them with the blood" (1 Samuel 14:32).

Eating of meat with the blood was forbidden (Genesis 9:4, Leviticus 17). When Saul heard of it he recognized that the people had committed a grave sin. So, he told them to bring a large stone that would serve as an altar and commanded them,

> "Let every man bring his ox or his sheep and slaughter them here and eat, and do not sin against the LORD by eating with the blood" (1 Samuel 14:34).

Again, Saul usurped the role of a priest and offered unauthorized sacrifices to the Lord, hoping to incur the Lord's mercy. In the midst of that sacrifice Saul found out that Jonathan had eaten, contrary to Saul's vow that his army would not eat. Jonathan confessed and was willing to die for his error. He had not known that Saul had forbidden it, and was willing to honor Saul's authority and receive death for his error, the consequence that Saul had pledged. Saul was grieved, but approved of Jonathan's death, pledging his own death as well. But the people intervened saying,

> "Shall Jonathan die, who has worked this great salvation in Israel? Far from it! As the LORD lives, there shall not one hair of his head fall to the ground, for he has worked with God this day" (1 Samuel 14:45).

The people usurped the authority of the king. This war with the Philistines was a comedy of errors, in that none of it comported with God's guidance or instruction. God was not in any of it. Saul had ignored God's word; he failed to "hear" it. Jonathan, the hero, had ignored Saul's orders, but won the battle. Then in an effort to honor Saul's authority Jonathan agreed to die in order to support Saul's usurped authority. But the people would not let the hero die, and ransomed Jonathan from death, in defiance of King Saul and God.

Agag

After this, Saul took up Joshua's call to rid the land of Israel's enemies. And Samuel authorized it.

> "The LORD sent me to anoint you king over his people Israel; now therefore listen to the words of the LORD. Thus says the LORD of hosts, 'I have noted what Amalek did to Israel in opposing them on the way when they came up out of Egypt. Now go and strike Amalek and devote to destruction all that they have. Do not spare them, but kill both man and woman, child and infant, ox and sheep, camel and donkey'" (1 Samuel 15:1-3).

Previously, the Lord had excluded the Amalekites from His list of people to exterminate, and here He seems to complete the list by adding them to it. Again, bear with the moral indignation you may feel because of God's suspected injustice here, and just allow the story to play out. Only then can we discover the lessons that God has for us regarding this story.

So, Saul gathered his army, invited the Kenites to separate from them and go to Egypt, and defeated the Amalekites.

> "But Saul and the people spared Agag and the best of the sheep and of the oxen and of the fattened calves and the lambs, and all that was good, and would not utterly destroy them. All that was despised and worthless they devoted to destruction" (1 Samuel 15:9).

When Samuel heard about it, the Lord said to him,

> "I regret that I have made Saul king, for he has turned back from following me and has not performed my commandments" (1 Samuel 15:11).

So Samuel went to Saul to confront him about it. And *Saul* responded,

> "Blessed be you to the LORD. I have performed the commandment of the LORD" (1 Samuel 15:13).

Saul thought that he had done what the Lord commanded. He had defeated the Amalekites. And Samuel responded,

> "What then is this bleating of the sheep in my ears and the lowing of the oxen that I hear?" (1 Samuel 15:15).

Saul replied that the *people* had spared the best of the sheep and oxen in order to provide sacrifices to the Lord, and they destroyed everything else. Saul shifted blame to the people, claiming that he (Saul) had been faithful to the word of the Lord. But Samuel disagreed and replied:

> "Has the LORD as great delight in burnt offerings and sacrifices, as in obeying the voice of the LORD? Behold, to obey is better than sacrifice, and to listen than the fat of rams. For rebellion is as the sin of divination, and presumption is as iniquity and idolatry. Because you have rejected the word of the LORD, he has also rejected you from being king" (1 Samuel 15:22-23).

This is the message that will be repeated *ad nasuem* by the Prophets in response to the faithlessness of the kings. Speaking through Samuel, God said that burnt offerings and sacrifices, what we call *liturgy*, is not the main thing that God wants. God wants hearts and minds, not liturgical performance. God is not opposed to liturgy, but only when it becomes the fruit of obedience.

Saul then saw that he had transgressed the commandment of the Lord and had followed the lead of the people, which made the people sovereign. So Saul asked Samuel for forgiveness, but Samuel would not give it. In a moment of passion as Samuel turned to leave, Saul grabbed him and tore his robe. Samuel responded by saying that God had torn the kingdom from Saul just as Saul had torn his robe. Saul again begged for forgiveness. So Samuel said:

> "'Bring here to me Agag the king of the Amalekites.' And Agag came to him cheerfully. Agag said, 'Surely the bitterness of death is past.' And Samuel said, 'As your sword has made women childless, so shall your mother be childless among women.' And Samuel hacked Agag to pieces before the LORD in Gilgal (1 Samuel 15:32-33).

Yikes! Saul had treated Agag as he himself wanted to be treated. There was honor among kings. Saul had received Agag's surrender, and thought that that was what the Lord had wanted. But it was not what the Lord had said! God's long range plan was to rid the world of the religion of vengeance, not to simply defeat one man's army. Samuel never saw Saul again.

> "The LORD said to Samuel, 'How long will you grieve over Saul, since I have rejected him from being king over Israel? Fill your horn with oil, and go. I will send you to Jesse the Bethlehemite, for I have provided for myself a king among his sons.' And Samuel said, 'How can I go? If Saul hears it, he will kill me.' And the LORD said, 'Take a heifer with you and say, "I have come to sacrifice to the LORD." And invite Jesse to the sacrifice, and I will show you what you shall do. And you shall anoint for me him whom I declare to you.'" (1 Samuel 16:1-3).

Saul had been the choice of the people whom God had ratified in order provide a lesson for Israel about rejecting God. They wanted a king like the pagans had, and they got one. This is the king that they chose. Here, at this point, early in Saul's reign the Lord rejected Saul as king and sent Samuel to find David.

DAVID

At the time Samuel did not know David. God had simply said that He would alert Samuel when Samuel found the right person to anoint as king. Samuel's only instruction was

> "Do not look on his appearance or on the height of his stature, because I have rejected him. For the LORD sees not as man sees: man looks on the outward appearance, but the LORD looks on the heart" (1 Samuel 16:7).

Samuel's anointing of David was perfunctory. David was the least expected to be qualified, even by Samuel. He was but a boy who had been out tending the sheep. He hadn't even been invited to interview with Samuel. Nonetheless, the Lord immediately recognized him, and Samuel poured oil over his head.

> "And the Spirit of the LORD rushed upon David from that day forward. And Samuel rose up and went to Ramah (1 Samuel 16:13).

At the same time

> "the Spirit of the LORD departed from Saul, and a harmful spirit from the LORD tormented him (1 Samuel 16:14).

And in order to assuage Saul's troubled spirit a musician was sought who could calm Saul's vexed spirit with soothing music. David happened to be a skilled lyre player and was assigned to Saul's court to be Saul's musician and armor bearer. Fortunately, David's music was able to soothe Saul when he was troubled.

The story of Goliath (1 Samuel 17) is one of the most familiar biblical stories. The little guy defeated the big guy. True enough, but the real biblical lesson is in the details. In order to avoid a larger battle, Goliath challenged the Israelites to send out their best soldier to fight one-on-one. The winner of that fight would determine the winning army. No Israelite would step forward, so Goliath taunted them day after day, belittling the God of the Israelites, who, rumor had it, was the source of the military strength of the Israelites.

David, who was bringing food for his brothers at the front lines where the army was arrayed against Goliath and the Philistines, heard Goliath belittle God. And David was incensed by it. So he volunteered to take on Goliath, knowing that he had experience slaying great beasts that had threatened his sheep. David was so insistent that he convinced Saul to send him out to fight Goliath. Saul tried to arm him in his (Saul's) armor, but it wouldn't fit. So David went out to meet Goliath with his weapon of choice—his sling and five smooth stones from the brook. His only armor was the protection of God. David's agility and his mastery of the sling would go against Goliath's brute strength, weight, and corresponding clumsiness.

The story drips with allegory and allusion. Everything about David was different than Saul. The old ways (symbolized by Saul's armor) would not work for David. He faced Goliath with nothing but the glory of the Lord, who had been grooming David for this day. David easily defeated Goliath and, as his reputation blossomed, Saul grew jealous.

> "The next day a harmful spirit from God rushed upon Saul, and he raved within his house while David was playing the lyre, as he did day by day. Saul had his spear in his hand. And Saul hurled the spear, for he thought, 'I will pin David to the wall.' But David evaded him twice" (1 Samuel 18:10-11).

Saul could no longer stand to have David in his presence playing his lyre, for every note inflamed Saul's jealousy. So he made David a commander of a thousand to both accede to David's growing popularity and to get him out of his immediate court. David had become a national hero over the Goliath incident, which irritated Saul to no end. Saul could not fail to reward David as a national hero because the people demanded it, but it galled him. So Saul then gave his daughter, Michal, to David as a public symbol of his appreciation of David. By bringing David into his family, Saul was able to share in David's heroism. But he secretly planned to send David to fight the Philistines, hoping that he would be killed.

But to Saul's frustration, David was successful at everything he did. The ensuing relationship between Saul and David provides grist for the story. Saul's troubled spirit comes to dominate him as David's successes and popularity continued to grow. Jonathan, Saul's son, developed a close and enduring friendship with David, and Jonathan helped David navigate Saul's court and his temper, even saving his life.

David's experience with Saul provided many lessons about what it takes to be a king, and Saul provided many examples of how *not* to do it. It was a time of job training for David. God caused David's deteriorating relationship with Saul to become the source of David's success. The more Saul pursued David with ill in mind, the more the people were able to see the difference between David and Saul.

David was careful not to usurp Saul's authority as king, even when he had clear opportunities to do so. David was able to hold the fledgling kingdom together while Saul grew increasingly out of favor with the people. At Saul's death David was thrust into kingship by popular vote. The stories are many and valuable so don't neglect studying them on your own.

However, as great a king as David would be, and as much as God was with David, we must remember God's admonition to Israel about establishing a kingdom that would be like other kingdoms of the world. God had called the whole idea of such an Israelite kingdom *apostate*. By seeking such a king, Israel turned her collective back on the Lord, who alone was intended to be the *only* King of the Israelites. Nonetheless, as Israel slid into her kingdom chapter, God did what he could to help make the apostate kingdom as good and faithful as it could be because it would mean that David would be "hearing" Him and not simply regurgitating Moses—at least he would hear some of what God was saying.

Again, God's intention was to provide future (or historic) lessons for His people regarding David's kingdom. The pagan idea of kings and kingdoms, which were mostly about vengeance and wars, was so far from God's plan for humanity that even with God's help the pagan model would prove to be a colossal failure. Nonetheless, important lessons would be taught in hindsight.

The key to understanding God's perspective about the kingdom of Israel is to keep in mind the two historic events that bracket the kingdom story that we find in the Bible as we have it today. The first was Samuel's response to the people when they called for a king like the other nations had. Samuel told them that God opposed the idea because such a king would surely become just like the other kings of the world—greedy, self-centered, apostate, etc. And second was the destruction of Jerusalem and the Temple in A.D. 70, which ended the story of the Jewish kingdom in history. God said that it would be a failure and a tragedy, and eventually it was.

So, why did God bother taking Israel through its kingdom phase? In order to teach historic lessons that proved God's Word to be true. Experience is the best teacher. The demand of the people brought Saul to power, and nothing about that process honored God. Yet, God did not give up on Israel, and recommitted Himself to continue to work with them in order to bring them to the best possible resolution given their horrible choices and their failure to "hear" the Lord—and to teach them a lesson about worldly kings.

As Saul began plotting David's death, his son, Jonathan, grew close to David, and warned him of his father's plot. David fled to Nob, where Ahimelech the priest fed him and gave him Goliath's sword. From there David went to Gath, Goliath's home, and sought refuge with King Achish. But Achish and his court did not trust David. So David fled to the cave of Adullam with his family. He next sought refuge in Moab, but the prophet Gad warned him of danger, so he went to the Forest of Hereth, and then to Keilah, where he was involved in a battle against the Philistines. When Saul learned that David was in Keilah, he planned to send an army to Keilah to capture and expose David as a traitor, or kill him. In order to protect Keilah from siege, David fled to the Wilderness of Ziph. During all of the various movements of David he was developing personal relationships with various clans and leaders throughout Israel and beyond, relationships that would serve him well during his future kingship.

The Philistines renewed their campaign against Saul, which diverted his attention for a time, while David found some respite in Ein Gedi. During Saul's pursuit of David in Ein Gedi he entered a cave where David and his supporters were hiding, but did not find them (1 Samuel 24:3-4). While in the cave, David cut off a corner of Saul's robe. In an effort to demonstrate that he had no malice toward Saul, David greeted Saul the next morning and told him that, while he had an opportunity to kill Saul, he did not. And to prove the story, he showed Saul the piece of his robe. The two were reconciled, and Saul began to recognize that David would become his successor.

Scripture provides several stories about Saul and David reconciling, which suggests that it happened more than once, and the stories are presented from more than one perspective. Another time David infiltrated Saul's camp at night and removed Saul's spear and water jug. In this story Abishai counseled David to kill Saul, but David refused, saying that he would not stretch out his hand against the Lord's anointed (1 Samuel 26:11). When Saul learned what David had done he confessed that he had been wrong to pursue David, and blessed him.

Another tradition recounts the story differently, or adds to it. Here Saul permitted David to reside in Ziklag, from where David led raids against the Geshurites, the Girzites, and the Amalekites, while leading Achish to believe that he was attacking the Israelites, the Jerahmeelites, and the Kenites. Achish believed that David was a faithful vassal. Achish instructed David to guard the rear flank in an invasion against Saul. David returned to Ziklag, and Jonathan and Saul both died in battle.

Gilboa

The story of Saul's death provides a key element in the long story of the Bible.

> "Now the Philistines were fighting against Israel, and the men of Israel fled before the Philistines and fell slain on Mount Gilboa. And the Philistines overtook Saul and his sons, and the Philistines struck down Jonathan and Abinadab and Malchi-shua, the sons of Saul. The battle pressed hard against Saul, and the archers found him, and he was badly wounded by the archers. Then Saul said to his armor-bearer, 'Draw your sword, and thrust me through with it, lest these uncircumcised come and thrust me through, and mistreat me.' But his armor-bearer would not, for he feared greatly. Therefore Saul took his own sword and fell upon it. And when his armor-bearer saw that Saul was dead, he also fell upon his sword and died with him. Thus Saul died, and his three sons, and his armor-bearer, and all his men, on the same day together.

> And when the men of Israel who were on the other side of the valley and those beyond the Jordan saw that the men of Israel had fled and that Saul and his sons were dead, they abandoned their cities and fled. And the Philistines came and lived in them" (1 Samuel 31:1-7).

Saul's army was defeated and Saul was wounded. He knew that he would be captured and tortured, so he endeavored to take his own life. Saul's kingship ended in utter defeat, but the story is not over. It picks up in the next chapter.

> "After the death of Saul, when David had returned from striking down the Amalekites, David remained two days in Ziklag. And on the third day, behold, a man came from Saul's camp, with his clothes torn and dirt on his head. And when he came to David, he fell to the ground and paid homage. David said to him, 'Where do you come from?' And he said to him, 'I have escaped from the camp of Israel.' And David said to him, 'How did it go? Tell me.' And he answered, 'The people fled from the battle, and also many of the people have fallen and are dead, and Saul and his son Jonathan are also dead.' Then David said to the young man who told him, 'How do you know that Saul and his son Jonathan are dead?' And the young man who told him said, 'By chance I happened to be on Mount Gilboa, and there was Saul leaning on his spear, and behold, the chariots and the horsemen were close upon him. And when he looked behind him, he saw me, and called to me. And I answered, "Here I am." And he said to me, "Who are you?" I answered him, "I am an *Amalekite*." And he said to me, "Stand beside me and kill me, for anguish has seized me, and yet my life still lingers." So I stood beside him and killed him, because I was sure that he could not live after he had fallen. And I took the crown that was on his head and the armlet that was on his arm, and I have brought them here to my lord'" (2 Samuel 1:1-10, italics added).

Saul had tried to kill himself by falling on a sword, but he even failed at that and lingered, when an Amalekite happened upon him. Remember that Saul had been commanded to utterly destroy the Amalekites, but here this Amalekite—against whom the Israelites were fighting—killed King Saul as an act of mercy. The Amalekite knew that he had slain King Saul because he took Saul's crown and amulet in order to bring them to David, whom he somehow recognized as Saul's successor. David was flabbergasted!

> "Then David took hold of his clothes and tore them, and so did all the men who were with him. And they mourned and wept and fasted until evening for Saul and for Jonathan his son and for the people of the LORD and for the house of Israel, because they had fallen by the sword. And David said to the young man who told him, 'Where do you come from?' And he answered, 'I am the son of a sojourner, an Amalekite.' David said to him, 'How is it you were not afraid to put out your hand to destroy the LORD's anointed?' Then David called one of the young men and said, 'Go, execute him.' And he struck him down so that he died. And David said to him, 'Your blood be on your head, for your own mouth has testified against you, saying, "I have killed the LORD's anointed."'" (2 Samuel 1:11-16).

Thus, Saul was killed as a result of his own disobedience because he had failed to completely obey God's command to utterly destroy the Amalekites.[1]

David was then anointed King of Judah, the southern part of Israel. But Saul's son, Ish-Bosheth, was anointed King of Israel in the north. War ensued between them until Ish-Bosheth was murdered. Here we find a premonition of the divided kingdom, and the seed of the division issuing from the spirit of the apostate Saul through his son, and which would carry into David's kingship.

The death of Ish-Bosheth brought the elders of Israel to Hebron where David was anointed King of all Israel. David's first exploit as King of Israel was to conquer Jerusalem and make it his capital. David brought the divided kingdom together and then brought the recovered Ark of the Covenant to Jerusalem, where he planned to build a temple for God. But Nathan the

---

1 See the Appendix: Amalekites, p. 290, to see how Christians today are to understand this awful Old Testament episode, and the necessity of seeing the Old Testament in the light of the New.

prophet said that the temple was to be built by David's son because David's sins were too heinous. Nathan also announced that God was making a covenant with the house of David that would be established forever (2 Samuel 7:16).

DAVID'S KINGSHIP

Like David's assent to the throne, his kingship was messy—sinful and bloody. As king of Israel he defeated the Philistines, and received tribute from the Moabites, Edomites, Amalekites, Ammonites, and Aram-Zobah, which began to fill his treasury.

At one point, Israel was flourishing when David remained in Jerusalem during a siege against Rabbah, the Ammonite capital. Looking out from his palace window one day, he saw a woman bathing on a nearby rooftop. Bathsheba was summoned, and David impregnated her. In order to hide his indiscretion, David called her husband, Uriah the Hittite, home, hoping that he would have sex with her so that the baby would be presumed to be his. Uriah then returned to Jerusalem, but not to his wife. So David conspired to have Uriah killed in battle. And with Uriah dead, David married Bathsheba.

Soon after, Nathan the prophet confronted David with a story about a shepherd mistreating a lamb, which incensed David to anger at the shepherd's insensitivity. Nathan then revealed that the story was about him and Uriah, whom he had killed. David recognized his own folly and repented. Regardless, Nathan prophesied that war and violence would never depart from David's house (2 Samuel 12:10). That prophecy was fulfilled during David's lifetime, and continued throughout the Old Testament kingdom period of Israel's existence, as we shall see. The fact that David "heard" and accepted Nathan's accusation, and repented of his sin is a good thing, a God thing. Nathan told him that he was forgiven and that he would not die, but the child would die. And David was emotionally devastated when the child died.

David's success as King was great, and much wealth poured into his treasury as he secured alliances through marriage and war. Toward the end of his reign, David's son, Absalom, declared himself king because he thought David had grown soft.

Absalom's army was defeated in Ephraim, where Absalom had been caught in the branches of a tree by his excessively long hair. Contrary to David's order, Joab, the commander of David's army killed Absalom. Absalom's death devastated David again.

Later, as David was bedridden with old age, his eldest surviving son, Adonijah, declared himself king. When Bathsheba and Nathan heard about it, they went to David and secured an agreement to crown Solomon as King to fulfill David's earlier promise. Adonijah's rebellion was then put down, and David would die at the age of 70, having reigned for forty years. On his deathbed David counseled Solomon to walk in the ways of the Lord, and to take revenge on his enemies (1 Kings 2:1-10). David, who loved the Lord and had served him all of his life, still failed to see the contradiction of his own life's testimony. David failed to see that God's long range plan was to replace the ancient religion of vengeance with a religion of love and forgiveness. But David had made progress toward God's plan, and God honored that.

To this day David is considered to have been Israel's greatest king, but his greatness was seriously flawed by his own sinfulness. He had built a great kingdom for Israel, but it was built on the foundation of apostasy, with the tools of vengeance, war, and intrigue, and the materials of sin and corruption. Yet, David acknowledged and listened to God throughout his life, authored many Psalms, was genuinely repentant, and did his best to live in obedience to God. His accomplishments were significant and many. Yet, those very accomplishments brought sin and corruption to his court, and ruined his family.

David's greatest accomplishment was to bring the long story of God and His people to the forefront of human history. However, the story of David was not a story of success, but was the story of the failure of Israel to be faithful to God, in spite of all of the grace and help that God had provided. The kingdom that David built is the story of death, destruction, and apostasy—punctuated by moments of David actually hearing and responding to God's lead—that culminated in history's greatest failure as the Temple was destroyed and Jerusalem sacked eons later in A.D. 70. David did not simply and woodenly apply the law of Moses to the establishment of the Temple. Rather, he adjusted Moses' law to the needs of the fledgling kingdom. However, his kingdom was not what God wanted for Israel according to Samuel. God loved David because David was able to "hear" God, but only intermittently. Nonetheless, it was a start; it moved God's ball down field. This is what made David special in God's eyes.

This understanding comes from carefully considering the whole story of the Bible, Old Testament and New, and then reading that understanding back into the text. The reason that this is important is that it reflects God's perspective. God stands outside of time and history, which means that He sees the whole sweep of history all at once. By considering the whole of the biblical story we are able to get a better understanding of God's perspective. However, at this point those involved in the Old Testament story didn't know what we know today. This perspective adds much to the story of Solomon coming to power.

Following the death of his elder brothers Amnon and Absalom, Adonijah considered himself the heir to the throne. Although David was aware of Adonijah's selfish desires and sinful actions, he never rebuked him. David's silence was interpreted by Adonijah and others as consent. In anticipation of David's imminent death, Adonijah invited various court officials to a solemn sacrifice in order to announce his claim to the throne. However, he did not invite Solomon or any of his supporters. Nathan then warned Bathsheba of the intrigue, and counseled her to remind the king of his previous promise to make Solomon his successor.

They convinced David to give orders that Solomon be immediately proclaimed king. Adonijah then fled and took refuge at the altar, where he received pardon for his conduct from Solomon on the condition that he showed himself a worthy man (1 Kings 1:5-53). He later made a second attempt to gain the throne by trying to marry David's last concubine, Abishag from Shunem. But Solomon denied authorization for such an engagement, even though Bathsheba now pleaded on Adonijah's behalf. Adonijah was then put to death (1 Kings 2:13-25).

Solomon

Solomon's first venture as King was to make an alliance with Pharaoh, King of Egypt, symbolizing the alliance by taking Pharaoh's daughter as a wife. The symbolism of this alliance drips heavy with irony, as Egypt had been a long standing enemy of Israel, representing everything Israel was *not* to become. And to top the irony off, Solomon then asked God for wisdom,

> "to govern your people, that I may discern between good and evil, for who is able to govern this your great people?" (1 Kings 3:9).

After marrying an Egyptian queen in complete defiance of Moses' law regarding foreign women and alliances, Solomon asks God for wisdom! Oy vey! And yet, in response God showered Solomon with grace. God was willing to work with Solomon.

> "And God said to him, 'Because you have asked this, and have not asked for yourself long life or riches or the life of your enemies, but have asked for yourself understanding to discern what is right, behold, I now do according to your word. Behold, I give you a wise and discerning mind, so that none like you has been before you and none like you shall arise after you. I give you also what you have not asked, both riches and honor, so that no other king shall compare with you, all your days. And if you will walk in my ways, keeping my statutes and my commandments, as your father David walked, then I will lengthen your days" (1 Kings 3:11-14).

It might be argued that Solomon's alliance with Egypt happened before God had given Solomon wisdom. Perhaps, but it didn't stop him from obtaining many wives and concubines throughout his life. In response, Solomon went to Jerusalem, where the Temple had yet to be built, and

> "offered up burnt offerings and peace offerings, and made a feast for all his servants" (1 Kings 3:15).

He left Gilgal, where the Tabernacle was, and went to Jerusalem, where there was no Temple, and offered sacrifices, as if he were a priest, committing the same sin that Saul and David had committed. Where exactly were these sacrifices offered? The only option suggests that they were offered on "high places," a term that usually referred to pagan worship—but not always. The positive spin here would be to understand this particular high place to be the chosen place of the future Temple. A seldom seen point here is that Solomon continued the kingly role of priest-king that Saul had usurped and David had established. However, God had not authorized the king to offer sacrifices, though He consented to it. Again, David had usurped that function, and God had conceded, of course. Solomon then continued that tradition, which cemented the pattern for the rest of Israel's kings.

Solomon's first test of his newly acquired wisdom came when two prostitutes came to him claiming to be the mother of the same child. The two women had their respective babies at the same time at the same place, but one child died in the night. In the morning both mothers claimed the living child. Solomon called for a sword so he could divide the child, and give half to each mother as an equitable solution. One mother agreed, and one declined because she valued the life of the child. Solomon then identified the declining mother as the true mother because she truly loved the child. Whether or not she was the biological mother, she would be the best mother because her concern was for the child, not for herself. This story began Solomon's fame as the wisest king the world has ever known.

Solomon prayed for wisdom because he knew he did not have it. It is curious that the wisdom that Solomon practiced, a wisdom rich in the fruits of the book of Proverbs would become what the Apostle Paul would call works righteousness (Romans 3:28). Solomon's wisdom was worldly wisdom, a wisdom that built successful kingdoms. And of course, that is exactly what God planned for him at this point in the story. It was necessary for Solomon to teach worldly wisdom so that Paul could teach that God justified the righteous by faith rather than by works. But at this point in the story God was teaching a lesson about the success of worldly kingdoms, the kind of kingdom that Israel had wanted, according to Samuel's report.

> "Now Hiram king of Tyre sent his servants to Solomon when he heard that they had anointed him king in place of his father, for Hiram always loved David" (1 Kings 5:5).

Solomon then entered into another significant alliance with King Hiram, a pagan king who would provide much labor and material for the Temple. Through this alliance, Hiram gained access to major trade routes to Egypt, Arabia, and Mesopotamia. The two kings also jointly opened a trade route over the Red Sea, connecting the Israelite harbor of Ezion-Geber with Ophir (2 Chronicles 8:16-17). Both kings benefited greatly as money and trade goods poured into their kingdoms. Israel would soon become the wealthiest kingdom in the Middle East. And with that wealth came all of wealth's accouterments—first and foremost among them being spiritual pride, apathy, and apostasy. The connection between wealth and apostasy would be illustrated over and over again through the history of Israel's kings.

In order for Solomon to amass the necessary materials to build the Temple he would need a workforce.

> "King Solomon drafted forced labor out of all Israel, and the draft numbered 30,000 men. And he sent them to Lebanon, 10,000 a month in shifts. They would be a month in Lebanon and two months at home. Adoniram was in charge of the draft. Solomon also had 70,000 burden-bearers and 80,000 stonecutters in the hill country, besides Solomon's 3,300 chief officers who were over the work, who had charge of the people who carried on the work. At the king's command they quarried out great, costly stones in order to lay the foundation of the house with dressed stones. So Solomon's builders and Hiram's builders and the men of Gebal did the cutting and prepared the timber and the stone to build the house" (1 Kings 5:13-18).

Forced labor equals slavery. Israel had reengaged itself with slavery, but this time as master. God then responded:

> "Concerning this house that you are building, if you will walk in my statutes and obey my rules and keep all my commandments and walk in them, then I will establish my word with you, which I spoke to David your father. And I

will dwell among the children of Israel and will not forsake my people Israel" (1 Kings 6:12-13).

God's intention has always been to establish His Word, to demonstrate His integrity, to prove Himself graceful and trustworthy. God did all He could to guide Solomon in the ways of wisdom and mercy, and did so in the face of Solomon's failure to sufficiently demonstrate either. But Solomon did establish the efficacy of works righteousness. Solomon had succeeded greatly and his worldly success was understood to be God's blessing. Solomon's success meant that the Temple that he built would be excessively extravagant beyond the imagination of even David, his father.

The new Temple towered over David's old palace. So, Solomon also built a new palace for himself. Then he built a palace for his first wife, Pharaoh's daughter. Scholars argue various reasons for the movement of Pharaoh's daughter to a new palace, or out of the old palace that had been consecrated by the presence of the Ark of the Covenant. A simple explanation is also available. In spite of Solomon's proclaimed "wisdom," he married into Egyptian tradition. And because his primary weakness was a fondness for women and power, it could be that Pharaoh's daughter wanted to be as important to Solomon as was his God. It could well have been that the building of her palace had been *her idea*. There is certainly sufficient historical precedent for such a thing among royalty.

So Solomon finished building the Temple, his own palace, and the palace of the queen, and then brought the Ark of the Covenant to the Temple. In conclusion, he prayed a long, eloquent prayer and sacrificed to the Lord "22,000 oxen and 120,000 sheep" (1 Kings 8:63). Following the celebrations the Lord appeared to Solomon a second time, consecrating the new Temple but delivering the same message. God would honor all that Solomon had done *if* Solomon would be faithful and walk

> "with integrity of heart and uprightness, doing according to all that I have commanded you, and keeping my statutes and my rules" (1 Kings 9:4).

For The Whole World

Only *then* would God establish his throne. As a warning and a premonition God then said:

> "But if you turn aside from following me, you *or your children*, and do not keep my commandments and my statutes that I have set before you, but go and serve other gods and worship them, then I will cut off Israel from the land that I have given them, and the house that I have consecrated for my name I will cast out of my sight, and Israel will become a proverb and a byword among all peoples. And this house will become a heap of ruins" (1 Kings 9:6-8, italics added).

At the end of the story of Solomon's many construction projects we find this ironic note:

> "All the people who were left of the Amorites, the Hittites, the Perizzites, the Hivites, and the Jebusites, who were not of the people of Israel—their descendants who were left after them in the land, whom the people of Israel were unable to devote to destruction—these Solomon drafted to be slaves, and so they are to this day. But of the people of Israel Solomon made no slaves. They were the soldiers, they were his officials, his commanders, his captains, his chariot commanders and his horsemen" (1 Kings 9: 20-22).

As Egypt had enslaved the foreigners in its land long before (i.e., the Israelites), so Solomon had enslaved the foreigners in Israel. Solomon, in spite of his wisdom and in spite of God's help and guidance, had become a king like the kings of Israel's neighbors. The visit by the Queen of Sheba and her luxurious gifts suggests the further expansion of empire that Solomon and Hiram had built, which brought even more wealth into Solomon's treasures.

> "Thus King Solomon excelled all the kings of the earth in riches and in wisdom. And the whole earth sought the presence of Solomon to hear his wisdom, which God had put into his mind" (1 Kings 10:23-24).

Idolatry

> "When Solomon became old, his wives shifted his allegiance to other gods; he was not wholeheartedly devoted

to the LORD his God, as his father David had been.
Solomon worshiped the Sidonian goddess Astarte and the
detestable Ammonite god Milcom. Solomon did evil in the
LORD's sight; he did not remain loyal to the LORD, like his
father David had. Furthermore, on the hill east of Jerusalem
Solomon built a high place for the detestable Moabite god
Chemosh and for the detestable Ammonite god Milcom.
He built high places for all his foreign wives so they could
burn incense and make sacrifices to their gods" (1 Kings
11:4-8).

Finally the writers of Solomon's history present what they had been hinting at all along—Solomon's idolatry. In fulfillment of God's previous warning, God said:

> "Because you insist on doing these things and have not kept
> the covenantal rules I gave you, I will surely tear the king-
> dom away from you and give it to your servant. However,
> for your father David's sake I will not do this while you are
> alive. I will tear it away from your son's hand instead. But I
> will not tear away the entire kingdom; I will leave your son
> one tribe for my servant David's sake and for the sake of my
> chosen city Jerusalem" (1 Kings 11:11-13).

Solomon, the wisest and most successful king the world had ever known, fell prey to idolatry in spite of the fact that the Lord warned him, and had made available to him all the wisdom the world could provide. In spite of God's help and nurture, in spite of God speaking directly to him, Solomon succumbed to idolatry. Thus, idolatry was cooked into the ancient nation of Israel very early in its history. This is an important lesson that Paul will harp on in his letters to the Corinthians,[2] a lesson we today must not overlook or minimize.

> "For the wisdom of this world is folly with God. For it is
> written, 'He catches the wise in their craftiness'" (1
> Corinthians 3:19).

---

2 *Arsy Varsy—Reclaiming The Gospel in First Corinthians*, 2008; *Varsy Arsy—Proclaiming The Gospel in Second Corinthians*, 2009, Phillip A. Ross, Pilgrim Platform, Marietta, Ohio.

ANCIENT KINGDOM

While the transfer of the kingship from David to Solomon was full of sin and intrigue, the transfer from Solomon made it seem like a trivial matter in comparison. While the transfer from David to Solomon had been finally settled with Solomon on the throne, the transfer from Solomon set a civil war in motion that lasted four hundred years, without any final resolution.

The first disagreement was between Rehoboam, Solomon's son, and Jeroboam, one of Solomon's previously trusted officers who had become disillusioned and previously fled to Egypt to escape Solomon's oppressive regime. With Solomon's death he returned to challenge Rehoboam for the throne. Rehoboam's mother, Naamah, was an Ammonite, and thus one of the pagan wives whom Solomon had married. As Israel gathered to coronate Rehoboam, whose kingship would continue the family lineage of David, Jeroboam appeared in order to bring an issue to Rehoboam on behalf of the people.

> "Your father made our yoke heavy. Now therefore lighten the hard service of your father and his heavy yoke on us, and we will serve you" (1 Kings 12:4).

King Rehoboam then met with his counselors and asked them how he should answer.

> "And they said to him, 'If you will be a servant to this people today and serve them, and speak good words to them

when you answer them, then they will be your servants
forever'" (1 Kings 12:7).

But Rehoboam, unhappy with the counsel of these wizened elders, solicited the counsel of "young men," who advised him:

> "Thus shall you speak to this people who said to you, 'Your father made our yoke heavy, but you lighten it for us,' thus shall you say to them, 'My little finger is thicker than my father's thighs. And now, whereas my father laid on you a heavy yoke, I will add to your yoke. My father disciplined you with whips, but I will discipline you with scorpions'" (1 Kings 12:10-11).

Rehoboam took this advice, fulfilling the prophecy

> "which the LORD spoke by Ahijah the Shilonite to Jeroboam the son of Nebat" (1 Kings 12:15).

And this in turn set the civil war in motion. The ten tribes of the Northern Kingdom in Samaria rebelled against Rehoboam's kingship in the Southern Kingdom of Judah. Lest we think that this struggle was against the "good" king, Jeroboam, and the "bad" king, Rehoboam, Scripture tells us more about Jeroboam.

> "And Jeroboam said in his heart, 'Now the kingdom will turn back to the house of David. If this people go up to offer sacrifices in the temple of the LORD at Jerusalem, then the heart of this people will turn again to their lord, to Rehoboam king of Judah, and they will kill me and return to Rehoboam king of Judah.' So the king took counsel and made two calves of gold. And he said to the people, 'You have gone up to Jerusalem long enough. Behold your gods, O Israel, who brought you up out of the land of Egypt.' And he set one in Bethel, and the other he put in Dan. Then this thing became a sin, for the people went as far as Dan to be before one. He also made temples on high places and appointed priests from among all the people, who were not of the Levites. And Jeroboam appointed a feast on the fifteenth day of the eighth month like the feast that was in Judah, and he offered sacrifices on the altar. So he did in Bethel, sacrificing to the calves that he made. And he placed in Bethel the priests of the high places that he

had made. He went up to the altar that he had made in Bethel on the fifteenth day in the eighth month, in the month that he had devised from his own heart. And he instituted a feast for the people of Israel and went up to the altar to make offerings" (1 Kings 26-33).

While Rehoboam, following Solomon, sorely oppressed the people, Jeroboam led them astray by establishing pagan worship among them. These are the two sides who fought the civil war in ancient Israel. Close attention to the details indicates that Rehoboam's sin of oppression and Jeroboam's sin of false worship were cooked into the opposing sides of this struggle in ancient Israel from the beginning. What is little recognized is the fact that there were three sides in this civil war—Rehoboam, Jeroboam, and God, who opposed them both.

What we find in Kings and Chronicles provides some opposing stories. Chronicles I & II tries to clean up the many failures of the kings, especially Solomon, and is in general conformity with the historical trajectory established by Rehoboam (oppression by the Temple establishment). Here we find the idea that the existence of the Temple justified the oppression because the Temple establishment considered themselves to be on the "right side of history." They did this by following the law, by imposing the law upon their society. Here we in the twenty-first century must remember Paul's teaching that the law cannot save. The law leads to death because it demands what human beings cannot of themselves provide. And the biblical history of Israel demonstrates this.

Kings I & II shows us that Solomon was guilty of idolatry (false worship), and was in general conformity with the historical trajectory of Rehoboam, his son. So, Jeroboam rejected the Temple and the king who reigned over it by establishing Baal worship in Samaria. Jeroboam, like so many antinomians[1] today, abandoned the law because its social imposition lead to oppression. We see much of this today.

---

1 Antinomianism: Literally "against law or norms;" the theological doctrine that by faith and God's grace a Christian is completely freed from all laws, including the moral standards of the culture, and even the Bible.

We are very accustomed to seeing this as a two-way struggle, in part because that is an easy reading of the text. The struggle between strict enforcement of the law on one side, and the abandonment of the law on the other creates a false dichotomy. We need to pay closer attention to the text. There is an unseen character involved. God opposes both the strict enforcement of the law and the abandonment of the law (according to Paul's New Testament teaching). Israel's prophets, who argued God's position (God being the unseen character) of holding the demands of the law and the freedom of grace together, in tension. The prophets consistently staked out a position that opposed both the oppression by the religious establishment in Judah that followed Rehoboam, and the false worship (Baalism) by the religious establishment in Samaria that followed Jeroboam. This is precisely what Jesus and Paul did. This character of the Northern tribes in Samaria and the Southern tribes in Judah continued to play out throughout the subsequent history documented in the Old Testament (found in I & II Kings and I & II Chronicles, and elsewhere). It's all there, but it's a more complex, subtle, and disturbing story than we are used to hearing. We have been blinded by our simplistic Sunday School mentality, thinking that the conflict is between good and evil, which hearkens back to the Fall.[2]

This perspective is little recognized today, and was less recognized in ancient Israel, because God's weapons are not like our worldly weapons of warfare.

> "Put on the whole armor of God, that you may be able to stand against the schemes of the devil. For we do not wrestle against flesh and blood, but against the rulers, against the authorities, against the cosmic powers over this present darkness, against the spiritual forces of evil in the heavenly places" (Ephesians 6:11, continue through verse 18).

God plays the long game, and was setting up the history of Israel in the Old Testament so that Israel could learn the impor-

---

2   See "False Dichotomy," *Ephesians—Recovering the Vision of a Sustainable Church In Christ*, Phillip A. Ross, Pilgrim Platform, Marietta, Ohio, 2014, p. 391.

tance of following God from their own personal and national experience. God expects people to learn from history. In this case it would be the negative historical experiences and consequences of not following God. The ultimate biblical consequence was the destruction of Jerusalem and the First Temple in 586 B.C., and again in A.D. 70. Civil war forces people to choose sides, and in this case neither side was with God. Again, this story provides an important lesson for our contemporary world that we must stop missing.

TEMPLE

The central issue of the civil war in ancient Israel according to the overarching story of the Bible as a whole was the defense and maintenance of the Temple. King David conceived it, and King Solomon built it. However, according to Samuel, while God approved, supported, and encouraged it, the kingdom and its Temple were not what God thought best for humanity. It was Israel who demanded a king and a kingdom like the pagan nations had. That desire, according to God through Samuel, amounted to the rejection of God's kingship. This central point must not be lost in the midst of the long story of the splendor and passion of Israel's ancient kingdom. That kingdom required a temple because the other pagan kingdoms had temples, and to compete in the world of pagan kingdoms the role of the temples was central. So, David conceived of and planned a Temple worthy of his God, worthy in his mind, though not so much in God's. And as we know, Christ later re-identified the Temple as His body. The ancient Temple of Israel was never intended by God to be anything other than an object lesson about idolatry for Israel and eventually for the whole world.

God, who told Moses that He would work with the stubborn Israelites, worked with David to design the Temple. God would use the Temple as an historical, pedagogical object lesson that would point to Him. Thus, the Temple and its accouterments provide very good and useful information about God. They did then, and they still do today. However, neither the Temple nor the liturgy were to become a substitute for God. Worshipers were not to idolize the Temple, nor were the kings to use it to justify themselves, their policies, or their kingdoms. Which, of course, is exactly what happened! The Temple became (even in its conception and construction) an idol, a substitute for God. This is the long, historic lesson that God was teaching through the destruction of the Temple, a lesson that Israel did not want to learn. It is a lesson that is still difficult today. Nonetheless, this was the central conflict in ancient Israel's civil war, and remains a central lesson to be learned today.

The biblical text tells us that *all* of the kings of Israel (Northern Kingdom) "did evil." The pattern had been set by Jeroboam, who might have rightly understood that the idolatry of the Temple was wrong, but mistakenly tried to correct it by abandoning the God of the Temple and turning to other idolatries (Baalism). The kings of Israel followed Jeroboam's lead. Their error was thinking that the remedy for Temple idolatry could be solved by the engagement of idolatry of a different sort. And the text is right to denounce it.

The problems in Judah were more complex because the Temple was in Judah. Because Israel (the Northern tribes) rejected the Temple, Judah (the Southern tribes) likely believed that they needed to defend it. Here the pattern had been set by Rehoboam, who doubled down on the enforcement of Temple practices, which had been oppressive to begin with. Remember that Solomon had built the Temple with slave labor.

In order to examine the various kings in a meaningful way we will look in some limited detail at the "good" kings because they are fewer in number and share a commonality. All of the "bad" kings suffer the same general problem: they fell into various forms of idolatry, mostly Baalism or worshiping in "high places," that is, not worshiping God, and not worshiping God in the Temple. The bad kings did not support the Davidic cultural, social, kingly, and religious traditions. Because David set the standard we need to begin with David.

DAVID

David, in spite of his many sins, established the biblical prototype of a godly king. Good kings were compared to David, evil kings were contrasted with David. Throughout Scripture we see the deep respect shown for this man after God's own heart (1 Samuel 13:14, Acts 13:22). The story of David's ascension from an overlooked shepherd to reigning king is well-known. Rather than rehearse the history of that ascent, we will look at the reasons for God's special regard and David's success.

Chronicles tells us that David was universally beloved, that everyone in Israel respected David. There were many significant doubts and problems regarding Saul, but according to Chronicles *no one* failed to swear allegiance to David. A simple review of some of the biblical details about David's life and reign proves this to be an overstatement, but it is important because it reveals the perspective of the Chronicler, who was spinning history in David's favor in order to grow the kingdom.

This does not mean that the Bible contradicts itself. Rather, everything in the Bible is true and provides important information about both God and humanity, about God's eternal truth and the tragedy of human sin. Here, the deeper truth reveals that the ancient Israelite establishment was intent on maintaining the Temple and its culture—come hell or high water, which is a key element in the unfolding story of the Bible. Some examples include (italics mine):

> "All these, men of war, arrayed in battle order, came to Hebron with a *whole heart* to make David king over all Israel. Likewise, all the rest of Israel were *of a single mind* to make David king" (1 Chronicles 12:38).

> "And David and *all Israel* were celebrating before God with all their might, with song and lyres and harps and tambourines and cymbals and trumpets" (1 Chronicles 13:8).

> "And David assembled *all Israel* at Jerusalem to bring up the ark of the LORD to its place, which he had prepared for it" (1 Chronicles 15:3).

> "So David reigned over *all Israel*, and he *administered justice and equity to all* his people" (1 Chronicles 18:14).

> "Yet the LORD God of Israel chose me from all my father's house to be king over Israel forever. For he chose Judah as leader, and in the house of Judah my father's house, and

among my father's sons he took pleasure in me to make me king over *all Israel*" (1 Chronicles 28:4).

"Then the people rejoiced because they had given willingly, for with a *whole heart* they had offered freely to the LORD. David the king also rejoiced greatly" (1 Chronicles 29:9).

The thrust of David's kingship was the unification of Israel. According to 2 Samuel, during David's ascension Saul's son Ish-Bosheth declared himself king in Samaria, and struggled with David for the throne of all Israel. Ish-Bosheth was eventually killed by his own people, which set David free to be king of the whole country. From that point forward, David united the many factions that he had been cultivating during Saul's reign. He could do so because of his previous involvement with them during Saul's kingship, and because David had become an outcast to Saul's court.

This is the central political reason for God's special regard: David unified the nation of Israel, which was a foundational step for the larger, historical lesson that God was teaching about kings and nations. The failure of Israel's nationalism could not be understood apart from the prior establishment of the nation that provided the best possible opportunity for success—Israel.

But David was a very flawed man, an adulterer and a murderer who ruined his own family in the pursuit of his kingship. David had several wives and each wife had various children. So some siblings were half-brother or half-sister. Absalom's and Tamar's mother was Maacah, daughter of Talmai, king of Geshur (2 Samuel 3:3). Ammon, first born and heir apparent, was a child of Ahinoam of Jezreel.

"Now Absalom, David's son, had a beautiful sister, whose name was Tamar. And after a time Amnon, David's son, loved her. And Amnon was so tormented that he made himself ill because of his sister Tamar, for she was a virgin, and it seemed impossible to Amnon to do anything to her. But Amnon had a friend, whose name was Jonadab, the son of Shimeah, David's brother. And Jonadab was a very crafty man. And he said to him, 'O son of the king, why are you so haggard morning after morning? Will you not tell me?' Amnon said to him, 'I love Tamar, my brother Absalom's sister.' Jonadab said to him, 'Lie down on your bed and pretend to be ill. And when your father comes to see you, say to him, "Let my sister Tamar come and give me bread to eat, and prepare the food in my sight, that I may see it and eat it from her hand."'

"So Amnon lay down and pretended to be ill. And when the king came to see him, Amnon said to the king, 'Please let my sister Tamar come and make a couple of cakes in my sight, that I may eat from her hand.' Then David sent home to Tamar, saying, 'Go to your brother Amnon's house and prepare food for him.' So Tamar went to her brother Amnon's house, where he was lying down. And she took dough and kneaded it and made cakes in his sight and baked the cakes. And she took the pan and emptied it out before him, but he refused to eat. And Amnon said, 'Send out everyone from me.' So everyone went out from him. Then Amnon said to Tamar, 'Bring the food into the chamber, that I may eat from your hand.' And Tamar took the cakes she had made and brought them into the chamber to Amnon her brother. But when she brought them near him to eat, he took hold of her and said to her, 'Come, lie with me, my sister.' She answered him, 'No, my brother, do not violate me, for such a thing is not done in Israel; do not do this outrageous thing. As for me, where could I carry my shame? And as for you, you would be as one of the outrageous fools in Israel. Now therefore, please speak to the king, for he will not withhold me from you.' But he would not listen to her, and being stronger than she, he violated her and lay with her" (2 Samuel 13:1-14).

Tamar argued that raping her would be an outrageous breach of the law of Israel, would disgrace her publicly, would harm Amnon's reputation, and was not necessary, since if he asked the king, David could grant Amnon's request to marry her legally. But Amnon didn't listen to reason. He overpowered and raped her. David's reaction:

"When King David heard of all these things, he was very angry. But Absalom spoke to Amnon neither good nor bad, for Absalom hated Amnon, because he had violated his sister Tamar" (2 Samuel 13:21-22).

Some early versions of the text add a sentence to verse 21 that could well have been in the original, but was omitted by a copyist from the Masoretic text:

> "But he did not curb the excesses (literally, 'spirit') of his son Amnon; he favored him because he was his firstborn."[3]

Amnon was heir to the throne, and that was more important to David. Amnon probably knew the story of David and Bathsheba where David sinned and seemed to get away with it, if you ignore the death of the bastard son of David's sin with Bathsheba. In today's world such a miscarriage would be easy to ignore. Perhaps it was for Amnon as well. No doubt Amnon grew up thinking that the king can do whatever he wants, which is still a common folly among kings and leaders.

However, Absalom was incensed, and hatched a plot to kill Amnon. He invited all of his brothers and sisters to an event in the country, and instructed his servants to get Amnon drunk and kill him. He told them to fear no incrimination because "have I not commanded you?" (2 Samuel 13:28). Again, Absalom, who would be in line as heir to the kingship, believed that the king could do as he liked.

This story indicates the troubles (sin) that had been baked into David's family, likely as a consequence of Nathan's curse, the consequence of David's sin:

> "'Now therefore the sword shall never depart from your house, because you have despised me and have taken the wife of Uriah the Hittite to be your wife.' Thus says the LORD, 'Behold, I will raise up evil against you out of your own house. And I will take your wives before your eyes and give them to your neighbor, and he shall lie with your wives in the sight of this sun'" (2 Samuel 12:10-11).

While it is true that David repented of his sin with Bathsheba, and the murder of Uriah, his repentance did not cure him of his sinfulness nor absolve him of its consequences, nor the consequences for the kingdom of Israel. So, when we believe

---

3 Found in the *Septuagint* and the Samuel manuscript from Qumran Cave IV, quoted by Anderson, *2 Samuel*, p. 176.

that David was a man after God's own heart because he willingly repented, we have only a half-truth. This is true, of course, but it is not the whole story about God's special regard for David. God was also pleased because David united Israel and inaugurated the kingdom, which set up the central lesson of the Bible. And David's repentance adds poignancy to the story of his sins and the ultimate failure of the Temple/Kingdom project.

SOLOMON

It is commonly believed that Solomon was faithful at first, but went astray later in life. The primary reason for this belief is that Solomon prayed for wisdom rather than wealth or success. However, examination of the text in the order that it has been given (the story line) provides a somewhat different understanding. Solomon's prayer is described in 1 Kings 3:1-15:

> "Solomon made a marriage alliance with Pharaoh king of Egypt. He took Pharaoh's daughter and brought her into the city of David until he had finished building his own house and the house of the LORD and the wall around Jerusalem. The people were sacrificing at the high places, however, because no house had yet been built for the name of the LORD.
>
> Solomon loved the LORD, walking in the statutes of David his father, only he sacrificed and made offerings at the high places. And the king went to Gibeon to sacrifice there, for that was the great high place. Solomon used to offer a thousand burnt offerings on that altar. At Gibeon the LORD appeared to Solomon in a dream by night, and God said, 'Ask what I shall give you.' And Solomon said, 'You have shown great and steadfast love to your servant David my father, because he walked before you in faithfulness, in righteousness, and in uprightness of heart toward you. And you have kept for him this great and steadfast love and have given him a son to sit on his throne this day. And now, O LORD my God, you have made your servant king in place of David my father, although I am but a little child. I do not know how to go out or come in. And your servant is in the midst of your people whom you have chosen, a great people, too many to be numbered or counted for multitude. Give your servant therefore an understand-

ing mind to govern your people, that I may discern between good and evil, for who is able to govern this your great people?'

It pleased the Lord that Solomon had asked this. And God said to him, 'Because you have asked this, and have not asked for yourself long life or riches or the life of your enemies, but have asked for yourself understanding to discern what is right, behold, I now do according to your word. Behold, I give you a wise and discerning mind, so that none like you has been before you and none like you shall arise after you. I give you also what you have not asked, both riches and honor, so that no other king shall compare with you, all your days. And if you will walk in my ways, keeping my statutes and my commandments, as your father David walked, then I will lengthen your days.'

And Solomon awoke, and behold, it was a dream. Then he came to Jerusalem and stood before the ark of the covenant of the Lord, and offered up burnt offerings and peace offerings, and made a feast for all his servants."

Notice first that Solomon married the daughter of Pharaoh and made a pact with the king of Egypt, the very nation that had enslaved Israel. Had Egypt ceased being an enemy of God? Not according to the text, which means that Solomon violated God's command to

"make no covenant with them and their gods" (Exodus 23:32).

"You shall not do as they do in the land of Egypt, where you lived, and you shall not do as they do in the land of Canaan, to which I am bringing you. You shall not walk in their statutes" (Leviticus 18:3).

And he made such a covenant before he asked for wisdom. Solomon "loved the Lord," walked in the statues of David—but seems to have ignored some very important statues of God, "only (read: except) he sacrificed and made offerings at the high places" (1 Kings 3:3). Was he guilty of idolatry? Or did he have to worship at the high places (consistently identified as places of idolatry) because there was no Temple? David had abandoned the Tabernacle and brought the accoutrements of worship to

Jerusalem, where he (King David) offered sacrifices, contrary to God's limitation of such to the priests. And Solomon followed suit.

But Solomon also advanced this practice by uniting his worship with the worship of the "high places." Everything about this story is wrong in that it violates so much of God's instructions to Israel through Moses. Solomon went to Gibeon, an ancient pagan city where Joshua made the sun stand still (Joshua 10:12), a city that had a "great high place ... to offer a thousand burnt offerings on that altar" (1 Kings 3:4). Clearly Solomon was up to his neck in syncretism, the blending or attempted amalgamation of different religions, in violation of the First Commandment.

And at Gibeon the Lord appeared to Solomon in a dream, asking Solomon what *He* (God) could give *him* (Solomon). It wasn't Solomon asking God for something; it was God who wanted to give Solomon whatever *he* wanted. Solomon responded by praising God for David's faithfulness and for providing himself (Solomon) with succession to the throne. Solomon referred to himself as a child compared to David, and then gave accolades for the people of Israel, who were "great" and "chosen"—the people that God had called stiff-necked, stubborn, and sinful. And finally Solomon asked God for the wisdom to know the difference between good and evil, hearkening back to Adam and the Fall, so that he could govern "this your great people."

The Lord was so pleased with Solomon's request that the Lord said that He would "do according to your (Solomon's) word" (1 Kings 3:12). Note that Solomon was not doing according to God's word, but the Lord was doing according to Solomon's word. God gave Solomon the desires of his (Solomon's) heart. The whole thing is reminiscent of Romans 1:24 where "God gave them up in the lusts of their hearts to impurity." God gives people the desires of their hearts. And Solomon received the desires of his heart. He got "wisdom," and in addition he would get wealth and fame.

He got what *he* wanted, the greatest, most successful kingdom in Israel's history. But now remember that God told Samuel that the institution of such a kingdom for Israel would end in disaster. Such a kingdom was not God's ideal plan for Israel. So, God gave success to the kingdom to show Israel what it would become.

The story ends with Solomon waking up and going to Jerusalem where he "offered up burnt offerings and peace offerings, and made a feast for all his servants" (1 Kings 3:15). He brought this story of his dream and encounter with God to Jerusalem where he offered sacrifices celebrating his syncretism. The whole thing sounds like a political speech, filled with nuance, innuendo, and self-accolades.

The text tells us that immediately following all this two "prostitutes" came before him each claiming a child to be theirs. Solomon's first case, his first opportunity to use his newly granted wisdom was to determine the real mother among two prostitutes. We know the story well. Solomon offered to cut the child in two, and the real mother gave up the child to save its life. And Solomon awarded her with the child because her love for the child was true.

> "And all Israel heard of the judgment that the king had rendered, and they stood in awe of the king, because they perceived that the wisdom of God was in him to do justice" (1 Kings 3:28).

Solomon was then lionized for saving the bastard child of a prostitute. Again, this story is soaked in sinfulness that seems to go unrecognized. The story has genuinely redeeming value, but it also reveals that the great King Solomon's greatest decision was rendered by sorting out bickering prostitutes arguing over a bastard son. There is nothing in the story that functions as righteousness according to God's Word. The united kingdom under Solomon "ate and drank and were happy" (1 Kings 4:20). The kingdom was awash in success. They had riches, food, and all of their needs were met. The kingdom grew as Solomon added foreign wives to his harem, wives that secured covenantal arrangements with various pagan nations and peoples, bringing them into Solomon's kingdom. The text tells us that the world had never seen such success, such worldly greatness. Indeed,

Solomon was faithful to David's vision, and was far more successful than David could even conceive.

Because Solomon added the God of the Bible to his syncretistic religion, his success grew renown the world over,

> "surpass(ing) the wisdom of all the people of the east and all the wisdom of Egypt" (1 Kings 4:30).

And at the height of this "wisdom" Solomon arranged a deal with Hiram, king of Tyre, to supply cedar wood for the construction of the Temple. Tyre! This alliance resulted in a very lucrative partnership which benefited both parties. According to the historian Richard Miles,

> "Commercially, this deal not only gave Tyre privileged access to the valuable markets of Israel, Judaea, and northern Syria, it also provided further opportunities for joint overseas ventures. Indeed, a Tyrian-Israelite expedition traveled to the Sudan and Somalia, and perhaps even as far as the Indian Ocean."[4]

And Solomon got the best wood for the new Temple from a pagan king. Would God approve the construction of the Temple with foreign help, slaves no less? Of course He did. But God was playing the long game, setting up an historical lesson of biblical proportion.

This is not an argument that Solomon was a bad king, or that the Lord disapproved of the Temple. God ordained Solomon and his Temple to be exactly what they were in order to demonstrate the folly of syncretism, even when one of the elements of the syncretistic religion genuinely involved the God of the Bible. God provided the fullness of His genuine help with the accomplishment of David's vision. What didn't happen was complete obedience to God's Word. The vision of the kings trumped God's vision for Israel. But before we blame the kings for their shortsightedness, we need to assess whether our own vision of God has trumped God's vision of us, God's vision for a world where His righteousness reigns.

---

4   Mark, Joshua J. "Tyre." *Ancient History Encyclopedia*. Last modified September 02, 2009. https://www.ancient.eu/Tyre/.

Asa

> "And Asa did what was right in the eyes of the LORD, as David his father had done. He put away the male cult prostitutes out of the land and removed all the idols that his fathers had made. He also removed Maacah his mother from being queen mother because she had made an abominable image for Asherah. And Asa cut down her image and burned it at the brook Kidron. But the high places were not taken away. Nevertheless, the heart of Asa was wholly true to the LORD all his days. And he brought into the house of the LORD the sacred gifts of his father and his own sacred gifts, silver, and gold, and vessels" (1 Kings 15:11-15).

Asa (913-910 to 873-869 B.C.) reigned for forty-one years, supported the Temple establishment, and opposed false worship (other gods), even when his own mother had fallen into idolatry. While 1 Kings testifies that Asa was "*wholly* true to the LORD *all* his days" (1 Kings 15:14, italics added), 2 Chronicles tells us that the prophet Hanani accused Asa of relying on the king of Syria rather than the Lord, which caused him to loose a battle; and reminded him that when he relied on the Lord he won battles. Hanani then prophesied that that one discretion would cause Asa to have war "from now on" (2 Chronicles 16:9). The Chronicler reported that Asa put Hanani in prison for it and "also oppressed some of the people at that time" (2 Chronicles 16:10). While Asa was defined as a good king, oppression was an issue in the midst of his kingdom success.

Jehoshaphat

Jehoshaphat (873-869 to 849-847 B.C.) was the son of Asa and reigned twenty-five years. His zeal in suppressing the idolatrous worship of the "high places" is commended in 2 Chronicles 17:6. In the third year of his reign he sent out priests and Levites throughout the land to instruct the people in the Law, as prescribed in Deuteronomy 31:10-13 for the Tabernacle. The kingdom enjoyed peace, prosperity, and the blessings of God for a time.

However, Jehoshaphat also pursued alliances with the Northern Kingdom, and his son, Jehoram, married Ahab's daughter, Athaliah. Ahab was the worst of the bad kings of Israel. The prophet Jehu, son of Hanani, reproached Jehoshaphat over this alliance. 2 Chronicles 19:4–11 tells us that Jehoshaphat repented and resumed his faithful prosecution of idolatry. But there are differing accounts of this alliance between Israel and Judah for the trade of gold with Ophir (1 Kings 22:48–49 vs. 2 Chronicles 20:35–37). The disagreement seems to be about who initiated the alliance.

Later Judah and Israel joined forces in a war against the Moabites, who were under tribute to Israel. The Moabites aligned against Jehoshaphat at Ein Gedi where Jehoshaphat prayed,

> "O our God, will you not execute judgment on them? For we are powerless against this great horde that is coming against us. We do not know what to do, but our eyes are on you" (2 Chronicles 20:12).

The voice of Jahaziel the Levite then announced that the next day this great host would be defeated. And they were, because they quarreled among themselves and slew one another, leaving the people of Judah to simply gather their spoils. The Moabites had been subdued, but seeing Mesha's act of offering his own son as a human sacrifice on the walls of Kir of Moab filled Jehoshaphat with horror, and he withdrew and returned to his own land (2 Kings 3:4–27).

Jehoshaphat maintained the Temple establishment by both cleansing the Temple of idolatry and protecting the kingdom from the pagan hordes. He united the kingdom under the Temple establishment, as David had done. Unification and oppression seemed to go hand-in-hand.

JOASH

Joash (801- 798 to 786-782 B.C.), not to be confused with Jehoash king of Israel, reigned forty years. He was almost killed by his grandmother, Athaliah, but was whisked away in his infancy and raised in the Temple for seven years. He was seven years old when he became king (what could possibly go wrong?!). Here we see evidence that Judah's kings had "handlers." The Temple establishment strove to manage the kings. Once on the throne, Joash restored God's house to its former glory by collecting money for Temple repair.

> "And Jehoash did what was right in the eyes of the LORD all his days, because Jehoiada the priest instructed him. Nevertheless, the high places were not taken away; the people continued to sacrifice and make offerings on the high places" (2 Kings 12:2).

At one point King Hazael of Syria threatened to attack Jerusalem. Joash had no stomach for battle and sought to bribe Hazael not to attack by sending him Temple money and treasures. It worked for a while, but such easy booty led Hazael back for more. A few seasons later Hazel sacked Jerusalem (1 Chronicles 24:23-24). This loss then set his servants (managers) against him, and they finally murdered him in order to put his son, Amaziah, on the throne.

Again, we note that while he did right in his support of the Temple, he also did evil by being a catalyst for its sacking by Hazel.

Amaziah

Amaziah (797-796 to 768-767 B.C.) reigned twenty-five years, twenty-four years of which were with the co-regency of his son, Uzziah. His first action was to execute the murderers of his father, but strict obedience to the Mosaic laws permitted their children to live.

He employed a mercenary army of 100,000 Israelite (Northern Kingdom) soldiers in his attempt to reconquer Edom, which had rebelled during the reign of Jehoram, his great-grandfather. An unnamed prophet commanded him to send the mercenaries back, and he did so (2 Chronicles 25:7–10, 13), much to the vexation of the mercenaries. His obedience to this command led to a decisive victory over the Edomites. (2 Chronicles 25:14–16).

Amaziah then worshiped some of the Edomite idols he had captured. Once again an unnamed prophet rebuked him for this idolatry, and the king threatened him with violence. His inflated pride led him to challenge Jehoash, grandson of Jehu, king of Israel to combat. His prideful desire for vengeance led Amaziah into a disastrous battle at Beth-shemesh that resulted in a humiliating defeat. The king was captured, the wall of Jerusalem was broken down; the city, the Temple, and the palace were looted, and hostages were carried to Samaria. Like his father, his defeat brought on another conspiracy that took his life. Nonetheless,

> "He did what the LORD approved, but not with wholehearted devotion" (2 Chronicles 25:2).

> "...Amaziah turned from following the LORD... (2 Chronicles 25:27).

He was appreciated for his efforts to defend the Temple, and scorned for failing to defend it.

Each of the "good" kings carried forward the agenda of the Temple establishment inaugurated by David. The "evil" kings succumbed to idolatry, either by rejecting the Temple or merging false gods and false worship into the Temple.

THE PROPHETS

The earliest prophets arose in response to the Northern Kingdom (Israel), which had followed the lead of Jeroboam, who had rejected the oppression of Rehoboam and the Temple establishment in Jerusalem. Jeroboam had turned to Baal in outright rebellion against the way that Rehoboam represented God. Again, Rehoboam simply doubled down on the sinful pattern established by Solomon, his father, the pattern of oppression through the divine right of the king. Because God established kings and kingdoms, Rehoboam, like Solomon, believed that whatever he did was justified by God. Rather than the king following God, the king justified his own decisions and actions by attributing his decisions and actions with divine sanction.

Jeroboam was right to reject Rehoboam's oppression, but he was wrong in his total rejection of the God of the Old Testament Temple. Similarly, Rehoboam was right to honor the God of the Old Testament Temple, but was wrong in his wooden embrace of Mosaic culture. Rehoboam was following Solomon, who was following David. In the same way, David had been right to adapt Mosaic culture to the new situation of Israel's occupation of the Promised Land.

The old culture of the Tabernacle had failed to produce a Godly culture for a landed people. This should have been no surprise because the Tabernacle culture was not designed for a landed people. The Tabernacle was fore a nomadic people, and was intended to break the pagan habits and traditions Israel had gained in Egypt. God would not allow the generation who left Egypt to settle the Promised Land because God needed a fresh start. So, only after Moses and that generation had died did God give the Promised Land to Israel. Prior to that point the wilderness culture was inadequate for the establishment of Israel. But at that point, the people also rejected God's plan, and sought a king like the other nations. God agreed to work with that rejection by establishing David as king in order to provide an historic lesson to His people.

David was able to hear God, but only in fits and starts. David "heard" God's vision for the Temple and a truly Godly life, as we see through his various writings. But he was unable to live out what he knew. In spite of David's sin he heard God's voice, and codified much of what he heard in the Psalms. But the consequences of his sin were so great that God forbade him from building the Temple. That job would fall to Solomon, his son.

David's example should have led Solomon to appreciate both David's concern for tradition and his openness to hearing God adapt tradition to the new situation of life in the Promised Land. But he didn't. Rather, Solomon took David literally, which was important for the building of the Temple. However, unlike David's wisdom which had led to various adaptations of the culture of the Tabernacle for life in the Temple era, Solomon's wisdom led to worldly success. Solomon's wisdom was worldly wisdom, and did in fact bring great worldly success to the Israelite culture of the Temple.

Rehoboam's error was to continue in Solomon's footsteps, while Jeroboam's error was to reject the God of Scripture. Rehoboam believed that a wooden reading of Scripture was the true reading, and imposed it upon his kingdom. Jeroboam believed that a wooden reading of Scripture was the true reading, and rejected it. And this pattern has continued to motivate warring factions throughout history, beginning with the ancient biblical civil war between the Southern Kingdom and the Northern Kingdom. The prophets arose in response to this stalemate and provided a fresh, faithful, yet dynamic reading/hearing of God's Word.

AHIJAH

Ahijah the Shilonite, a Levite prophet of Shiloh during Solomon's reign prophesied that the kingdom would be divided as a result of Solomon's sin and that Jeroboam would become king. He was able to do this because he was able to "hear" the Lord; and he spoke for the Lord saying, "thus says the Lord" (1 Kings 11:31). The prophets rejected both sides of the civil war because they rejected the wooden, static reading of Scripture. Yet, they did not introduce anything unbiblical, but rather simply and correctly adapted and applied God's original intention (found in Israel's history) to their current circumstances.

Ahijah, whose book of prophecy has been lost, was the first of the prophets (chronologically).

> "Then he told Jeroboam, 'Take ten pieces, for this is what the LORD God of Israel says: "Look, I am about to tear the kingdom from Solomon's hand and I will give ten tribes to you. He will retain one tribe, for my servant David's sake and for the sake of Jerusalem, the city I have chosen out of all the tribes of Israel. I am taking the kingdom from him because they have abandoned me and worshiped the Sidonian goddess Astarte, the Moabite god Chemosh, and the Ammonite god Milcom. They have not followed my instructions by doing what I approve and obeying my rules and regulations, like Solomon's father David did. I will not take the whole kingdom from his hand. I will allow him to be ruler for the rest of his life for the sake of my chosen servant David who kept my commandments and rules. I will take the kingdom from the hand of his son and give ten tribes to you. I will leave his son one tribe so my servant David's dynasty may continue to serve me in Jerusalem, the city I have chosen as my home. I will select you; you will rule over all you desire to have and you will be king over Israel. You must obey all I command you to do, follow my instructions, do what I approve, and keep my rules and commandments, like my servant David did. Then I will be with you and establish for you a lasting dynasty, as I did for David; I will give you Israel. I will humiliate David's descendants because of this, but not forever" (1 Kings 11:31-39).

His prophecy was against the Temple, against Solomon, and against Rehoboam who would double down on the oppression that Solomon had used in building the Temple with slave labor. Solomon had been guilty of both idolatry and oppression. Ahijah, speaking for God, spoke in defense of

> "David who kept my commandments and rules ... so my servant David's dynasty may continue to serve me in Jerusalem (1 Kings 11:34, 36).

At first glance it sounds like David had been faithful to Deuteronomic Law. However, we have seen above that David's faithfulness was checkered—intermittent, partial.

My thesis is that David adapted Deuteronomic Law, which had originated with Moses for the Tabernacle in the wilderness, to *his* vision of the Temple and its kingdom. God needed to let Israel play out her vision for a kingdom in order to demonstrate that it would not work, even with God's help. Clearly, David's faithlessness in many areas is well-attested, which lobbies for a less than strict reading of Ahijah's testimony to David's faithfulness. God had directly given David instructions for the Temple and kingdom, but again, the existence of the kingdom came from the rejection of God by the people. God would use that rejection and its fruit (the Temple and its kingdom) to provide an historic lesson for Israel about the consequences of rejecting God as the true King. Because those consequences would take time to unfold, God needed to establish a "lasting dynasty" that followed David's example.

Keep in mind that following King David involved the rejection of God's kingship, according to Samuel. Ahijah said that David's descendants would be humiliated "because of this" (v. 39). Because of what? Because of the "lasting dynasty" of David, "but not forever" (v. 39). The humiliation and the Davidic dynasty would come to an end. The vision of the end of David's kingdom provided a premonition of the gospel of Jesus Christ, who brought an end of the Kingdom of Israel in A.D. 70.

The other prophets who prophesied against the Northern Kingdom were Jehu, Elijah, Micaiah, Elisha, Amos, and Hosea. The central sin that these prophets highlighted was idolatry, the abandonment and rejection of God, turning to false gods and false worship. Jeroboam had set that pattern.

Isaiah

Isaiah was an eighth century B.C. prophet, a Temple priest during the reign of Uzziah in Judah, the Southern Kingdom. Most of the earlier prophets hailed from Samaria, the Northern Kingdom. The traditional understanding, prior to the modern period of history, was that all sixty-six chapters of the book of Isaiah were written by one man, Isaiah, possibly in two periods roughly between 740 B.C. and 686 B.C., separated by approximately fifteen years. This view includes dramatic prophetic declarations regarding Cyrus the Great in the Bible, acting to restore the nation of Israel from Babylonian captivity. The problem with this view is that Isaiah mentioned the name "Cyrus" (Isaiah 44:28; 45:1), but there was no king named Cyrus at that time, as far as we know. Cyrus lived from 600 to 530 B.C.

Another widely-held view is that chapters 1–39 originated with the historical prophet, interspersed with prose commentaries written in the time of King Josiah, who had initiated the Deuteronomic Reform,[1] and that the remainder of the book dates from immediately before and immediately after the end of the exile in Babylon, almost two centuries after the time of the historic prophet.

While this issue has caused great consternation in the history of biblical scholarship, my intention is to deal with the text as it is presented. My concern is the content and meaning of the text, not its authorship. My assumption is that God has authorized the text as it is presented, and that there is value and meaning in the content. For those who want some explanation of the authorial problem, assume that the Bible has had several editors at various times in history whose identities have been lost, and that the Holy Spirit has continued to faithfully guide the production and preservation of Scripture over the ages, guiding the various editors as well as the original authors. This is not a lot different from what we do today with our various versions of the Bible. We

---

1 See *Galatians—Backstory/Christory*, Phillip A. Ross, Pilgrim-Platform, Marietta, Ohio, 2016, p. 138-9.

know that there was a major edit during the Babylonian captivity.[2]

We trust that the Spirit continues to guide faithful editors today. In addition, it is likely that the prophets taught and developed a following or a school of thought during their lives, people who preserved their work and their perspective. It was common literary practice of the day for students to speak and write in the name of the prophet, as if they were the original prophet, as a way of maintaining his teaching. Later generations collected their writings in a common collection because the various prophetic schools of thought had common concerns.

This scenario suggests that what Isaiah had been preaching and prophesying in the eighth century B.C. had similarities and application to the conditions of the sixth century B.C. In the eighth century the idolatry of the Northern Kingdom had reached and contaminated the Temple establishment of the Southern Kingdom, where Isaiah was a priest. The Northern Kingdom was sacked in 722 B.C. by the Assyrian army which captured the Israelite capital at Samaria and carried away the citizens into captivity. The kings of Judah then worked to extend their influence and protection to those who had not been exiled, some of whom had fled to Jerusalem. They also sought to extend their authority northward into areas previously controlled by the Kingdom of Israel.

Isaiah's prophecy of destruction and hope fit both the fall of the Northern Kingdom in 722 B.C. *and* the fall of the Southern Kingdom in 586 B.C. Perhaps the Spirit's purpose of melding the two-part authorship of the book of Isaiah was to emphasize the fact that the sins of the Northern Kingdom and the sins of the Southern Kingdom were common to both, that both Kingdoms had been deaf to God in similar ways, and that such deafness consistently leads to destruction. After all, this has been a perennial problem for humanity throughout history. And it still is!

Uzziah reigned in Judah during Isaiah's life. He was sixteen when he became king and reigned for fifty-three years. Pride led to his downfall when he entered the Temple to burn incense on

---

[2] *Adam as Israel: Genesis 1-3 as the Introduction to the Torah and Tanakh*, Seth D. Postell, Wipf & Stock, Eugene, Oregon, 2011.

the altar. Azariah, the High Priest, saw this as an attempt to usurp the prerogatives of the priests and confronted him about it with a band of eighty priests, saying,

> "It is not proper for you, Uzziah, to offer incense to the LORD. That is the responsibility of the priests, the descendants of Aaron, who are consecrated to offer incense. Leave the sanctuary, for you have disobeyed and the LORD God will not honor you"(2 Chronicles 26:18).

Then a great earthquake shook the ground and damaged the Temple. The rays of the sun shone on the king's face through a crack in the wall and immediately gave him leprosy. He was then driven from the Temple and compelled to live in "a separate house" until his death (2 Kings 15:5, 27; 2 Chronicles 26:3). The kingship was then given to his son, Jotham in 740 B.C. (2 Kings 15:5).

During this same time the kingdom of Judah enjoyed a time of success and wealth that led to self-satisfaction and spiritual apathy among both the rulers of the establishment and the people. And this was the situation in which Isaiah prophesied. Few people listened to him, and fewer yet believed him as he predicted the downfall of the nation that would result from their apathy. Isaiah lived through the fall of the Northern Kingdom, and it is possible that many people concluded that *that* was the destruction he prophesied.

And this may be the reason that the editors conflated Isaiah's prophecy with the fall of the Southern Kingdom as well, in that the fall of the Temple in Jerusalem would bring Isaiah's message home, underscoring its ongoing value. It wasn't just about "those other people" in the North many years earlier, it was also about those in Jerusalem at that time, as well. The destruction(s) of the Temple set up a pattern in history, a pattern of success, apathy, and destruction that has played out over and over again to varying degrees in Israel and beyond. This is the lesson that God was teaching Israel, though Israel—and all humanity, really—has had great difficulty getting and remembering.

Reading Isaiah today seems like his prophecy pertains to us in the twenty-first century—and it does! It pertains to every society that fails to learn what God is teaching. No doubt those who read it during the time of the Babylonian captivity felt the same way. So much so, that they conflated the earlier Isaiah with the same prophecy for themselves, which led to the combining of the first Isaiah with the second. Same problem, same lesson, same prophecy, same result.

Our contemporary problem with the authorship of Isaiah was not an issue for previous generations because of the centrality and universality of the message. In contrast, contemporary scholars are tempted to dismiss or belittle the content of the message because of the issues of authorship. But if the Holy Spirit truly guided Isaiah's writings, then the same Spirit was still alive two hundred years later—and still today! It is not the various authors of the Bible who give it credibility. Rather, the credibility of the Bible comes from the reality and veracity of the Holy Spirit. This is the truth that still shines through the book of Isaiah *because* of the authorship issues. What many people think of as a biblical error, God uses to establish the persistent reality and veracity of the Holy Spirit and His ability to communicate God's message.

HOSEA

Hosea was also an eighth century prophet in Israel, the Northern Kingdom. His ministry lasted about sixty years and he was the only prophet of Israel of his time whose written prophecy has survived the destruction of the Northern Kingdom. Hosea was a contemporary of Isaiah and an inspiration for Jeremiah (who lived in the sixth century).

Hosea's writings focus on his relationship with his wife, Gomer, who had been habitually unfaithful to him. Their relationship parallels the relationship between God and Israel, and Israel's adulterous and idolatrous relationship with pagan gods. In spite of the fact that Gomer ran away from Hosea several times to sleep with another man or men, he loved her in spite of her faithlessness. He could not stop loving her. Similarly, even though the people of Israel worshiped and idolized false gods, God continued to love them and did not abandon his covenant love for them. This is Hosea's essential message of hope, though he prophesied destructive consequences of their faithlessness. In spite of the pain and destruction coming to the Northern Kingdom, God would not give up on Israel as a people, but would continue to love and care for them. Thus, in the full light of the whole story of God, Hosea was a prophet of grace and mercy.

Hosea accused the Northern Kingdom of apostasy because they had turned away from God in order to follow Jeroboam and Baal, a Canaanite god. Hosea declared that unless they repented of these sins, God would allow them to be destroyed, and be taken into captivity by Assyria. Hosea wrote about his initial disgust with Gomer, and God's analogous disgust with Israel, that resulted in divorce. Their covenant had been broken, not by Hosea or God, but by the unfaithfulness of Gomer, and analogously by the unfaithfulness of Israel.

Gomer gave birth to a son whom Hosea named Jezreel, a name that refers to a valley in which many wars had been fought in Israel's history, especially by the kings of the Northern Kingdom. It is possible that the father of the child Jezreel was not Hosea, perhaps someone from the north. The child may have been the fruit of Gomer's faithlessness, which would make him a bastard son. This would strengthen the analogy to Israel's faithlessness.

Later Gomer had a daughter, whom Hosea named *Lo-ruhamah*, which means "unloved" or "pitiful." Again, Hosea was probably not the father. This name again analogously points to Israel and suggests that God will no longer have pity on the Northern Kingdom because its destruction was imminent. The message is that the fruit of faithlessness leads to destruction.

Gomer then had another son, who was named *Lo-ammi*, meaning "not my people," or "not mine," again suggesting that Hosea was not the father. It was a name of shame and rejection to show that the Northern Kingdom would also be shamed and rejected. Its people would no longer be known as "God's People." The Northern Kingdom had been rejected by God because of their faithlessness to the covenant.

Early in the book of Hosea we find his prophecy of restoration:

"Therefore, behold, I will allure her, and bring her into the wilderness, and speak tenderly to her. And there I will give her her vineyards and make the Valley of Achor a door of hope. And there she shall answer as in the days of her youth, as at the time when she came out of the land of Egypt. 'And in that day, declares the LORD, you will call me "My Husband," and no longer will you call me "My Baal." For I will remove the names of the Baals from her mouth, and they shall be remembered by name no more. And I will make for them a covenant on that day with the beasts of the field, the birds of the heavens, and the creeping things of the ground. And I will abolish the bow, the sword, and war from the land, and I will make you lie down in safety. And I will betroth you to me forever. I will betroth you to me in righteousness and in justice, in steadfast love and in mercy. I will betroth you to me in faithfulness. And you shall know the LORD. And in that day I will answer, declares the LORD, I will answer the heavens, and they shall answer the earth, and the earth shall answer the grain, the wine, and the oil, and they shall answer Jezreel, and I will sow her for myself in the land. And I will have mercy on No Mercy, and I will say to Not My People, "You are my people"; and he shall say, "You are my God"' (Hosea 2:14-23).

The book of Hosea represents a covenant lawsuit, where God accused Israel of breaking their previous covenant. God's disappointment towards Israel is analogously expressed through the broken marriage covenant made between Hosea and Gomer. Hosea taught that faithfulness to God was paramount, emphasizing the moral side of God's nature. Israel's ongoing faithlessness, despite all warnings, led to the fall of the Northern Kingdom. It wasn't that God had abandoned them, but that they had abandoned God. Hosea considered infidelity as the chief sin, reflecting the authenticity of the First Commandment.

In the light of Christ, Paul made much of Hosea's prophecy of restoration and grace.

"What if God, desiring to show his wrath and to make known his power, has endured with much patience vessels of wrath prepared for destruction, in order to make known

the riches of his glory for vessels of mercy, which he has
prepared beforehand for glory—even us whom he has
called, not from the Jews only but also from the Gentiles?
As indeed he says in Hosea, 'Those who were not my people I will call "my people," and her who was not beloved I
will call "beloved." And in the very place where it was said
to them, "You are not my people," there they will be called
'sons of the living God'" (Romans 9:22-26).

Here Paul was teaching that Christ brought the restoration of
God's Old Testament covenant with humanity, that God's
covenant concerned all humanity. God was bringing restoration
of His original covenant to humanity through Jesus Christ. The
gospel of Jesus Christ is in perfect alignment with the message of
Hosea: God is always gracious, but there are worldly consequences to sin.

JEREMIAH

Jeremiah (~650-570 B.C.) lived during a time of transition in
the ancient Near East. The dominant Assyrian empire had declined and fallen. Nineveh, the capital of Assyria, had been
captured in 612 by the Babylonians and Medes. But the new
world power was the Neo-Babylonian empire, ruled by king
Nebuchadnezzar. Judah had been a vassal of Assyria and, when
Assyria declined, Judah wavered in its allegiance between Babylonia and Egypt, but ultimately became a province of the Neo-
Babylonian empire. It was a time of world transitions.

Jeremiah's early messages were condemnations of false worship and social injustice, with a summons to repentance.
Jeremiah's ministry began before Josiah's reform (621 B.C.), and it
is likely that Jeremiah would have supported the reform movement because of the apostasy of Judah and the Temple culture.
However, it appears that over time Jeremiah became increasingly
troubled by and even opposed to Josiah's reform because it dealt
with the externals of religion and not with the inner spirit and
ethical conduct of believers. Indeed, that is exactly what law-
based religion does and is exactly what the Temple culture became under Josiah's reform. We can see this today because we
have read the Apostle Paul.

Jeremiah may have fallen into a period of silence for several years because of the failure of the reform to effect the spiritual condition of the people, and the failure of his prophecies concerning the foe from the north to happen. Many scholars have failed to understand that Jeremiah's contribution to the biblical story was to see that the law-based Deuteronomic Reform had failed to accomplish what Josiah hoped it would accomplish. We would do well not to miss this point because it is the major point of the Old Testament that led to the coming of Christ and the New Testament teaching of grace.

Jeremiah most clearly prefigured this New Testament scenario by suggesting that God would provide new hearts of flesh. He incorporated this vision into his prediction of their captivity and eventual return to Jerusalem. Jeremiah hoped that the Babylonian captivity would show them their error so that when they returned they could do so with God's original plan for them, the original plan that did not include the kind of king and kingdom that the people had asked Samuel to inaugurate. Did they learn this lesson? We will examine this when we come to the rebuilding of the Temple under Nehemiah.

Early in Jeremiah's ministry he called the people and the Temple to God's ancient (original) plan.

> "Thus says the LORD: 'Stand by the roads, and look, and ask for the ancient paths, where the good way is; and walk in it, and find rest for your souls.' But they said, 'We will not walk in it'" (Jeremiah 6:16).

The old King James Version better translates this verse.

> "Thus saith the LORD, Stand ye in the ways, and see, and ask for the old paths, where is the good way, and walk therein, and ye shall find rest for your souls. But they said, We will not walk therein."

It's better because it does not engage a literal interpretation of some of the words. The ESV makes it sound like Jeremiah was asking them go stand in or by an actual road. The KJV helps us to see that he was calling them to examine their way of life, and to correctly evaluate it from God's perspective, to "see" it rightly.

And finally, Jeremiah called them to ask for God's ancient ways, to *desire* God's old path, God's original way. Would that have been the way of the Deuteronomic Reform? Perhaps, initially it was. But over time Jeremiah "saw" that a strictly law-based reform produced a culture that resulted in religious oppression based on a literal interpretation of a law code that had been developed for a previous time, Israel's wilderness journey. It didn't work, and quickly became oppressive in the effort to make it work, to impose it.

The Temple establishment became self-righteous, defined as the righteous demands of their reform movement. This oppression then caused Jeremiah to change his mind about the Deuteronomic Reform, to "see" the failure of the law to change hearts and minds. He likely saw this as it became clear in the reign of Jehoiakim, whose reign was an active and difficult period in Jeremiah's life. Jehoiakim was very different from his father, Josiah, whom Jeremiah had commended for wanting the kind of justice and righteousness proposed in Deuteronomy. By the time Jehoiakim took the throne, the reform had clearly manifested its foul fruit, the fruit of oppression, the fruit of legalistic imposition. Thus, Jeremiah denounced Jehoiakim, who, no doubt, had justified his oppression in the name of righteousness and justice based on the Deuteronomic Reform.

To correctly assess Jeremiah's ministry we must keep in mind what we have learned from the Apostle Paul, who shined the light of Christ back onto the Old Testament. Christ had removed the veil that had blinded the Jews to the true lessons of their own history, and Paul was able to "see" the Old Testament without the veil, with the light of Christ. The ancient pagan temples were bastions of law and order—and vengeance or justice when that law was breached. Such authoritarian peacekeeping was even more necessary in ancient times than it is today, because Christ has significantly affected our contemporary world.

God's grand plan has always been to teach Israel, and eventually the whole world, that, while law is necessary for human culture, it is not sufficient. The law is good and has a purpose, yet the social imposition of law by one group upon another always produces oppression because the leaders use the law to justify their own self-centered beliefs and actions. Over time, the self-evident nature of the law becomes the self-righteousness of successful leaders.

Psalm 137

Traditionally this psalm is attributed to the prophet Jeremiah, and the Septuagint version of the psalm bears the superscription: "For David. By Jeremias, in the Captivity." The immediate context is the early arrival of the captive people of Israel in Babylon. Jerusalem had been under siege (starved for a long period of time), the Babylonian troops sacked and burned the city, including the Temple. Whatever was of value had been taken from homes and from the Temple, and the people were in slavery in Babylon.

> "By the waters of Babylon, there we sat down and wept, when we remembered Zion. On the willows there we hung up our lyres. For there our captors required of us songs, and our tormentors, mirth, saying, 'Sing us one of the songs of Zion!' How shall we sing the LORD's song in a foreign land? If I forget you, O Jerusalem, let my right hand forget its skill! Let my tongue stick to the roof of my mouth, if I do not remember you, if I do not set Jerusalem above my highest joy!" (Psalm 137:1-6).

The command to sing joyfully for those who just destroyed their world was an expression of highest mockery and contempt. The intensity of the visceral disgust that Israel had for their Babylonian captors at that point would have been off the charts. And yet as we look back on this Psalm, this event from the twenty-first century, we need to remember and proclaim God's sovereignty over history. We must acknowledge that it was God who destroyed Jerusalem and the Temple, using Babylon as His hammer. It wasn't Babylon who was responsible for their destruction, it was God!

Why did God destroy Jerusalem and the Temple? That's what the Bible is about. That is the main theme of the long story of the Bible. We know that Jesus is the reason, that the Old Testament set up the coming of Jesus Christ and the New

Testament. But the ancient Jews did not know that. From their perspective, they were supposed to understand that the Temple had been destroyed because they had turned it into an idol. God destroyed it because of their faithlessness and His faithfulness. This was the lesson of God's sovereignty for them at that time. The destruction of the Temple was an expression of their own corruption, their own idolatry—in the name of Yahweh!

In fact, it was God who caused the Babylonian captors to demand a song of joy from them! God was orchestrating this event. He was using the Babylonians to test their mettle, to see if they had learned to exercise the new religion of forgiveness. Did they understand that it was God who was doing this to them? Or would they blame the Babylonians and fall back on the old religion of vengeance? So the captive Jews composed and sang a song to the Babylonians:

> "Remember, O LORD, against the Edomites the day of Jerusalem, how they said, 'Lay it bare, lay it bare, down to its foundations!' O daughter of Babylon, doomed to be destroyed, blessed shall he be who repays you with what you have done to us! Blessed shall he be who takes your little ones and dashes them against the rock!"

The tenor of their song demonstrated that they had *not* learned to exercise the new religion of forgiveness, but were still stuck in the old religion of vengeance. In fact, through their liturgical use of this Psalm they institutionalized their desire for vengeance into the new liturgies that were used during their captivity in Babylon. God had destroyed their world *because* they could not or would not let go of their desire for vengeance.

The Temple had been destroyed because of their corruption, their failure to hear God's message of forgiveness. They were still psychologically and culturally stuck in the ancient religion of vengeance. This Psalm stands as a testimony that they would institutionalize—and did in fact institutionalize—this same spirit of vengeance into the new Temple that they would build following their captivity. It was also a message to God that they had not yet learned what He was teaching them.

To this day, Psalm 137 is traditionally recited before the Birkat Hamazon (Grace After Meals). And verses 5-6 are customarily said by the groom at the Jewish wedding ceremony before breaking a glass as a symbolic act of mourning over the destruction of the Temple. Verse 7 is found in the repetition of the Amidah on Rosh Hashanah.

This Psalm exhibits a kind of blindness that disassociates the blessings of God's grace, good memories of Temple worship, and ancient Jewish culture that is praised in the first half of this Psalm, from the ancient spirit of vengeance in the second half. But in Christ believers can see that the first half of the Psalm is a celebration of faithfulness, but that faithfulness is abandoned in the second half. And this means that the "faithfulness" celebrated in the first half was not true faithfulness. In Christ we can see that they did not learn what God was teaching them in the Temple. And failing to learn God's forgiveness, they doubled-down on *their* commitment to God (a feigned faithfulness), rather than seeing *God's* commitment to them (to teach them the blessings of mercy and forgiveness). In essence, they committed themselves to a regurgitated vision of the past, and neglected God's vision for the future.

EXILIC PROPHETS

Several other prophets were active contemporaries of Jeremiah: Zephaniah, Habakkuk, Ezekiel, Daniel, and Obadiah.

Zephaniah was likely composed during the period of the kings, which means that it is about Judah's (Jerusalem and the Temple establishment's) refusal to obey its covenant obligations rediscovered by Josiah (the Deuteronomic Reform) regarding Yahweh. Josiah's reform began well, but as it morphed into oppression the people resisted and rejected it. So, despite having seen Israel's (the Northern Kingdom's) exile a generation or two earlier, and despite the fact that the Temple establishment attributed the fall of the Northern Kingdom to God's anger against Israel's disobedience and idolatry, Zephaniah urged Judah to conform to the Deuteronomic law, saying that God *might* forgive them if they did so.

Zephaniah repeatedly used the expression, the "day of the Lord," The "day of the Lord" tradition also appears in Amos, Isaiah, Ezekiel, Obadiah, and Joel. This tradition prophesied that the Lord would wreak vengeance on unrighteousness, resulting in great destruction and cataclysm in order to purify God's people of various sins. The idea was that God's patience has a limit, and at a certain point the many sins of God's people push God beyond that limit. The fall of the Northern (Israel) and Southern (Judah) Kingdoms fit this pattern, as did the destruction of Jerusalem and the Temple in A.D. 70.

Habakkuk is generally believed to have lived in the seventh century B.C., prior to the Babylonian siege and capture of Jerusalem in 586 B.C. The first two chapters describe a dialog between God and Habakkuk, suggesting that Habakkuk was able to "hear" God. Habakkuk lived in a time of apostasy and unrighteousness, and asked God why He didn't destroy the disobedient. The central message, famously cited by Martin Luther, was that "the righteous shall live by his faith" (Habakkuk 2:4). This idea has played a central role in Christian thought. Paul used it in his letters to the Romans, Galatians, and Hebrews as the starting point for his discussions about faith. The third chapter of Habakkuk is a liturgical song.

Habakkuk is the least biographically known of the prophets. His only biblical mention occurs in his own book. This fact should suggest some relationship with Melchizedek, who also stands out among biblical characters because he too had no known lineage. This is important because Paul suggested that Christ was a priest in the order of Melchizedek (Hebrews 7), not in the order of Aaron or Levi. According to Paul, Christ, the great messenger of faith, also brought an end to the oppression of law. The law had failed to bring God's kingdom. This was the overarching story of the Old Testament. So, Christ would bring it about through faith.

Ezekiel was exiled in Babylon for twenty-two years (593–571 B.C.) where he wrote six visions comprising three themes: 1) judgment on Israel (chapters 1–24), 2) judgment on the nations (chapters 25–32), and 3) future blessings for Israel (chapters 33–48). Ezekiel explained to the captive Jews that the Babylonian destruction of the Temple and the captivity of God's people had been a punishment for their faithlessness. Ezekiel was trying to make sense of Israel's failure to implement God's kingdom and her Babylonian captivity.

His initial vision of God, described in fantastic images of lights and jewels, of a wheel within a wheel, etc., points to a vision of God as a great warrior. The purpose of this vision, addressed in his second theme, was to let Israel know that it was *God* who had brought about their destruction and captivity. It was not that God had abandoned them, but that God Himself had brought about their calamity because of their faithlessness, but was still with them in the midst of it. Ezekiel's final theme or vision prophesied that their exile would eventually come to an end, Jerusalem and a new Temple would be rebuilt—and that great blessings would result from that new Temple. Those blessings pointed to Christ, who is God's eternal Temple.

Ezekiel wrote of the destruction of Jerusalem as a purification sacrifice upon the altar that was necessary because of the "abominations" in the Temple. Those abominations included idolatry and false worship described in chapter 8. The burning of Jerusalem and the Temple was seen as a sacrificial fire of purification. He then announced that a small remnant would remain true to God in exile, and would return to rebuild the purified city. The image of the valley of dry bones returning to life in chapter 37 signifies the restoration of a purified Israel.

Ezekiel described God's promise that the people of Israel would maintain their covenant with God, and following their purification by fire (destruction and captivity), would receive a "new heart" to enable them to observe God's commandments and live in proper relationship with God and with others. However, according to Paul, the veil of Moses would not be lifted until the advent of Jesus Christ. So, Ezekiel's vision was also constrained by the veil that occluded God's whole plan from the time of Moses.

Nonetheless, Ezekiel provided a vision of hope in the midst of Israel's calamity and despair as they endured captivity in

Babylon. Ezekiel was fundamentally concerned with the presence (*shekhinah*) of God. Interestingly, the Hebrew word *shekhinah* does not appear in the Bible. The Jewish rabbis coined this extra-biblical expression which literally means "he caused to dwell," signifying that it was a divine visitation of the presence or dwelling of the Lord God on this earth.

God had spoken to Moses in the midst of the pillar of cloud in Exodus 33 to assure him that His Presence would be with the Israelites (v. 9) as they set out into the Wilderness. God spoke to Moses "face to face" (v. 11) out of the cloud, but when Moses asked to see God's glory, God said, "you cannot see my face, for man shall not see me and live" (v. 20). This suggests that the visible manifestation of God's glory (*shekhinah* or presence) was muted, hidden, or veiled. When Moses asked to see God's glory, God hid Moses in the cleft of a rock, covered him with His hand, and only then passed by. When He removed His hand Moses saw only God's back.

This is the veil that Paul mentioned (2 Corinthians 3:13-16), a veil that hid God's ultimate purpose of the law from the ancient Israelites. Paul taught that the law cannot save, but only provides damnation for those who impose it as a condition of salvation. In contrast, the gospel of grace teaches that salvation comes through God's personal love of humanity and a reciprocal desire to please Him. Furthermore, that desire is only dispatched by the presence or *shekhinah* of the Holy Spirit in the lives of believers. God had not abandoned His people, rather, His people had abandoned God long before their captivity.

Furthermore, God had not abandoned His people in their captivity. His mission was to maintain Israel's place as the people of God. God would restore them, so they had to hold on to God's presence in their midst. The challenge of their captivity was to maintain by adjusting their traditions without a Temple. Again, rather than regurgitating Moses, they would need to adapt God's law to their current circumstance of captivity in Babylon, which would require changes to their Temple-centered social traditions. However, they would not be able to make such changes without the *shekhinah* of the Holy Spirit, which we know would only be fully manifest in the light of Christ.

Christ came in the context of or as a response to the Old Testament, and He cannot be understood properly apart from that context. So, knowing the overarching story of the Old Testament is essential to knowing Christ as the *shekhinah* of the Holy Spirit. That story, which began at Creation, focused on the people of Israel through Abraham. The story of God's presence with His people began with the conversion of Abraham and Abraham's son (Isaac) and grandson (Jacob), and great grandson (Joseph), which took them into slavery in Egypt. Moses then led them out of Egypt into the Wilderness. And only after that generation had perished in the Wilderness, did God send them into the Promised Land. But the Promised Land had been occupied by people, who like the Israelites in the Wilderness, could not receive or "hear" God. When the culture of the Tabernacle failed to establish peace in the Promised Land (the period of the Judges), the people wanted to establish a kingdom like the kingdoms of the pagans whom they failed to defeat. God advised against it, but they wanted it anyway. So, God gave it to them.

They would have a kingdom like their pagan neighbors. The people chose Saul to be king, but God chose David. Solomon built the Temple and established the kingdom as a great world nation. But following Solomon's death his sons plunged the kingdom into civil war. That war ended with the defeat and capture of both sides—the Northern Kingdom and the Southern Kingdom. Ezekiel's context was the capture of the Southern Kingdom by Babylon. Ezekiel provided a renewed vision of God, who would be with Israel during their captivity. During that time Israel needed to adjust her religious and cultural traditions because they had lost the Temple, which had been the center of those traditions.

God's original intention was to be the King of Israel Himself through His *shekhinah* glory, through His Holy Spirit. But He knew that Israel needed a model by which to understand how to live in God's kingdom. That model or Messiah had not yet come in fullness. So, rather than looking forward, Israel looked back to her former glory. David had been their most faithful king, and had established their most successful period. So, they looked back to David and their former glory, and sought to rebuild Jerusalem and the Temple as it had once been, forgetting or denying the Godless past of the Temple. That idea, like their original idea of having a king like their pagan neighbors, was not God's idea of what would be best for them. But they were a stubborn and resourceful people, so God decided to work with them once again.

DANIEL

> "In the third year of the reign of Jehoiakim king of Judah, Nebuchadnezzar king of Babylon came to Jerusalem and besieged it. And the Lord gave Jehoiakim king of Judah into his hand, with some of the vessels of the house of God. And he brought them to the land of Shinar, to the house of his god, and placed the vessels in the treasury of his god" (Daniel 1:1-2).

Daniel and his friends had been taken to Babylon to serve in the court of King Nebuchadnezzar. In preparation for that service they were taught the culture of Babylon, and they were to eat Babylonian food and study Babylonian culture and religion. They were taught the "literature and language of the Chaldeans" (Daniel 1:4). However, Daniel and his friends refused to eat the king's recommended diet, but preferred a simple diet of vegetables and water. Daniel suggested that the health of he and his friends be compared to others who ate the king's diet.

> "At the end of ten days it was seen that they were better in appearance and fatter in flesh than all the youths who ate the king's food. So the steward took away their food and the wine they were to drink, and gave them vegetables" (Daniel 1:15-16).

The test went so well that all of the youth who were in training to serve the king's court were given vegetables and water rather than the king's diet. These four—Daniel, Shadrach, Meshach, and Abednego—excelled in "learning and skill in all literature and wisdom" (Daniel 1:17), and became the leaders or models for all Israel.

While this story is literally true, it also has symbolic meaning of a deeper truth. It wasn't just the Babylonian food that was rejected. While they studied Babylonian religion and culture, they did not "digest" it. They maintained their Jewish identity, their Jewish God and Jewish culture, even though they were immersed in Babylonian traditions. Remember that Jeremiah told Israel to

> "Build houses and settle down. Plant gardens and eat what they produce. Marry and have sons and daughters. Find wives for your sons and allow your daughters get married so that they too can have sons and daughters. Grow in number; do not dwindle away. Work to see that the city where I sent you as exiles enjoys peace and prosperity. Pray to the LORD for it. For as it prospers you will prosper" (Jeremiah 29:5-7).

It almost sounds like Jeremiah was telling the exiled Jews to adapt themselves to Babylonian culture. And no doubt, some Jews likely understood it this way. Daniel then provided a correction to that potential misunderstanding of Jeremiah. Daniel taught that there were limits to their Jewish cultural adaptation in Babylon. They were not to forget or neglect the fundamentals or basic elements of their Jewish identity as God's people. But because their Temple had been destroyed and could no longer serve as the centerpiece of their corporate life together, they would need to make some adjustments to their traditions.

Ezekiel's ministry and teaching centered on the adjustments they needed to make. Their corporate traditions had been severely hampered by the loss of the Temple, so Ezekiel taught them to focus on their individual morality. God had appointed Ezekiel to be a watchman over Israel in their captivity, to warn them that if they did not repent and turn back to God He would execute the final stage of His judgment on them. Ezekiel called Israel to corporate regeneration through his vision of "dry bones" (Ezekiel 37). That vision accused Israel of being dried up spiritually, which had led to their captivity, but it also prophesied that God would resurrect them as a faithful people. This prophecy pointed to Jesus Christ, but they did not and could not know that yet. So, they misunderstood (and misapplied) the prophecy to be about the rebuilding of the Temple in Jerusalem. They were partly right in that it was about the Temple, but the lesson as we now understand it was about Christ as the Temple of God

(John 2:19) rather than the rebuilding of the Temple in Jerusalem.

The Old Testament community continued to understand Ezekiel's prophecy in Old Testament terms, as the Temple in Jerusalem, until Jesus came to set the record straight. We must not fault them for that understanding because it contributed to the rebuilding of the Temple, which gave Christ the opportunity to clarify the issue for us.

God's intent was never to create a worldly kingdom like the other kingdoms of the pagans. Rather, God's Kingdom would enthrone Himself as the *shekhinah* glory or presence of the Holy Spirit in the lives of His people. God Himself would be their King, and His people would enact the will of God in the world by giving their personal and corporate attention to God. God's Kingdom would not be like any kingdom ever known in the history of the world. God was doing a new thing, not regurgitating an old thing.

The book of Daniel is composed of various court tales (chapters 1–6) and various apocalyptic visions (chapters 7–12). In addition, some chapters were originally written in Hebrew (chapters 1 and 8–12), while others were written in Aramaic (chapters 2–7). There is also a chiastic arrangement[3] of the Aramaic chapters, and a chronological progression in chapters 1–6 that moves from Babylonian to Median times, and from Babylon to Persia in chapters 7–12. Scholars have made various suggestions to explain these oddities, but it appears that the language division and concentric structure of chapters 2–6 are literary devices designed to bind the two halves of the book together. This fact does not damage the veracity or reliability of the content of the material. It simply links divergent information, which should encourage us to find out why they are linked. Something common is shared between them.

There is much confusion about the book of Daniel, which can be clarified by understanding its historical context. The prophecies of Daniel are fairly accurate history down to Anti-

---

3   A chiastic pattern is a literary technique. An example of chiastic structure would be two ideas, A and B, together with variants A' and B', being presented as A, B, B', A'.

ochus IV Epiphanes, king of Syria, but not in its prediction of his death. The text alludes to the two campaigns of Antiochus in Egypt (169 and 167 B.C.), the desecration of the Temple (the "abomination of desolation" in Matthew 24:15), and the fortification of the Akra (a fortress built in Jerusalem). However, there is no mention of the reconstruction of the Temple, or about the actual circumstances of the death of Antiochus (164 B.C.). This suggests that chapters 10–12 were likely written or edited between 167 and 164 B.C. Yet there is no evidence of a significant time lapse involved. So, all of this means that Daniel's historical context was around the Maccabean revolt, a Jewish rebellion (167-160 B.C.), led by the Maccabees against the Seleucid Empire and the Hellenistic influence on Jewish life.

The two parts of the book that were linked by the literary device appears to link two historic periods: the Babylonian captivity of Israel, and the Maccabean revolt. Though centuries apart, these two events or periods have something significant in common. Both describe important defeats or failures of the Israelite kingdom project. Both involve the "doubling down" by the Jewish establishment regarding strict observance of former laws and customs that were thought to be foundational contributors to an imagined "golden age" of the Temple. And both ended in destruction and failure.

Daniel is particularly difficult for Protestants to understand because, unlike the Roman Catholic Bible, the Protestant Bible does not include the Apocrypha, which is composed of various intertestamental works related to that revolt. Protestants consider these books to be historical, but not inspired. The decision not to include them was made during the Protestant Reformation (sixteenth century), and resulted in a failure to study them. Much of the millennial debates (premillennial vs. amillennial vs. postmillenial) originated from various attempts to fit Daniel into the long biblical story without consistent reference to the Maccabean revolt.

Nonetheless, the Spirit has given us the book of Daniel as it is, so we must not neglect its content because of editorial concerns. Rather, we are to understand Daniel to have made a significant contribution to the long story of the Bible. We see

For The Whole World

that Daniel was written during the captivity, but was added to and/or edited much later, as Isaiah had been. And again, this suggests the continuing vitality of the Holy Spirit through history.

Daniel was an interpreter of dreams, and his book begins with Nebuchadnezzar's dream. Nebuchadnezzar was king of Babylon from 605 to 562 B.C. Immediately, we see that the book of Daniel, which received its final editing during the 160s B.C., involves events from much earlier. This should not challenge the veracity of Daniel's work or integrity, but should compel us see that he was telling God's overarching story from the captivity to the Maccabean revolt. Again, the conflation of historical eras suggests a consistent theme that ran through these ages. Nebuchadnezzar's dream was about the development of the pagan world from the Babylonian captivity to the Maccabean revolt, and beyond. Nebuchadnezzar's kingdom would be divided, but the spirit of the pagan nations would continue. And it did.

Daniel's fiery furnace story constituted a promise of preservation through various struggles and opposition to living faithfully in pagan Babylon. God would preserve Daniel and his friends, and all who followed them, no matter how bad it got.

Chapter 4 detailed Nebuchadnezzar's second dream, his madness, and his subsequent conversion.

> "At the end of the days I, Nebuchadnezzar, lifted my eyes to heaven, and my reason returned to me, and I blessed the Most High, and praised and honored him who lives forever, for his dominion is an everlasting dominion, and his kingdom endures from generation to generation; all the inhabitants of the earth are accounted as nothing, and he does according to his will among the host of heaven and among the inhabitants of the earth; and none can stay his hand or say to him, 'What have you done?' At the same time my reason returned to me, and for the glory of my kingdom, my majesty and splendor returned to me. My counselors and my lords sought me, and I was established in my kingdom, and still more greatness was added to me. Now I, Nebuchadnezzar, praise and extol and honor the King of heaven, for all his works are right and his ways are just; and those who walk in pride he is able to humble" (Daniel 4:34-37).

Here we see Daniel's vision of pagan nations and rulers coming to faith in Christ. God's great plan was to save the whole world, the human genome, from self-destruction through unbridled sin. And the story of Nebuchadnezzar's restoration prefigures the ultimate conversion of all nations. That day is yet to come, but significant progress has been made since the days of Daniel.

Haggai

Haggai (521-516 B.C.) urged the people to proceed with the rebuilding of the Second Temple. Haggai attributed a recent drought to their prior refusal to rebuild the Temple, which he saw as key to God's glory. Of course, God had not changed His mind about the outcome of the Jewish kingdom that had been communicated through Samuel. Two facts propelled the Second Temple project forward: 1) Israel had not yet seen the folly of the Temple and were committed to restoring it to its "former glory," and 2) the Messiah had not yet come to provide the true model for human flourishing.

The book of Haggai ends with the prediction of the downfall of kingdoms because of the continued failure of Israel in particular and humanity in general to deal with sin. Here we find a consistent theme of human history. He asked the priests,

> "'If someone carries holy meat in the fold of his garment and touches with his fold bread or stew or wine or oil or any kind of food, does it become holy?' The priests answered and said, 'No'" (Haggai 2:12).

Then he asked them,

> "'If someone who is unclean by contact with a dead body touches any of these, does it become unclean?' The priests answered and said, 'It does become unclean'" (Haggai 2:13).

Then Haggai said,

> "So is it with this people, and with this nation before me, declares the LORD, and so with every work of their hands. And what they offer there is unclean" (Haggai 2:14).

He then suggested that they were not qualified to build the Temple because they were full of sin. Haggai taught that their own sin had brought down the first Temple, according to the prophets. And their stay in Babylon had only further corrupted them, and they would therefore carry that sin into the project to rebuild the Temple. Nonetheless, said Haggai, God would bless them. Here again we hear the gospel of God's amazing grace. We need to note two things about Haggai's teaching: 1) they would build their sin into the Second Temple project, and 2) God is gracious and merciful toward sinners.

Interestingly, Haggai ends by pointing to Zerubbabel, governor of Judah. Zerubbabel, the grandson of Jehoiachin, the penultimate king of Judah (not counting David), led the first group of Babylonian Jews to Jerusalem to begin the rebuilding project. 42,360 Jews returned from the Babylonian captivity in the first year of the reign of Cyrus, King of Persia (538-520 B.C.). Zerubbabel then laid the foundation of the Second Temple in Jerusalem.[4] This, then, provided the fulfillment of Ezekiel's prophecy.

ZECHARIAH

Zechariah was a prophet of Messiah, of the coming of the Lord to complete or fulfill His Kingdom project among His people. The return of Israel to Jerusalem from exile is the theological premise of Zechariah's visions in chapters 1–6. Chapters 7–8 address the quality of life that God wants his renewed people to enjoy. He then provides encouraging promises regarding the blessings of faithfulness. Chapters 9–14 comprise two visions of the future, visions that the writers of the New Testament applied to Jesus Christ. Zechariah began by telling them not to emulate their fathers, meaning the traditions of their immediate ancestors, those who preceded the Babylonian captivity (the corruption of the Judges and the First Temple) and those who were currently in Babylon—those who could not see the Temple in the light of the coming Messiah.

---

4   For more on this perspective see: *Galatians—Backstory/Christstory*, Phillip A. Ross, Pilgrim Platform Books, Marietta, Ohio, 2016, "Backstory," The Second Temple, p. 25-ff.

> "The LORD was very angry with your fathers. Therefore say to them, Thus declares the LORD of hosts: Return to me, says the LORD of hosts, and I will return to you, says the LORD of hosts. Do not be like your fathers, to whom the former prophets cried out, 'Thus says the LORD of hosts, Return from your evil ways and from your evil deeds.' But they did not *hear* or pay attention to me, declares the LORD. Your fathers, where are they? And the prophets, do they live forever? But my words and my statutes, which I commanded my servants the prophets, did they not overtake your fathers? So they repented and said, 'As the LORD of hosts purposed to deal with us for our ways and deeds, so has he dealt with us'" (Zechariah 1:2-6, italics added).

The fall of Jerusalem and the Temple that led to the Babylonian captivity was the result of the practices and traditions of the First Temple. Former prophets (Isaiah, Jeremiah, etc.) had railed against those practices and traditions, and the faithlessness that animated them. Note Zechariah's concern about "hearing" the Lord (Zechariah 7:13).

Zechariah's vision of a horseman suggests travel. His vision of horns, craftsmen, and a measuring line suggest construction. His vision of Joshua as High Priest suggests two things: 1) Joshua's mission to conquer the Promised Land, and 2) the coming of a new Joshua. Jesus' name is a variant of Joshua, and Paul described Jesus Christ as the great High Priest (Hebrews 4:14-16).

The vision of the golden lampstand is curious in that Zechariah seems to not recognize them or their function. This may suggest that the Israelites in Babylon did not recognize Temple imagery. Did it suggest some confusion about the Temple that Jesus would clarify (John 2:19-21)? Perhaps. Zechariah also alluded to Zerubbabel's role in the rebuilding of the Temple. Notice also the role of grace in the placing of the keystone of the Temple.

> "And those who are far off shall come and help to build the temple of the LORD. And you shall know that the LORD of hosts has sent me to you. And this shall come to pass, if you

will diligently obey the voice of the LORD your God"
(Zecharah 6:15).

Israel was then called to hearken to the "voice" of the Lord, not the "word." "Voice" suggests an active, dynamic relationship with God, where "word" would be a call to heed the traditional texts. It is not that God was somehow denying the validity or veracity of the Hebrew texts or traditions. They were not to deny or ignore them. By no means! Rather, God was building His Temple (Christ) on the foundation of His historic Word. Building or establishing the Kingdom is an ongoing project. It is dynamic, not static. God doesn't change, but we do, and we must adjust our understanding of God's unchanging Word as *we* grow. Understanding God requires a fundamental continuity from seed to flower to fruit. While our historical seasons change, we are always who we were created to be in Christ.

Zechariah's call for mercy and justice reflects such development. He criticized their fasting, which represented their traditions, and called them to a higher personal morality.

> "Thus says the LORD of hosts, 'Render true judgments, show kindness and mercy to one another, do not oppress the widow, the fatherless, the sojourner, or the poor, and let none of you devise evil against another in your heart.' But they refused to pay attention and turned a stubborn shoulder and stopped their ears that they might not hear. They made their hearts diamond-hard lest they should hear the law and the words that the LORD of hosts had sent by his Spirit through the former prophets. Therefore great anger came from the LORD of hosts. 'As I called, and they would not hear, so they called, and I would not hear,' says the LORD of hosts, 'and I scattered them with a whirlwind among all the nations that they had not known. Thus the land they left was desolate, so that no one went to and fro, and the pleasant land was made desolate'" (Zechariah 7:12-14).

Here Zechariah told them why the First Temple had been destroyed, and then gave them a message about the preservation of the Second Temple that would come into play later, when Messiah would come. Chapters 9-14 then provide prophecies about Messiah and the Day of the Lord, the judgment that would accompany Him. Zechariah wove the coming of Christ into his vision of the Second Temple. Israel still labored under the veil of Moses. Only the advent of Christ would remove the veil. So, the veil remained in the Second Temple.

Malachi

The book is commonly attributed to a prophet by the same name, but the Hebrew meaning of *Malachi* is "my messenger" (or "his messenger" in the Septuagint) and may not be the author's name at all. Scholarly debates rage about the identity of the author. Some scholars argue that Malachi originally consisted of three independent and anonymous prophecies, two of which were subsequently appended to Zechariah, and are sometimes called Deutero-Zechariah, with the third becoming the book of Malachi. From the *Catholic Encyclopedia:* "We are no doubt in presence of an abbreviation of the name *Mál'akhîyah*, that is Messenger of Elohim."

The dating of Malachi appears to be post-exilic because it uses a Persian term for governor (*pehâ*), and because Judah had a king before the exile. The book of Malachi was apparently known to the author of *Ecclesiasticus* early in the second century B.C. But most scholars say Malachi was written between Haggai and Zechariah, slightly before Nehemiah came to Jerusalem in 445 B.C. Again, note that this book also appears to be related to vastly different historical periods. However, the discrepancies in the dating do not mean that the text is unreliable. Rather, it suggests an enduring problem or concern regarding God's people that was being addressed.

Malachi was written to correct the negligence of the Israelite priests in post-exilic Jerusalem. The Jews had returned to Jerusalem and the Temple had been rebuilt. Clearly, the prophets urged the people of Judah and Israel to understand the destruction of the First Temple and their exile as punishment for failing to uphold their covenant with God. Malachi's context, then, was life in the Second Temple era, when commitment to God was again waning. This same pattern of behavior regarding Temple worship kept resurfacing over many centuries.

Malachi charged the priests with failing to respect God as God deserved. He accused them of using substandard sacrifices when God demanded animals "without blemish" (Leviticus 1:3). The priests, who were supposed "to determine whether the animal was acceptable,"[5] were offering blind, lame and sick animals for sacrifice because they thought nobody would notice or care. This idea fueled Jesus' passion when He cleansed the Temple.[6]

He accused *Judah* of faithlessness and profanation.

> "Judah has been faithless, an abomination has been committed in Israel and in Jerusalem. For Judah has profaned the sanctuary of the LORD, which he loves, and has married the daughter of a foreign god" (Malachi 2:11).

If this was written at the earlier date, the accusation pointed to the Northern Kingdom as a justification for their Assyrian captivity. And if it was written at the later date, it pointed to the priests of the Second Temple for their Babylonian captivity. The argument I am making is that this accusation fit both scenarios and was a perpetual problem. Again, the conflicting dates don't suggest a faulty text, but rather point to an ongoing failure among God's people, and the intentional editorial conflation of divergent periods as a testimony to the tenacity of the ongoing problem.

> "You have wearied the LORD with your words. But you say, 'How have we wearied him?' By saying, 'Everyone who does evil is good in the sight of the LORD, and he delights in them.' Or by asking, 'Where is the God of justice?'" (Malachi 2:17).

Malachi addressed the issue of divorce, and while marriage was likely a problem, the greater analogous issue was religious covenant abandonment. Just as the priests offered unacceptable sacrifices, so the people had neglected to offer their full tithe to God. The author assured the faithful that the differences between

---

5   *The Cambridge Bible Commentary on the New English Bible.*, "The Books of Haggai, Zechariah and Malachi," Rex Mason, New York, Cambridge University Press, 1977.

6   See *Galatians—Backstory/Christory*, "Jesus & The Temple," Phillip A. Ross, Pilgrim Platform, Marietta, Ohio, 2016, p. 37.

those who served God faithfully and those who did not would bring serious consequences. Malachi's threats of judgment against unfaithfulness are many, and yet he also rang a note of grace and mercy.

> "Then those who feared the LORD spoke with one another. The LORD paid attention and heard them, and a book of remembrance was written before him of those who feared the LORD and esteemed his name. 'They shall be mine, says the LORD of hosts, in the day when I make up my treasured possession, and I will spare them as a man spares his son who serves him. Then once more you shall see the distinction between the righteous and the wicked, between one who serves God and one who does not serve him'" (Malachi 3:16-18).

It is important to note that God does not treat all people the same, just as a secular judge today does not treat everyone the same. Law abiders are treated differently than law breakers. While the law is the same for all people, people will experience different consequences of their behavior. The consequences will be markedly different for those who obey the law from those who break the law.

The book concludes by calling people to remember the law of Moses (the Ten Commandments), and the "statues and rules" (Malachi 4:3, which points to Deuteronomy and Leviticus), and by promising that Elijah would return. Elijah had defended the worship of God over Baal, the ancient Canaanite deity. God also performed many miracles through Elijah, including resurrection, bringing fire down from the sky, and entering Heaven alive "by fire" (2 Kings 2:11). Ahab, the worst of the bad kings of Israel was king during Elijah's time. Ahab had built a temple for Baal, and his wife, Jezebel, brought an entourage of priests and prophets of Baal and Asherah into the king's court.

Most scholars believe that Malachi's reference to Elijah pointed to Jesus as being one like Elijah. And the allusion is fruitful. But another perspective is that Malachi's allusion to Elijah pointed to the character of the Second Temple, that things were just like they had been during the administration of Ahab. Malachi's use of Elijah pointed to the idea that the Second Temple establishment had or would become as bad as, or worse than, the Temple establishment that Elijah confronted, and that God would need to send one like Elijah or greater than Elijah to sort it out.

This idea better explains Malachi's final threat that God would soon "come and strike the land with a decree of utter destruction" (Malachi 4:6). These are the final words of the Old Testament, the Jewish Bible. It is most significant that the Jewish Bible ends with a threat of utter destruction, particularly in the light of the destruction of Jerusalem and the Second Temple in A.D. 70, which fulfilled the long arc of the story of the Old Testament.

The destruction of A.D. 70 was not the end of the story of the Bible, but was the end of the story of the Old Testament Temple. However, the story of Jesus Christ intervened before A.D. 70 in order to provide, not only hope for the future of the world, but the historical reality of God's presence in the world and His commitment to the manifestation of His Kingdom in the world in spite of human sin.

The beginning of the New Testament marks the end of the Old Testament. The final prediction in Malachi was double-edged in that Malachi predicted both the coming of One who

> "will turn the hearts of fathers to their children and the hearts of children to their fathers," *and will* "strike the land with a decree of utter destruction" (Malachi 4:6).

Jesus Christ is the great heart restorer, and He is also the One who brought the Temple to destruction in A.D. 70. Why did both of these things happen? Because not all hearts were turned to God, and this fact revealed the

> "distinction between the righteous and the wicked" (Malachi 3:18).

THE ADVENT

The biblical promise of Messiah, a prophet or great human figure who would establish the Kingdom of God is very ancient. The first reference to Christ is found in the Protoevangelium:[1]

> "I will put enmity between you and the woman, and between your offspring and her offspring; he shall bruise your head, and you shall bruise his heel" (Genesis 3:15).

Much has already been written about this, so further information is readily available.

Melchizedek significantly prefigured Christ, but little is known of him.[2] Moses made explicit reference to Christ in Deuteronomy 18:15-19:

> "The LORD your God will raise up for you a prophet like me from among you, from your brothers—it is to him you shall listen—just as you desired of the LORD your God at Horeb on the day of the assembly, when you said, 'Let me

---

[1] Strictly speaking, the protevangelium refers to the last part of Genesis 3:15. According to H. C. Leupold, this passage uses a zeugma in the word *bruise*, which may be translated "it shall crush thy head and thou shalt bruise his heel."

Because of the grave nature of the context, the fall of man, this passage describes more than just a man stepping on a snake's head. The reference to the seed of the woman as Christ is believed to relate to the Virgin birth of the Messiah, as well as the Hypostatic union of the Divine nature with the Human nature of Christ (https://wiki2.org/en/Protevangelium).

[2] Previously discussed, p. 58.

not hear again the voice of the LORD my God or see this great fire any more, lest I die.' And the LORD said to me, 'They are right in what they have spoken. I will raise up for them a prophet like you from among their brothers. And I will put my words in his mouth, and he shall speak to them all that I command him. And whoever will not listen to my words that he shall speak in my name, I myself will require it of him."

Here we see Moses taking refuge in the veil where he asked God not to speak to him anymore. The veil, though used by women in ancient times, was originally used by Moses. After speaking with God, Moses' face was radiant, and it frightened the people. So Moses veiled his face. The function of a veil is to obscure or partly hide something (Exodus 34:29-35). Isaiah understood the veil to allude to the idea that God hid the fullness of His truth from the ancient Israelites in order to later reveal a greater truth through their own history, a history that had not at that point sufficiently unfolded.

> "They know not, nor do they discern, for he has shut their eyes, so that they cannot see, and their hearts, so that they cannot understand" (Isaiah 44:18).

God did this in order to set up the advent of Jesus Christ in a way that would reveal the fullness of the truth of Jesus Christ through the history of the world that was yet to come (from the perspective of the Old Testament). God made the advent and ministry of Jesus Christ a matter of historical record in order to demonstrate its reality and effectiveness.

REVIEW AND PREVIEW

Much later Paul spoke to the reality of this veil:

> "Since we have such a hope, we are very bold, not like Moses, who would put a veil over his face so that the Israelites might not gaze at the outcome of what was being brought to an end. But their minds were hardened. For to this day, when they read the old covenant, that same veil remains unlifted, because only through Christ is it taken away. Yes, to this day whenever Moses is read a veil lies

over their hearts. But when one turns to the Lord, the veil is removed" (2 Corinthians 3:13-15).

The idea expressed here is foundational to the biblical perspective being articulated in these pages. Paul was shining the light of Christ back onto the pages of the Old Testament, back into the history of ancient Israel, in order to reveal what the old priests and prophets could not clearly see. Of course, many of the old prophets and teachers alluded to Messiah, to the coming fullness of the revelation of God. But they also knew that they were only pointing to a reality that they did not fully comprehend.

The primary idea of the Old Testament is the giving of the Law, first through the Ten Commandments after the Israelites escaped from slavery in Egypt, then through its further clarification through Leviticus and Deuteronomy by Moses and the elders. This was the period of the Tabernacle, a movable tent that provided a location in which to worship God. However, God's people at that time, though they had escaped from Egypt, could not escape the cultural and religious habits they had gathered in Egypt during their four hundred year captivity. And because God was creating a new culture for humanity, beginning with Abraham and the people of Israel, He needed to begin with a culturally clean slate. So, none of the generation who had escaped Egypt were allowed to enter or be part of the new culture in the Promised Land. Consequently, they wandered in the desert for forty years so that none of them were alive when Israel entered the Promised Land—not even Moses.

Once in the Promised Land they failed to obey God completely by failing to completely rid the Promised Land of pagan influence.[3] And the rest of the Old Testament story is about them wrestling with those pagan influences. The story of the Old Testament is about Israel's failure to live in complete obedience to God. We (humanity) cannot live with ourselves apart from obedience to God's Law. God's Law protects humanity from tearing human culture apart. The key to life in the Kingdom of God is the proper understanding and application of God's Law to our present circumstance. And the chief difficulty

---

3   See Agag, p. 148.

related to the Law arises because, while God's Law does not change, human culture does. This means that God's Law must be appropriately and correctly interpreted in the midst of the dynamics of human culture, human growth and maturity.

The first major cultural failure of the ancient Israelites in this regard is found in the book of Judges. Israel had inhabited the Promised Land, which meant that they were no longer nomads. However, the culture of Moses had been nomadic. Moses had interpreted the Ten Commandments for a nomadic people. The period of the Judges added to the difficulties that had occurred from the failure to rid the Promised Land of pagan influences. What was added was the additional difficulty of adjusting their nomadic Law and cultural practices to the needs of a landed society.

At the height of the failure of the Judges the people asked Samuel to appoint a king like the pagan nations had. It is important to see that, while this was not God's idea, He allowed it because He could use it to teach an important lesson to humanity. This means that the whole history of the Temple and its Old Testament kingdom would be developed in order to provide an historic object lesson about the importance of obedience to God's Law, rightly interpreted. So God directed the design (through David) and construction (through Solomon) of the Temple in order to later use the story of the Temple to point to the real Temple—Jesus Christ (Hebrews). The symbolism of the Old Testament Temple, and its historical failure to establish the Kingdom of God, pointed to the reality and necessity of Jesus Christ. We turn, now, to His Advent.

THE PROMISED BIRTH

The synoptic gospels (Matthew, Mark, and Luke) recount the story of the birth of Jesus Christ as a human being. However, the gospel of John, written much later, begins with the story of the Word as God, who created the whole universe. John's gospel argues for the preeminence of the Spirit of Christ in the fleshly man called Jesus. Jesus taught His followers to submit to the preeminence of the Spirit over their own thoughts, ideas, and desires. So, it is no surprise that John wrote about and followed that model.

While it is essential that the Messiah came in human flesh, the purpose of His birth and life was to demonstrate that God's Spirit, His Word, is able to conquer sin and death, that the character of God's story—God's man, Jesus Christ—could dominate and overcome the long story of human sin. And while it was essential that the story of Jesus Christ had a physical, bodily, historical reality, it is also important that He has a spiritual reality of even greater consequence.

The first disciples came into contact with the physical Person of Jesus Christ, everyone else comes into contact with the spiritual Person of Jesus Christ—the very Word and character of God through the Bible. While it is essential that Jesus Christ actually lived as a human being in history, those who lived after His ascention—including us—have no contact with Him as an actual, fleshly, human being. Our only contact with Him is spiritual, so His spiritual reality is essential for 99.9% of Christians. Today, Christ's spiritual reality inhabits both God's Word and His people.

The need to honor and defend the physical reality of the Person of Jesus Christ was absolutely essential to the first disciples —and to us, but more to them. The actual, physical reality of Christ's presence in the ancient world is the foundation for the actual, spiritual reality of Christ's ongoing presence in the world since that time, and for all time henceforth. Consequently, the Gospels focused attention on Jesus Christ as an actual Person in the world. The synoptic gospels laid the foundation for Jesus Christ as an actual human Person, and John laid the foundation for Jesus Christ as the actual Spirit of God, whom he refers to as the Word of God.

The gospel writers established Jesus Christ as the promised Messiah of the Old Testament, as the fulfillment of Old Testament prophecies. From the beginning the kingdoms of the world had been built on the foundation of sin—Adam's sin, Cain's sin, Enoch's sin, Lamech's sin, the great Tower of Babel, etc. God then called Abraham out of that world of sin, but because sin resides in the human heart, Abraham's extrication from that world was complicated. The complications of human extrication from sin comprise the story of the Bible.

God knew that it would take more than pulling sinful individuals out of that sinful world. It would take more than pulling various families and tribes out of that sinful world. As long as sin remained in the world it would threaten the stability of God's people because people are weak. Human beings, the most sensitive of God's creatures, are easily and effectively tempted to succumb to the pleasures of their sensitivity, to the narrowness of their self-concern, and the passions of their undisciplined imaginations. As long as sin remains, people will continue to wander into its bogs and swamps.

Jesus was born from a virgin mother. On the one hand Jesus had a human lineage, but on the other His lineage was spiritual.

JOHN'S PROLOGUE

Matthew and Luke began their Gospels by citing Jesus' human lineage to show that He was the fulfillment of the ancient Messianic prophecies, and to establish that His ministry was a continuation of God's intention in the Old Testament. Mark didn't mention lineage, but simply tied Jesus to the Messianic prophecies of Isaiah. In contrast, John provided the lineage of the Holy Spirit by beginning with Creation:

> "In the beginning was the Word, and the Word was with God, and the Word was God" (John 1:1).

John equated God's Word (λόγος) with the activity of the Holy Spirit in the world. Much has been said about the definition of the Greek word *logos*. Let me suggest that John intended it to represent the connection between language and reality. When words convey the truth of a thing those words are an expression of *logos*. God spoke His Creation into existence.

> "And God said, 'Let there be light,' and there was light" ...
> And God said, 'Let there be an expanse ... And God said,
> 'Let the waters ...'" (Genesis 1:3, 6, 9), etc.

God spoke what we call *reality* into existence. However, reality is not just the objective "matter" of the universe, but is also the linguistic structures and integrity that is needed to communicate that reality to others. This reality is also composed of ideas or thoughts that are fused to the "objective" aspects of "matter" through consciousness, and are contrasted with imaginary ideas or descriptions that have no corresponding physical reality. Apart from this communicable aspect of reality nothing could be said about anything. So the communicability of reality is essential to God's Creation—and especially to human beings because it facilitates the aspects of Creation that can be discussed.

While it is a matter of faith to believe that God spoke the world into existence, and Genesis clearly says this, John then suggested that what God spoke into existence is the reality of language itself, the integrity of language to accurately and adequately describe human existence, the reality in which human beings live. Plato called it the world of forms, and abstracted forms (or ideas) from substance (matter) as if reality is dualistic, as if forms have some sort of objective existence apart from the material things they represent.

But that is not what John was doing. John was arguing for the reality of the Holy Spirit, that the Holy Spirit is the glue that binds language to the reality of "matter." We can also call this reality the *universe*, the idea that language (verse) can be universally (uni) communicated among human beings. The universe is the communicable reality of humanity. Theologically, John was saying that in Christ God was reversing the curse of the ancient tower of Babel, when universal language and communication became divided or segmented. This language or *logos* was supposed to provide light, clarity, knowledge, and/or understanding in that it established the integrity of language and reality. A consequence of the integrity of language and reality has been the development of science and technology, a relatively recent phenomena in human history. Science and technology grew out of the seedbed of European Christendom, out of the principles of Trinitarian Christianity.

God has also been populating this linguistic reality with people who could understand what was being communicated. This is Christ's mission in the world. Eventually all people will be swept into this universe, this universal understanding of reality—at the fullness or completion of the eschaton. In the meantime, it is growing. And like a crop it grows through seasons, each season creates new seeds for further growth and expansion. Some seasons are more productive than others, and over time the crop will dominate humanity.

But we must be careful with the language of dominion (Genesis 1:28) and domination because God does not force people to do anything. That's not how God works. God pulls or draws (John 12:32), He doesn't push people into conformity. He leads but doesn't push people into His reality of language integrity or formality. Rather, He changes our desires to conform to His desires by giving us what we want. He tells us about the consequences of wanting the wrong things, and then gives us those wrong things when we want them in order to show us why He doesn't want them for us—because they have adverse consequences in this world.

Virgin Birth

The doctrine of the Virgin Birth attempts to solve the threefold problem of 1) Jesus' legitimacy, 2) His Davidic lineage, and 3) His divinity. Many unbelievers and scholars believe that Jesus was the bastard son of Mary who was adopted by Joseph, which would make Him illegitimate in Jewish society. But if He is to be understood as the promised Messiah He needed to be in the lineage of David, the model king. And as Messiah He needed a direct connection to God Himself.

The two lineage lists in Matthew and Luke vary at several points, which has caused much difficulty among theologians. Matthew began with Abraham, while Luke began with Adam. The lists are identical between Abraham and David, but differ following David. Various solutions have been suggested. A common explanation is that Luke traced the genealogy of Mary, with Eli being her father, while Matthew described the genealogy of Joseph. This view was advanced as early as John of Damascus (d. 749). Other explanations are more complex.

However, Israel's fixation on human lineage had a limited usefulness. As with circumcision, an intimately related institution, its purpose was to separate the culture of God from the culture of sin. Israel left Egypt and kept to herself because God

For The Whole World

was creating a new culture that was to be completely different from the culture(s) of the pagans. God was at the center of that new culture through His covenant relationship with them. God was grafting a Godly branch to an ungodly vine, and used the idea of covenant to bind them together. People could understand His covenant relationship with them because they understood the idea of marriage covenant.

The limit of the usefulness of the maintenance of Jewish lineage was reached when Israel failed to obey God's command to completely rid the Promised Land of pagan influences.[4] From that time forward, the Godly culture would need to evangelize pagans in order to bring them into God's new culture because God's plan would not be complete until all humanity was included. Had Israel perfectly obeyed God's command, over time everyone in the Promised Land would have been born into it. But because pagans continued to dwell in the Promised Land, they would need to be evangelized and converted to faithfulness to God's covenant. Consequently, God needed to work apart from human lineage, and used His grace and mercy to further the expansion of His Kingdom through the presence and power of the Holy Spirit. And this was why John traced the lineage of the Spirit (John 1), the lineage of grace and mercy in his gospel.

However, Israel lived under a veil. The ancient Israelites did not understand this because they persisted in their stubbornness, their pride of self-importance. Had they honored God through perfect obedience, God would have continued to honor them as His people. Had Israel lived in complete obedience to God, He would have set them on a pedestal as the model for Kingdom citizens. But because of their disobedience, He singled them out to become an object lesson to the world regarding their obstinance.

Matthew and Luke wrote in order to bridge the failed model of ancient Israel with the yet future Kingdom of Jesus Christ. In order to do this they needed to identify and establish Jesus Christ as the long promised Messiah of the Old Testament, and part of those prophecies had been couched in the faithful lineage idea.

---

4 See Agag, p. 148.

So, they scoured the Scriptures to produce such a lineage, but they had their proverbial fingers crossed because they also understood that Jesus Christ had ended for good the false ideas that God required a faithful blood lineage to accomplish His purpose. They had learned from Jesus that God worked through the Bread of heaven not the blood of lineage, through grace, not race. God's intentions for humanity have always been universal. God was saving humanity from self-destruction. He was out to save the human genome from extinction. The only lineage that God is now concerned about is the lineage of faithfulness, the family of grace.

So Matthew and Luke wrote a serious parody of Jesus lineage by tracing the lineage of faithfulness rather than biological progenation. John understood this and wrote his prologue as the lineage of the Holy Spirit in support of this idea. The parody involved making serious fun of the Jewish lineage obsession by breaking the rules: including women (Rahab the harlot), skipping generations, etc. It turns out that Jesus' lineage is actually the lineage of grace, not race.

Paul then identified Jesus Christ to be in the priesthood of Melchizedek, and one of the main things about Melchizedek was that he had no lineage. For the most part, the Christian church has yet to catch up with Matthew, Luke, John, and Paul.

Nonetheless, the serious aspect of the doctrine of the virgin birth is that it points to the divinity of Jesus Christ, where divinity implies something infinite, like one of the defining characteristics of God. It is necessary that humanity be intimately related to God. One way to think of this is that humanity can be considered to be a mathematical infinite set[5] because we are able to reproduce. Everything capable of reproduction is a potentially infinite set. In order to understand this, you must "do the math" (understand Set Theory).

---

5 Not infinitely large but infinitely open ended. Through reproduction humanity can increase in number. For the purposes of this analogy, consider the set of humanity (individual human beings) to be infinite with regard to the mathematics of Set Theory.

Christ is a kind of Aleph-null[6] with regard to humanity as a mathematical set. The Aleph-null represents the first and/or last element of an infinite series that completes the series in order to identify it as a complete ordered set. Without the Aleph-null an infinite set could not be considered to be complete because we could continue to identify additional elements that would be included in the set, from now to eternity. Thus, the Aleph-null is both like the other elements of the set, and very different from them because of the role it plays in the set. The similarities between the Aleph-null in set theory and Jesus Christ are fascinating. Please don't neglect studying them. The allusion here is that Jesus Christ plays the role of the Aleph-null in the well-ordered, infinite set of His Body, the Church.

The study of mathematical sets provides interesting and insightful information about several biblical issues that deal with issues of membership in the body of Christ. All membership issues are about the limits and boundaries of the set of people who belong to Christ.

This is a complex idea, but it will help to make John's gospel ring clear in ways that demonstrate the necessity of Jesus' divinity when we realize that divinity pertains to the ideas of infinity and eternity. Infinity has to do with size, i.e., the extent of Christ's efficacious salvation, and eternity has to do with time, which involves procreation. Paul described the church as the body of Christ. In other words, the church is the Spirit of Christ in individual Christians where the Spirit of Christ is defined as the character of Christ living or extant through those individuals, and the set of individuals is considered to be a group, kind, or unit. Again, divinity belongs to the realm of infinity. The math of the infinite is different from the math of the finite in some very interesting and enlightening ways. Mysterious things happen when we apply the logic of math to the infinite, and the math helps us better understand those mysteries—and John's Gospel!

---

6   https://wiki2.org/en/Aleph_number

WISE MEN

Three foreign, pagan kings were aware of the prophecies about Messiah, and determined that the birth of Jesus was the fulfillment of those prophecies, and decided to bring the infant Messiah gifts. Weird! When Herod heard about it he asked them to let him know when they found the infant Messiah so that he could also pay his respects. But Herod was lying. He actually wanted to kill the Messiah in order to protect himself from the popular claims of a rival authority. So, Herod ordered his soldiers to seek and kill all the male infants they could find in Bethlehem.

Everything about this story is outside of Israel, outside of the Temple establishment and Jewish tradition. None of the wise men of the story were faithful Jews, yet they recognized the reality and authority of Messiah. Of course, we know that their actions were predicted by Scripture, but they didn't know that. The very people who had prophesied and were eagerly anticipating the Messiah—the Old Testament Jews—were not the ones who recognized Him. Those who were outside the Jewish culture and Temple traditions were the ones who honored the birth of Messiah. Gentiles brought Him gifts.

> "Then, opening their treasures, they offered him gifts, gold and frankincense and myrrh" (Matthew 2:11).

"Opening their treasures" means that the gifts were costly, expensive, valuable. Those gifts endowed Jesus; they provided for his well-being and education. They also likely financed the trip to Egypt to escape Herod's wrath (Matthew 2:13–23). So, while ancient Israel escaped slavery by fleeing Egypt under the guidance of Moses, Jesus sought refuge from Herod in Egypt. Why didn't Jesus' family seek refuge with the Jews? They were His people. If anyone should have provided protection for the young Messiah it should have been the Jews! This scenario speaks volumes. It both condemns the Jewish establishment and honors the wisdom of pagan leaders and their pagan traditions. In addition, it communicates the idea that Jesus came for the whole world, and not just the Jews.

The term *Magi* likely refers to the Persian priestly caste of Zoroastrianism. And while the Magi are commonly referred to as kings, there is nothing in Matthew's account that implies that they were rulers. The identification of the Magi as kings is linked to Old Testament prophecies that describe the Messiah being worshiped by foreigners, pagans.

> "And nations shall come to your light, and kings to the brightness of your rising" (Isaiah 60:3, see also Psalm 68:29, Psalm 72:10).

Here again we see the universal mission of Christ: to bring the nations to the genuine worship of the only real God. The inclusion of the wise men in the story of Christ's birth served to condemn Jewish culture and the Temple establishment because they had lost this universal dynamic of God's mission to the world. The Second Temple Jews had "circled the wagons" and were in a protective mode against the world, and had been in that mode for many centuries, since before the rebuilding of the Second Temple.

Who were these wise men? Scripture doesn't identify them, but tradition does. Melchior was identified as a Persian or Arabian scholar; Caspar, an Indian scholar; and Balthazar, a Babylonian scholar. They were all intellectuals, academics, scientists, inasmuch as astrology was the science of stars and predictions. Science and academia has always dabbled in the art of prediction. These scholars represented the major kingdoms outside of Israel of the day.

We are told that they came from the East, which would have meant that they came from Persia and/or Arabia, the deserts East of Jerusalem. The desert people were tolerant of other religions, but the dominant religion of that area at the time was Zoroastrianism, with its priestly *magos* class. There were also Persian beliefs about the rising of a star as a prediction of the birth of a ruler, and Zoroastrian myths describing the manifestation of a divine figure in fire and light.

During the Jewish exile in Babylon King Nebuchadnezzar had captured the best and brightest of the defeated Jews and integrated them into his advisory body of wise men—stargazers, dreamers, intellectuals of the time. Daniel and his friends were added to his accumulation of *magi*.

> "And in every matter of wisdom and understanding about which the king inquired of them, he found them ten times better than all the magicians and enchanters that were in all his kingdom" (Daniel 1:20).

Here we find a connection to the Babylonian captivity of Israel, which tied into the prophecies of the Old Testament, and the character of the Second Temple establishment. At one point, Nebuchadnezzar put Daniel in charge of his *magi*, so it was likely that the wise men who had visited Jesus centuries later had come because they had been educated in the tradition of Daniel. Daniel had become the most successful Israelite evangelist in Babylon. And later Babylon had been captured by Persia about 539 B.C. So, the Persian intellectuals would have known about Daniel's predictions.

A number of factors led to the eventual fall of Babylon. The leadership of the Babylonian king, Nabonidus, led to much turmoil. The Babylonian Marduk priesthood hated Nabonidus because he had suppressed Marduk's priests and had elevated the priests of the moon-god Sin[7] in an effort to centralize Babylonian religion. Cyrus allowed the Jewish exiles to return to Jerusalem, and to take their sacred vessels and symbols. That permission was embodied in a proclamation (Ezra 1:1-11), whereby Cyrus the Persian justified his claim to the Babylonian throne. Tradition says that the Jews in Babylonian captivity initially greeted the Persians as liberators. Although the Jews never rebelled against the Persian occupation, they were restive under Darius I and Artaxerxes I of Persia, but never took up arms against the Persians.

Later, after the Temple had been rebuilt, the Second Temple establishment understood itself to be protecting Jewish culture and tradition through separation from various pagan influences. So, while the Second Temple establishment had been "circling the wagons" in Babylon and later in Jerusalem, Daniel and his followers had been busy educating the Persian elites in the Old Testament Scriptures.

---

7   *History of the Persian Empire,* A.T. Olmstead, Univ. of Chicago Press, 1948, p. 38

THE BAPTIST

John The Baptist preceded Jesus and anticipated His ministry. John had gathered a following and when he lost his head, Jesus took over leadership of his group of followers, which gave Jesus a jump start for His ministry. Jesus then compared John to Elijah.

> "For all the Prophets and the Law prophesied until John, and if you are willing to accept it, he is Elijah who is to come. He who has ears to hear, let him hear" (Matthew 11:14).

These are the words of Jesus, which makes them important. And the idea of having ears to hear alerts us to something subtle and widely overlooked.

What is still little understood or accepted today is the idea that the allusion to Elijah was not merely communicating something about John or Jesus, but that it also alluded to the idea that the character of the Second Temple establishment was similar to the reign of King Ahab, who was the worst of the bad kings. Thus, the meaning of the verse is that they expected that Elijah or a prophet like Elijah would be required to address such a high degree of Temple rot, that it would take someone with the prophetic skills of Elijah to address their situation. Such an expectation would have been understood by the Temple authorities to be insurrectionary, so Jesus' disciples would need to keep it under the radar. Thus, special ears were needed to understand the message.

The Gospels vary in their descriptions of John being like Elijah. Matthew and Mark describe John's attire to be like that of Elijah, who also wore a hair coat with a leather belt (2 Kings 1:8). Matthew said that John was "Elijah who is to come" (Matthew 11:14). This suggests not only that John was Elijah's successor, but again it meant that one like Elijah was needed to address the corruption of the Temple in Jesus' day. In the gospel of John, John the Baptist expressly denied being Elijah because John thought that the analogy was intended to point to Jesus.

In the annunciation narrative in Luke, an angel appeared to Zechariah, John's father, and told him that John would

> "turn the hearts of the fathers to the children, and the disobedient to the wisdom of the just"

and that he would

> "go before him in the spirit and power of Elijah" (Luke 1:16-17).

This then fulfilled Malachi's prophecy (Malachi 4:6). Elijah had acquired a mythological character in Israel because he had been mysteriously taken up to heaven by a whirlwind (2 Kings 2:11). And what goes up, must come down. So, the mythos of Elijah contributed greatly to the expectation of the coming of Messiah, conflating the long expected Messiah with the return of Elijah.

John The Baptist had come to accuse the Second Temple and her people of horrific corruption, and provide an opportunity for repentance. The fact that *he* baptized people *outside* of the Temple tells us that he believed that the Temple establishment had lost all religious authority, that renewal would need to come from outside the Temple culture. John provided a case study of the corruption by accusing Herod of illegally marrying his brother's wife, Herodius. While it might be argued that Herod was not part of the Second Temple establishment, it is now and was then common knowledge that Herod *controlled* the Second Temple establishment. The Jewish establishment was more Roman than Jewish, and that was John's point.

John was the last of the Old Testament prophets, and Jesus acknowledged John's prophetic significance.

> "And the disciples asked him, 'Then why do the scribes say that first Elijah must come?' He answered, 'Elijah does come, and he will restore all things. But I tell you that Elijah has already come, and they did not recognize him, but did to him whatever they pleased. So also the Son of Man will certainly suffer at their hands.' Then the disciples understood that he was speaking to them of John the Baptist" (Matthew 17:10-13).

Jesus acknowledged that John fulfilled the expectations for the return of Elijah, which would complete the Old Testament

For The Whole World

promise. But John also said that his only role was to point to Jesus Christ, the Messiah. This is important because it allows Jesus to stand outside of the Old Testament in order to provide the renewal that needed to come from outside the Second Temple establishment. Jesus Christ is both the fulfillment of the Old Testament predictions about Messiah, and He stands outside of the Temple culture. Jesus was not the return of Elijah because Elijah still represented the Old Testament, and his return would represent a return to the Old Testament system.

The "renewal" that Jesus Christ brings is not some sort of return to a former Jewish glory, but rather Christ marks the beginning of a worldwide glory that the Old Testament had failed to produce. This failure of the Old Testament was intentional on God's part because it provided the necessary context for the world-wide ministry of Jesus Christ. Jesus calls the whole world to God's future, not to some imagined past. Yet, at the same time, He does not call people to abandon the past because we cannot move forward without learning the lessons that history teaches.

THE CHRIST

JESUS' BAPTISM

His baptism is one of the five major aspects of the gospel narrative of the life of Jesus, the others being the Transfiguration, Crucifixion, Resurrection, and Ascension. In the gospels, the baptismal accounts of Luke and Mark record a voice addressing Jesus, "You are my beloved Son, in whom I am well pleased," but in Matthew the voice addressed the crowd, "This is my beloved Son...." (Matthew 3:13–17, Mark 1:9–11, Luke 3:21–23). Alternatively, John's Gospel provides a witness rather than a narrative.

> "I saw the Spirit descend from heaven like a dove, and it remained on him. I myself did not know him, but he who sent me to baptize with water said to me, 'He on whom you see the Spirit descend and remain, this is he who baptizes with the Holy Spirit.' And I have seen and have borne witness that this is the Son of God" (John 1:32-34).

John's focus is not on Jesus nor on the crowd, but on the Holy Spirit who descended upon Jesus. The idea here is that in Jesus the Holy Spirit has established a secure foothold or beachhead that has manifested in the identity of Jesus Christ as being divine, the second Person of the Trinity. John's witness tells us that the baptism of Jesus Christ provided an archetype or model for the sacrament of baptism. The important thing about baptism is not about the water or the ceremony, but about the symbolism that points to the reality of human identity getting caught up or raptured[1] into the reality of God.

The idea here is that the coming down of the Holy Spirit upon Jesus brought Him into the reality of God. And this is the reality of baptism for every baptized Christian. Baptism is about the Holy Spirit inhabiting the life of individuals, and changing their fundamental human identity by the power of the Holy Spirit.

Baptism is a ceremonial acknowledgment of the reality of regeneration. The sacrament of baptism is neither the beginning nor the end of the process of regeneration, but is simply a social, ceremonial recognition that Jesus Christ has inaugurated a new type, kind, or species of humanity, a new way of being human, and that the person baptized is being regenerated or re-identified as being in Christ. And the fact that it is a public celebration contributes to the reality that it represents.

John's description about what happened next is both interesting and instructive.

> "The next day again John was standing with two of his disciples, and he looked at Jesus as he walked by and said, 'Behold, the Lamb of God!' The two disciples heard him say this, and they followed Jesus. Jesus turned and saw them following and said to them, 'What are you seeking?' And they said to him, 'Rabbi' (which means Teacher), 'where are you staying?' He said to them, 'Come and you will see'" (John 1:35-39).

If we remove the comma from John's statement about the Lamb of God, it changes from a merely exclamatory statement like, "O look, the Lamb of God," to more of a command: "Take hold of and observe Jesus as the Lamb of God because He is someone of an especially remarkable or impressive nature." Two of John's disciples who heard John say this, then followed Jesus, as if they were responding to John's comment, John's directive.

Jesus asked them what they wanted, as if to say, "You seem to be following me. What do you want?" They then identify Je-

---

[1] The definition of rapture: "A feeling of intense pleasure or joy. Expressions of intense pleasure or enthusiasm about something."

sus as "Rabbi." There has been no previous indication that Jesus was an official Rabbi, one who had received significant training and had been granted social authority among the Jews. So John translated the term for us to tell us that they simply meant that they recognized Jesus to be a spiritual teacher who took on disciples. That simple word then suggested that they were asking Jesus if they could become His disciples, and because discipleship was an intimate relationship that would require close proximity, they asked Him where He was living because as His disciples they would need to be close to Him. And Jesus then invited them to come and see, which was a statement of acceptance of them to be His disciples.

One of the arguments in support of the historicity of the baptism of Jesus by John is that it is a story that seems to contradict the idea of the divinity of Jesus. The problem was that John The Baptist had baptized people for the remission of their sins, and Jesus was understood to be without sin. So the invention of this story would seem to contradict something important about Jesus—His sinlessness, and would have been an embarrassment because it positioned John above Jesus. The Gospel of Matthew offset this problem by describing John as feeling unworthy to baptize Jesus. So Jesus, asserting His authority, gave John permission to baptize Him (Matthew 3:14–15).

After John The Baptist was killed by Herod, John's followers became Jesus' disciples. And Jesus took up John's basic message,

> "Repent, for the kingdom of heaven is at hand " (Matthew 3:2; 4:17).

Following this, Matthew tells us that Jesus began calling His disciples and ministering to great crowds. Jesus took up John's mantle, John's message of repentance outside of the Temple. Jesus called people to regeneration outside of or apart from the Temple establishment. Later John will tell us that Jesus was calling people into an understanding of God's Temple that did not require buildings (John 2:21).

The Temptation

Jesus' baptism inaugurated His ministry, and the first milestone of His ministry involved His temptation in the desert. Like Job in ancient times, it was the Spirit of God who drove Jesus into the wilderness. Jesus did not choose to go of His own accord, but He did agree to go.

Jesus' three temptations in the wilderness involved 1) hedonism, pertaining to hunger and satisfaction, 2) materialism, pertaining to kingdoms and wealth, and 3) egoism, pertaining to power and might. John later wrote again of these temptations in a letter:

> "For all that is in the world—the desires of the flesh and the desires of the eyes and pride of life—is not from the Father but is from the world" (1 John 2:16).

The "desires of the flesh" refers to hedonism, the "desires of the eyes" refers to materialism, and the "pride of life" refers to egoism. Temptations can mislead and pervert three central human characteristics: thinking, desiring, and emotion. These are all subjective experiences, which are sometimes referred to as mind, soul, and heart. Jesus later named these when He defined the Greatest Commandment.

> "You shall love the Lord your God with all your heart and with all your soul and with all your mind" (Matthew 22:37).

Interestingly, these subjective experiences are related to what are called *transcendental ideas* or *ultimate ideals* in three important areas of human activity: 1) science (truth and thinking), 2) arts (desiring and creating beauty) and 3) justification (law and the pursuit of goodness, defined as righteousness or justice). Christians are called to live in faith, hope, and love, to pursue God, who Himself is the epitome of Truth, Beauty, and Justice.

There is much scholarly discussion about the historicity of Jesus' temptations, discussion about the literary genre of this story. Is it to be considered to be history, parable, myth, or a compound of various genres? Seeing it as a parable, it would speak to Jesus' inner experience of temptation. Seeing it as autobiographical, it would speak to the kind of Messiah Jesus was called to be. Because it is Scripture it is all of these various genres and more. For us to get distracted by literary analysis and concerns for its historicity will detract from the simple reading and meaning of the story. It's an old children's story about real struggles that people have, struggles that have real life and death consequences.

The most important thing is that the plain moral of the story comes right out of the text. In answer to each temptation Jesus quoted Scripture that defeated the various temptations. Jesus relied on Scripture for guidance in the face of temptation. Satan tempted Jesus to use supernatural powers, but each time Jesus relied on Scripture alone to resist the temptation. This demonstrated that ordinary people could do like Jesus did by relying on Scripture for guidance. This insured that ordinary people could follow Jesus' example.

THE CLEANSING

The story of the cleansing of the Temple occurs near the end of the Synoptic Gospels (Matthew 21:12–17, Mark 11:15–19, and Luke 19:45–48), but near the beginning in the Gospel of John (John 2:13–16). Some scholars believe that these refer to two separate incidents because the Gospel of John includes more than one Passover. John's Gospel is mostly about Jesus' teaching during the events of Passover.

I have argued in *Galatians—Backstory/Christory* that the Temple cleansing is central to the ministry of Jesus because it is central to the Old Testament story which ended in A.D. 70 with the destruction of the Temple and the loss of the Jewish kingdom (or homeland). All of Jesus' ministry was opposed to the Temple and the Temple culture. The Temple culture had instituted various practices that provided genuine analogical truth about the God/human relationship. But over time those practices and analogies became increasingly focused on the Temple itself rather than the Temple as an analogy. As interpretation and understanding became more literal, it lost the importance of its symbolic and analogical truths.

> "The cleansing of the Temple event was not about money, nor about selling stuff in the Temple, nor about changing money for a profit—none of that. The moneychangers were doing nothing wrong, according to Old Testament law. They had the blessing of the High Priest and the Temple establishment. Rather, Jesus attacked these things because they were simply manifestations (fruit) of Temple corruption, manifestations of the ongoing Jewish blindness. Jesus' whole ministry was focused on the origin or source of the corruption, not the particular ways that the corruption manifested. Jesus was after the root of the problem, not the fruit. The Temple cleansing provided a witness against 1) accommodation to Roman authority, 2) corruption of Temple worship as legalism focused on sacrifices rather than on God's calling, and 3) the injustice and idolatry of the Temple sanctioned system of mammon, a term that was used to describe gluttony, excessive materialism, greed, and unjust worldly gain" (*Galatians—Backstory/Christory*, p. 40).

NEW BIRTH

Jesus said to Nicodemus:

> "Truly, truly, I say to you, unless one is born again he cannot see the kingdom of God ... Truly, truly, I say to you, unless one is born of water and the Spirit, he cannot enter the kingdom of God (John 3:3, 5).

Nicodemus recognized that God was working with, in, or through Jesus when he said,

> "Rabbi, we know that you are a teacher come from God, for no one can do these signs that you do unless God is with him" (John 3:2).

So, when Nicodemus asked, "How can these things be?" (John 3:9) he was asking, *how can these things come to be? Or how can these things be facilitated?* And Jesus provided the answer: Those who "see" the Kingdom of God must speak about what they know about it. They must testify about heavenly things, about eternal life with, in, or through Christ.

Baptism is traditionally understood as an outward sign of the inward reality of regeneration or new life in Christ. The intended result of baptism is the living out of the gifts of the Spirit (Galatians 5:22-23) in obedience to Jesus Christ. Regardless of when baptism occurs, regardless of who performs it, this is God's intended result. And arguing about the details of the baptism ceremony runs counter to this intended result. The arguments over means and mode detracts from the true meaning of baptism.

While the Greek word for rebirth or regeneration (παλιγγενεσία) appears only twice (Matthew 19:28 and Titus 3:5), the idea of regeneration represents a broader theme of re-creation, spiritual rebirth, and/or being born again (John 3:3-8 and 1 Peter 1:3). The idea is as old as the Bible itself, as it occurs over and again throughout the Old Testament, especially in the prophets.

Unfortunately, most of the commentary about regeneration deals with *individual* regeneration and ignores social or community regeneration, not to mention the renewal of *all things* spoken about in Matthew 19:28 and Revelation 21:5. Individual regeneration or renewal is important, and must not be neglected, but so are the social aspects of it. In fact, regeneration cannot be properly understood or engaged apart from the social and ecological aspects.[2]

Just as physical birth produces a new person in the world, spiritual birth produces a new person in the heavenly realm (Ephesians 2:6) and a new kind in the earthly realm.[3] We could also call it a new *kind* of person, or a new *kind* of humanity. In this regard heaven is better understood as a realm or regimen than a place, where a regimen is a way of life, or a cluster of habits for the restoration and promotion of well-being. Heaven includes all the places where this regimen rules. Through regeneration people acquire "eyes to see" and "ears to hear" spiritual things. They see and hear things that they didn't notice before,

---

2 *Ephesians—Recovering the Vision of a Sustainable Church in Christ*, Phillip A. Ross, Pilgrim Platform Books, Marietta, Ohio, 2013.

3 *Galatians: Backstory/Christory*, Phillip A. Ross, Pilgrim Platform, Marietta, Ohio, 2015, "New Creation," p 294.

because their core values have changed, because they have new priorities, because they are new creatures in Christ. The born-again become partakers of Christ's divine nature or character (2 Corinthians 5:17).

God, not us, brings about this transformation (Ephesians 2:1, 8). God's great love and free gift, His rich grace and abundant mercy, are the cause or source of the rebirth. God leads and we follow. God initiates and we respond. The mighty power of God —the very power that raised Christ from the dead—is the power that causes the regeneration and conversion of sinners (Ephesians 1:19–20). Thus, regeneration is a kind of down payment, security deposit, or earnest payment for future resurrection in Christ. Regeneration is a kind of, or a beginning of, or a simile for resurrection. It helps us understand the idea of personal, bodily resurrection, and apart from an experience of personal regeneration the idea of the wholeness of biblical resurrection is a silly myth.

One of the reasons another apostle had to be chosen to replace Judas Iscariot was that "one of these men (the candidates for Judas' replacement) must become with us a witness to his resurrection" (Acts 1:22). And they did so

> "with great power the apostles were giving their testimony to the resurrection of the Lord Jesus, and great grace was upon them all" (Acts 4:33).

Paul had personally seen and talked with the resurrected Christ (1 Corinthians 9:1, 15:8; Acts 22:6-10), and because of this he enthusiastically confirmed the fact of Jesus' resurrection. He said to Agrippa, a high Roman official,

> "To this day I have had the help that comes from God, and so I stand here testifying both to small and great, saying nothing but what the prophets and Moses said would come to pass: that the Christ must suffer and that, by being the first to rise from the dead, he would proclaim light both to our people and to the Gentiles" (Acts 26:22-23).

The regeneration/resurrection idea has two senses, two poles or points of comparison, two applications. Personal regeneration in this life is given so that we can have some idea about the reality of the future resurrection of humanity. Clearly the resurrection of humanity will come when Jesus returns in glory to bring down from heaven and establish the Kingdom of God on earth. The "Holy City" or "New Jerusalem" (Revelation 21:1) points to a future event that will happen on earth. The promise is that those who have been regenerated before that time will be resurrected at that time in order to populate God's Kingdom on earth. All who put on the character of Christ are regenerated in this life, and will be resurrected into the next. This is the idea of the future application that exists today in the form of hope. Christians hope for God's Kingdom to manifest in this world.

Personal regeneration in this life, in this world, is necessarily and firmly linked to this future hope. Christians are called to live as if they are already in the Kingdom of God on earth by manifesting the characteristics of Jesus Christ, who best represents God's character in human flesh. While we are waiting for Christ's return in glory, we are to act out Christ's character, to live according to the fruits of the Spirit—love, joy, peace, patience, kindness, goodness, faithfulness, gentleness, and self-control, etc. (Galatians 5:22-23).

The secret of accomplishing this is to realize that it cannot be done apart from the Holy Spirit, who inhabits God's people in this life as a down payment, or earnest payment, or security deposit for bodily resurrection when Christ returns in glory. Each person who seriously engages this process contributes to the spiritual and social momentum that will be caught up with Christ's return in glory. Thus, we contribute to Christ's return in glory by manifesting the fruits of the Spirit in this life. Or we could also say that the Holy Spirit is bringing about Christ's return in glory by manifesting the fruits of the Spirit in the lives of born-again Christians today. He leads and we follow. He initiates and we respond, we agree.

The Old Testament talks a lot about harvesting and firstfruits, a term used to designate the first part of the harvest. In the Old Testament the fristfruits were holy and were to be dedicated and given to God, to the Temple. As God's people, born-again or regenerated Christians are the firstfruits of God's spiritual harvest according to James 1:18.

Of course, Jesus is the first of the firstfruits, and the most holy part.

> "But in fact Christ has been raised from the dead, the firstfruits of those who have fallen asleep (died)" (1 Corinthians 15:20).

The apostle Paul explained that Jesus is "the firstborn over all creation," "the firstborn from the dead" and "the firstborn among many brethren" (Colossians 1:15, 18; Romans 8:29). Clearly other fruits will follow as the harvest continues.

Paul and the Apostles spoke about a resurrection to everlasting life as a spiritual reality—something more than a physical body. There are many stories in the Bible about individuals who were restored to physical life and/or health prior to the crucifixion and promised resurrection of Jesus. This was helpful, but they all died again.

Paul, however, made an important distinction between these restorations or healings and the resurrection of God's firstfruits:

> "But our citizenship is in heaven, and from it we await a Savior, the Lord Jesus Christ, who will transform our lowly body to be like his glorious body, by the power that enables him even to subject all things to himself" (Philippians 3:20-21; compare 2 Corinthians 5:1-5).

The down payment or security deposit for this resurrection is the manifestation of Christ's characteristics by His people through regeneration in this life. This security deposit is not made by us into God's "bank," but is made by God who has dispatched His Holy Spirit to inhabit God's people, to live in their habits. It is the character of Christ manifested through the fruits of the Spirit in the lives of believers that constitutes what is more than our physical bodies. And it is the character qualities of the fruits of the Spirit that Christians will take into heaven when Christ returns in glory.

DISCIPLES

In the ancient world a disciple was a follower of a teacher, someone who put the teacher's teachings into practice. It is not the same as being a student today because a disciple in the ancient biblical world actively imitated both the life and teaching of the teacher. It was an apprenticeship that would eventually make the disciple become a living copy of the teacher.

There were many followers of Jesus during his ministry. Some were given a mission, such as the commission of the seventy in Luke 10:1, the Great Commission (Matthew 28:18-20) after the resurrection of Jesus, and the conversion and mission of Paul (Acts 9). The Apostles were the original twelve disciples who were charged with proclaiming the gospel to the world. The difference between disciples and apostles is subtle because we are all called to proclaim the gospel however we can. Apostles have a special calling and have special gifts for this purpose.

When Judas Iscariot, who betrayed Jesus to the Romans, committed suicide the other apostles decided to replace him, and cast lots and chose Matthias to replace Judas (Acts 1:26). Curiously, Matthias was not referred to again in the Bible. My understanding here is that Matthias was the choice of the apostles, but Paul was the choice of God. Paul's apostleship stretches the idea that the apostles were composed only of those first disciples who walked with Jesus. Paul testified that he met the resurrected Christ on the road to Damascus and was converted by Him. But because Paul's experience of Christ was spiritual it expands the idea of apostleship to include more than those who actually related directly to Jesus prior to His resurrection. Paul then went on to prove his apostleship by being the most prolific of the New Testament writers.

So, if we include Paul in the list of "original" apostles we have thirteen, assuming that Matthias was included as the replacement for Judas. This is a significant issue because it allows the Bible to claim both the traditional idea that the twelve apostles corresponded to the twelve tribes of ancient Israel, yet suggests that the New Testament expands the identity of God's people beyond the twelve tribes. The symbolism of Paul's inclusion as the apostle to the Gentiles maintains the biblical idea that God's original mission involved the whole world, for which God chose Israel to be an ancient case study. It also makes Paul's teaching foundational for all who are not of Jewish ancestry. Indeed, Jesus' mission was to reclaim God's original mission as a mission to the world, and not merely a mission to the Jews. So, Paul's mission was central to the mission of Jesus Christ, such that apart from Paul the mission of Jesus Christ cannot be properly and historically understood.

Jesus emphasized that being a disciple would be costly. Disciples desired to learn not only the teaching of the rabbi, but to imitate the practical details and habits of the teacher's life. One cannot be a disciple by merely sitting in a classroom and listening to lectures or reading books—or sitting in church listening to sermons. Disciples must interact with a real living teacher. Disciples literally follow a particular person in order to reproduce the habits, character, and thinking of their teacher, to eventually become the *kind* of person the teacher is.

Paul's role in opening up the opportunity for all people to become disciples was absolutely central because Paul claimed to have had a real relationship with the living—and resurrected—Christ. And the resurrected Christ is the only Christ that anyone since Jesus' crucifixion can relate to. The other side of this idea is that no one can be a disciple *unless* they have a real relationship with the living and resurrected Christ. And all such relationships issue out of personal regeneration by the power and presence of the Holy Spirit. Because the Holy Spirit is in unity with the Godhead—Father, Son, and Holy Spirit, three-in-one and one-in-three—contact with the Holy Spirit is contact with Jesus and with God. That contact is real, personal, and effective.

A Christian disciple is a believer who follows Christ in order to offer his or her own imitation of Christ as a model for others to follow, as Paul did (1 Corinthians 11:1). Disciples exercise or practice faith (Acts 2:38). Modern Christianity has focused on belief and faith in an overly abstract and intellectual way, as if thinking about certain ideas or believing certain things makes a person Christian. The difference between the modern idea and the ancient practice of discipleship is critical.

While belief is important, even critical, it must not be abstracted from actual practice, actual living. There is a sense in which discipleship can be taught and practiced without beginning with belief. People become Christian through the reality of personal regeneration by the Holy Spirit. The Spirit changes hearts and minds, and only when hearts and minds have been changed by the Holy Spirit do people have "ears to hear" and "eyes to see" the reality of the resurrected Christ. This means that regenerate people can begin with either belief about Jesus Christ or by simply practicing the fruits of the Spirit in their own lives. God calls us to "taste and see" (Psalm 34:8). Both Godly belief and Godly practice lead to the same thing: the unity of belief and practice. The reason for this is that genuine interest in Christ that leads to genuine practice of the fruits of the Spirit is the fruit of regeneration. The Holy Spirit works in people before they recognize or realize the presence of the Holy Spirit in their lives.

What keeps this from becoming works-righteousness is the presence of the Holy Spirit, because manifesting His fruits cannot be done apart from Him. It is not our own ability that allows us to manifest the fruits of the Spirit. Rather, it is the reality of the Spirit within us. The more we engage the fruits of the Spirit personally the more disciples grow in wisdom and understanding—or belief, or faith. You see, only real disciples actually *want* to genuinely manifest the fruits of the Spirit in their own lives.

MIRACLES

In order to understand biblical miracles we must first understand the difference between what is *natural* and what is *supernatural*. The most basic definition of supernatural indicates something other than, outside of, or above what is natural. *Super-* is a prefix, originally used in loanwords from Latin, and has the basic meaning of *above* or *beyond*. Words formed with *super-* have the following general senses: "to place or be placed above or over" (i.e., superimpose, supersede), "a thing placed over or added to another" (i.e., superscript, superstructure, supertax), "situated over" (i.e., superficial, superlunary) and, more figuratively, "an individual, thing, or property that exceeds customary norms or levels" (i.e., superalloy, superconductivity, superman, superstar). When applied to nature, *super-* indicates something that occurs outside of natural processes, something that would not otherwise exist in nature, or something that represents the highest degree of nature.

According to the biblical creation story, God created everything, and then created humanity as the crown of creation, meaning that humanity is God's best or highest creation in this world (Psalm 8). This makes humanity itself a supernatural kind or species. The idea of natural law suggests that the energy or momentum of creation continues to replicate life according to some set of rules or natural laws, as if a kind of momentum is involved. Natural law is defined as a body of law or a specific principle of law that is held to be derived from nature and binding upon human society in the absence of or in addition to positive law. Positive law is a term that refers to statutes that have been laid down by a legislature, court, or some other human institution and which can take whatever form the authors want. Natural law exists in nature, apart from humanity or positive law. Some basic examples are gravity, the laws of thermodynamics, the physics of motion, etc. These laws exist regardless of what we think about them.

Nature is often differentiated from human culture, such that nature governs in the absence of human culture. Nature is what happens in this world in the absence of humanity. A world without humanity would be purely natural. And humanity would be natural without God or apart from the knowledge of God's law. The revelation of God's law is, then, supernatural, by definition, because it comes from a supernatural source—God.

From this perspective, humanity, as the crown of creation or the highest expression of nature, represents or has contact with or produces what is supernatural. It is this last meaning of the word that I suggest for the biblical definition of *supernatural* because what humanity produces, our cultural artifacts and processes, would not exist in nature without language, human knowledge of God's Word (the integrity of language and reality). Humanity and human culture exist above nature or apart from nature or as the highest expression of the laws of nature. Consequently, and contrary to common understanding, in the light of God's Word humanity itself is supernatural, using the above definition of *super-* as a prefix. What humanity creates would not exist in the natural world without language, exposure to God's Word. In particular I'm referring literature and the fruit of human language, to science and technology and their fruits. Such fruits are supernatural, by this definition.

Understood in this way, the products of human culture are supernatural in that in nature alone, nature unaffected by God's Word and human involvement, they would not exist. This is particularly true of science and technology, which is a sort of human engine that produces cultural artifacts. In addition, the supernatural existence of the fruits of science and technology would be immediately understood to be magical or supernatural by people who lived before the development of modern science and technology. From this perspective, contemporary people live in a supernatural realm, a supernatural world, a world created by science and technology.

Biblical miracles served as a kind of precursor of this perspective, and when understood as such they provide deep and meaningful lessons that are not otherwise discerned. Contemporary people can continue to mine the Bible for nuggets of truth that are extremely valuable. From this perspective it is possible to read many of the biblical miracle stories from a naturalistic perspective and assign natural interpretations of the miracles, and still discover deeper meaning and understanding that is commensurate with contemporary thought.[4]

Indeed, those who dismiss the miracles of the Bible as crude rationalizations of primitive people do so because they interpret the Bible literally rather than literarily (symbolically, figuratively, allegorically, meaningfully, etc.).

Medieval theologians used a fourfold method of interpreting Scripture known as the *quadriga*, suggesting four senses or ways of interpretation: 1) as history, 2) as allegory, 3) as figurative, and 4) as analogical. But because Medieval theologians were accused of getting lost in their pre-scientific speculations, modern scholarship has rejected the *quadriga*. Modern theologians today mostly embrace the historical-grammatical method of biblical interpretation, a Christian hermeneutical method that strives to discover the Biblical authors' original intended meaning of the text.

---

4 See *John's Miracles—Seeing Beyond Our Expectations*, Phillip A. Ross, Pilgrim Platform, Marietta, Ohio, 2019.

There is nothing wrong with the historical-grammatical method of interpretation, except if it causes all other methods to be disallowed or ignored. It is helpful to try to understand the original intent of the author and the perspective of the original audience. But if biblical interpretation stops at that point it fails to understand and appreciate the idea that the Bible is an inspired document, that God Himself not only spoke to those who originally wrote and read it, but that God continues to speak through the Bible in every age, even today. While God is always conveying the same message and does not change, we—those to whom He is speaking—do change. And over time, people have changed a lot, as history testifies. The world has changed a lot in the last five thousand years. This means that in order for God's message to be the same over time, each generation of believers must read and understand it afresh, from their own personal and historical perspective. Otherwise we will be reading a dead message for people who are long gone. We do not share the cultural assumptions of our ancient ancestors. Additionally, history has an accumulated meaning that allows us to see historical patterns over long periods of time. And biblical interpretation has a similar kind of accumulated value that demonstrates the stability and continuity of God's Word over time.

Of course, in another sense people have not changed at all. We are still driven by the same basic needs and desires. We are still human beings and are subject to the vicissitudes of being human in a hostile world. Nonetheless, our historical context is fraught with very significant changes compared to ancient times. One such change has to do with population growth. As populations grow and massive cultures develop, the ways and means of dealing with basic human needs has changed dramatically, i.e., food production, housing, transportation, communication, sewage, etc. Older methods of cultural maintenance are simply inadequate to support contemporary populations. And these things affect human consciousness, habits, and culture. Yet, God still speaks the same message through the Bible, and to understand it like those who first heard it understood it, we must interpret and explain it in a way that produces the same original understanding to people who are quite different from its original audiences.

Interestingly, God has foreseen this scenario and provided for this practice within the biblical story itself. This is what I have been trying to say in these pages. In order for God's message to humanity to remain the same throughout history, it must be interpreted and understood dynamically. However, that dynamic is not without limits, rules, and patterns. It is more like a quadratic equation that traces a dynamic path over time, rather than a simple static equation that defines a particular shape or straight trajectory. It must remain true to the original pattern or trajectory.

This has special application to the occurrence and understanding of biblical miracles. The miracles point to the mystery of the Spirit and the mystery of life itself. However, it is not that the mystery means that the Spirit or life are beyond understanding, but rather that our understanding of them will continue to grow, mature, and develop without end. It is not that the Spirit somehow draws a line and says that beyond this line understanding cannot go. Rather, the Spirit continues to bring real and significant understanding without end.

Forgiveness

Christianity is primarily about the grace and mercy of forgiveness. Forgiveness is defined as an intentional and voluntary act by which a victim who has been harmed experiences a change in feelings and attitude toward the person who caused the harm. In addition, forgiveness eliminates negative emotions such as seeking revenge, and provides the ability to wish the offender well. Forgiveness must be differentiated from condoning (i.e., failing to see an action as wrong and in need of forgiveness), excusing (i.e., not holding the offender responsible for the action), forgetting (i.e., removing awareness of the offense from one's own memory), pardoning (i.e., allowing a person who has been convicted of a crime to be free and absolved of that conviction, as if they were never convicted), and reconciliation (i.e., restoration of a relationship).

Forgiveness may be considered from three perspectives: 1) the person who forgives, 2) the person forgiven, and/or 3) the relationship between the forgiver and the person forgiven. Genuine forgiveness is granted without the expectation of restorative justice, and without the expectation of a response on the part of the offender. With minor offenses the offender is often not aware that he or she has even caused an offense, and therefore won't offer an apology. It doesn't occur to them that an apology is needed. So the expectation of an apology prior to the issuance of forgiveness will not lead to forgiveness. Consequently, for forgiveness to be effective it must be given without expectations of any sort. Having expectations of someone who has offended you is the definition of a grudge, and a grudge is an unforgiven offense, an unmet expectation. The exercise of forgiveness is not merely for the sake of the person who caused the offense, it is primarily for the sake of the person who feels offended.

Forgiveness and justice are often thought of as opposites that can cancel each other, but they are not. Justice is usually confused with revenge, still today! The demand for justice is a demand for punishment as a way to "get even." But punishment for some crime or offense in no way restores anything to the person who has been harmed or offended. It only satisfies the demand for revenge. The only way to remove the demand for justice and revenge is to forgive. Seeking revenge, even in the name of justice, creates an escalating cycle of retributive violence and offense—which creates more demand for revenge.

The only way to break the cycle of offense that demands revenge and revenge that demands retributive violence and/or humiliation of the offender is to understand that justice is not something that one *receives*—not from a court, not from the state, not even from God. Rather, justice is something that one *gives* to others. Those who want justice must live justly themselves (Micah 6:8). And by living justly or righteously individuals contribute to the justice and righteousness of their community, which reduces the instances of them being the cause of offense or harm to others. When people live justly with genuine righteousness they will not cause harm or offense to others, which will reduce and eventually eliminate the need for revenge and the call for justice.

Humanity has been locked in an increasing cycle of revenge and retributive violence for a gazillion years, because people are sinners and sin against one another in a bazillion ways. The demand for justice is a self-centered demand that serves one's own honor and respect. The demand for justice comes out of one's own pride, thinking that others *owe* you honor and respect. Thus, justice becomes the payment of a debt owed to you by someone who has offended you. This is the most common understanding of justice. But it is wrong! And it is wrong precisely because it can never result in justice, where justice is understood as a balancing of accounts that requires someone else to make a payment to you in order to restore your account. This is a false understanding of real justice because it creates a debt in someone else's account that must be paid *to* you. And what is even worse, the payment of that debt to you in turn increases *your* pride, which is a sin and will eventually cause you to be the cause of someone else being offended with you (Isaiah 2:12, 23:9; James 4:6; Philippians 2:3; Proverbs 8:13, etc.).

The only way to break this cycle of offense that calls for justice and produces revenge, which causes offense, etc., is the issuance of the kind of forgiveness without expectation that completely cancels the debt. Such forgiveness must necessarily be given without any expectation.

The giving of such forgiveness will cause a feeling of great personal offense and harm to the one who gives it because their sense of being honorable (in the way described above) will suffer harm. Their pride will be offended from a perceived loss of honor thought to be due them. This is precisely what Jesus Christ has done by acting as God and living in perfect justice by refusing to be offended, which canceled all human debt owed to God because of human offense. This, then, allows God to issue forgiveness without expectation, which breaks the cycle. And the breaking of this cycle is God's great mission to the world. For the last five thousand years God has been working to replace the religion of vengeance with the religion of forgiveness. And, while much progress has been made, we still have a long way to go.

Beatitudes

The Beatitudes (Matthew 5:3-12, Luke 6:20-22) provide categories of people who are blessed (μακάριος). The biblical idea of being blessed is another way of describing people who have received God's grace. The structure of each Beatitude describes in the first part of the verse a category of people, and in the latter part of the verse indicates the fruit or consequence of their blessing. The unusual thing about the categories of people that are listed is that such people are not ordinarily thought of as being the recipients of God's grace or blessing. So, Jesus was using the Beatitudes as stories to teach people to see or find God's blessing in the midst of difficult circumstances.

The first,

> "Blessed are the poor in spirit, for theirs is the kingdom of heaven" (Matthew 5:3),

describes people who find themselves defeated by difficult circumstances that discourage them. Calvin says of this verse,

> "Christ pronounces those to be happy who, chastened and subdued by afflictions, submit themselves wholly to God, and, with inward humility, betake themselves to him for protection" (*Calvin's Commentaries*, Matthew 5:3).

Various translations render the Greek word as *happy*, which to me seems to be a little shallow. It's not wrong, but it fails to communicate the joy of being a recipient of God's grace. Yet to render it as *joy* would err on the overenthusiastic side because the discouragement of difficult circumstances is real. Most of the Beatitudes point to a future state of blessedness, i.e., "shall be comforted" (Matthew 5:4), "shall inherit the earth" (Matthew 5:5), "shall be satisfied" (Matthew 5:6), etc. In this regard the Beatitudes point discouraged people to hope in Christ because discouragement tends to undermine hope.

The purpose of the Beatitudes is to help people see God's grace where they don't usually expect it. Consequently, the Beatitudes don't simply provide comfort for discouraged people, but they teach people to look for God's grace where they least expect it. And as people learn to do this, they find God's grace everywhere! As a result, discouraged people find themselves to be awash in God's grace and mercy, even in the midst of personal discouragement. Thus, engaging the Beatitudes is an exercise of faith, and exercising faith strengthens and increases it. The exercise of faith in turn provides salt and light, not just for one's self, but for one's community as well.

FULFILLMENT OF THE LAW

Christ said that He came, not to abolish the law, but to fulfill it. And more than that, He said that

> "not an iota, not a dot, will pass from the Law until all is accomplished" (Matthew 5:18).

Many, if not most, people have interpreted this literally to mean that Christianity must literally and woodenly understand and apply all of the laws of the Bible, Old Testament and New, exactly as they are given, as if every verse of the Bible is universally applicable throughout history. Thus, many people think that Christians are not to mix fabrics (Deuteronomy 22:11), eat shellfish (Leviticus 11:9-10), or eat with sinners (1 Corinthians 5:11).

If you have understood the general thrust of this book so far and God's great mission to the world, you might think that I am arguing *against* the strict adherence to God's law. Or you might think that Jesus was arguing in Matthew 5:17-20 *for* strict adherence to God's law. In either case, you would be wrong. Rather, I'm trying to show that the Bible as a whole (Old Testament and New) is not simply about strict adherence to God's Law, but is about teaching people about God's intended purpose in giving His Law. God knew in advance that no mere individual[5] would be able to fulfill His law, and brought judgment upon ancient Israel over and over again because of their failure to live in conformity to His law, and finally He sent Christ as the fulfillment of His law. In order to understand God's mission, we

---

5 Again, see https://wiki2.org/en/Aleph_number. Set Theory and the role of the Aleph Null helps to explain a lot of biblical mysticism. Jesus was able to fulfill God's law because Jesus was more than a mere individual. He was both fully human and fully divine.

cannot begin with Christ because Christ is the answer to a global human problem, as well as the answer to an Old Testament problem. In addition, we each and all must understand that the problem is *ours*—in the twenty-first century, personally and collectively. What problem? The problem of survival, personal and collective. We need to be saved from extinction, as individuals and as a species.

Is salvation just a warm fuzzy story that God gives to people who love Him? Salvation is not icing on the cake or gravy for the meat. Salvation is the cake of celebration and the meat of the gospel. Before Christ can become the answer, we must determine—and actually and personally ask—the proper question. Asking the right questions is much harder than providing the right answers, because the answer is always embedded in the question. Questions and answers go together like love and marriage. The right question is: exactly what do you/we need to be saved from?

Sure, we are saved from hell and damnation and eternal torment in the fire of Sheol. But for most people all that stuff is mostly abstract, distant, other worldly, and not all that important right now. Sure, we'll need Christ later to keep us from all that, but that's in the next life. All that stuff is not a priority right now. It's easy to assent to Christ (or not), and intend to deal with that stuff later (or dismiss it). But right now we have more pressing concerns—work, play, some life goal, work, bills to pay, whatever.

In the Old Testament people did not talk about being "saved" until after some serious catastrophe. After the city burned, or after the raiding hoards plundered and left. Then people knew exactly what they had been saved from because they were still alive. While few people realize it or the importance of it, this was also true for people living in the New Testament times.

We tend to think that Paul's journeys were much like our mission journeys today. We commission our missionaries, have a potluck dinner, and sent them out. The missionary then goes to people who did not invite him to tell them about Christ, of whom they know nothing, and did not ask. But that is not the way it happened in the New Testament.

First of all Jerusalem was sacked and the Temple destroyed by Rome in A.D. 70, and most of the New Testament was written within a few decades on both sides of this event. And during the time that Rome was persecuting Jerusalem, the Temple establishment was persecuting Christians. So Christians were fleeing Jerusalem before and after A.D. 70 because it was not hospitable for them. Some who saw the proverbial writing on the wall, left before the destruction, and Paul wrote instructions to them. Others left during and after the destruction. All of this means that Christians were fleeing into the surrounding countries, fleeing for their lives, and looking for new opportunities for work and homes. And they gathered together as they fled because they had common concerns, common needs, and common language. Much of the New Testament was written for these people to help them understand what had happened to them, and to guide them in their new endeavors.

Evangelism was quite natural because people would ask them about why they were traveling or moving. "So, what brings you to these parts?" The answer would be the story about what had happened in Jerusalem, and because Jesus had played a central role in the Jerusalem difficulties, they would talk about Him. Paul and the Apostles wrote in order to help them explain it all. Evangelism was nothing more than making new friends by telling your story about why you left Jerusalem.

God's law played a central role in that story, as people tried to come to terms with the fact that God had caused the destruction of the Temple and the scattering of His people. Why would God do that? Why would He destroy what had been so important to Him for thousands of years? And was there a positive outcome to this story of destruction?

Christians generally understand that Christ's sacrifice on the cross was a better sacrifice and that it put an end to animal sacrifices. Christ's sacrifice has provided forgiveness "once and for all" (Romans 6:10, Hebrews 10:10). But what is less understood is the role of the Temple in God's great plan. There are two important things to remember about the Temple, things that set the context of the Temple.

First, the establishment of Israel's kings amounted to the rejection of God as King (1 Samuel 8:7), and second, it was King David who had envisioned the building of the Temple. Of course God went along with both of these developments, and even genuinely provided His best counsel for their success. And we can learn much of value from God's involvement! But He knew that Israel's kingship and Temple cult would end in destruction, as they did. The Temple was always intended by God to be a temporary institution that would set up the proper roll of the Messiah. Sending Jesus was not God's plan-B. While one of the purposes of God's Law is to show us our sin, one of the purposes of the Temple was to institutionalize our sin, to make us all feel the consequences of our sin—which then fully manifested in the destruction of Jerusalem and the Temple in A.D. 70.

Why would God do this? Because the nature of Original Sin required it. As previously described, the Garden sin was the rejection of God's counsel and the acceptance of the counsel of the Serpent, the deceiver. Rather than depending on God's counsel, Adam and Eve, following the Serpent's lead, determined good from evil for themselves (Genesis 3:6). Have you ever talked with someone who is convinced that he knows how to do something, but you know for sure that his way will not work? There is no convincing such a person with words alone. They will not believe you until they do it *their* way and see it fail. Only then are they open to hearing you. That was God's position with Adam and Eve—and Israel.

People have always been saved or accepted by God on the basis of God's grace through the counsel of the Holy Spirit. When people cut themselves off from the counsel of the Holy Spirit, they confront God's law, God's rules for living a satisfying and sustainable life on earth, on their own. But because people are designed to live by the counsel of the Holy Spirit and in harmony with God, life without that counsel ends in disharmony, disaster, and destruction.

Having cut themselves off from this counsel, Adam and Eve mistakenly believed that they could live in harmony with God by following their own counsel, which was actually the counsel of the deceiver. The language they used to interface with reality, to understand the world and to make a home in the world, was inadequate as a valid representation of the truth of the reality in which they actually lived. It gave them a false understanding of reality, of God, and of the world. They overestimated their own ability to understand the world, and underestimated the value and importance of God's counsel, God's wisdom, God's perspective.

Nonetheless, God agreed to help them by providing real wisdom and genuine counsel. The Bible is full of God's wisdom and counsel. However, the long story of the Bible is the story of God's people, living in the abundance of God's wisdom (the Old Testament), but whose assumptions about themselves precluded them from engaging fully or correctly with God's wisdom. They lived under a veil (2 Corinthians 3:13-15). The purpose of the law was hidden from them.

The mission of Jesus Christ was to fulfill God's law, God's counsel, in such a way as to provide for both justice and mercy. So He lived according to God's righteousness, but the wisdom and law of Jesus' day (both the corruption of ancient Rome and of the Second Temple establishment) condemned Him to death. The travesty of His death on the cross shocked many people into seeing the travesty of life apart from the counsel of the Holy Spirit. Suddenly they discovered that their own Bible, the Old Testament, had predicted and set up this very travesty: the death of a perfectly good and innocent man who lived according to God's counsel, who was condemned by their leaders, their laws, laws that depended on the very best wisdom that humanity had produced, both in Israel and in Rome. The best possible human wisdom ended in corruption because it denied the ongoing counsel of the Holy Spirit. The Old Testament Jews had God's Word, but did not listen to God's voice, God's counsel. They did not have ears to hear (Isaiah 35:5, Job 36:10, Matthew 13:15-17, Acts 7:51, etc.).

Today we understand that the presence and power of the Holy Spirit through regeneration, which provides access to God's voice, is necessary for the correct interpretation of God's

Word. However, this does not mean that every thought of the regenerate is inspired—far from it! It simply means that unbelievers who study God's Word, the Bible, are not able to understand it as God intends it to be understood.[6]

WHEAT & TARES

Jesus' parable (Matthew 13:24-13:30) teaches that we are not to try to remove evil or unsaved people in society or in the church. In response to the question about separating wheat (the saved) from the tares (the unsaved) Jesus said,

> "No, lest in gathering the weeds you root up the wheat along with them. Let both grow together until the harvest, and at harvest time I will tell the reapers, Gather the weeds first and bind them in bundles to be burned, but gather the wheat into my barn" (Matthew 13:29-30).

This runs counter to what most "faithful" churches have been doing for millennia. Most churches have been primarily concerned with gathering people to be church members who have some common beliefs (agreeing to some doctrine or statement of faith), and separating out those who don't share that belief. But here Jesus said to let them grow together until the final harvest, when the ultimate separation will be made. Most people fear that the tares (weeds) will take over the garden if they are allowed to grow together.

Elsewhere (Mark 4:3-9) Jesus said that good seed sown in a field of weeds will not produce, but that in general weeds are not a threat to a wheat field that has good soil. So, we must remember that Christianity is a field of wheat with some tares, not a

---

[6] "We may be moved and induced by the testimony of the Church to an high and reverent esteem of the Holy Scripture. And the heavenliness of the matter, the efficacy of the doctrine, the majesty of the style, the consent of all the parts, the scope of the whole (which is, to give all glory to God), the full discovery it makes of the only way of man's salvation, the many other incomparable excellencies, and the entire perfection thereof, are arguments whereby it does abundantly evidence itself to be the Word of God: yet notwithstanding, our full persuasion and assurance of the infallible truth and divine authority thereof, is from the inward work of the Holy Spirit bearing witness by and with the Word in our hearts" (*Westminster Confession of Faith*, 1647).

field of tares with some wheat. Thus, our priority and attention needs to be on growing good, strong, healthy wheat, and on soil improvement, not on eliminating the tares. We become what we pay attention to. Corruption grows by our paying attention to corruption, and goodness grows by our paying attention to

> "whatever is true, whatever is honorable, whatever is just, whatever is pure, whatever is lovely, whatever is commendable, if there is any excellence, if there is anything worthy of praise, think about these things" (Philippians 4:8).

Think about this as you watch television or surf the Internet. We need to fill our lives with what is true, honorable, just, pure, lovely, commendable, excellent, and worthy of praise. And eliminate the things that are not on this list.

PETER'S CONFESSION

> "Now when Jesus came into the district of Caesarea Philippi, he asked his disciples, 'Who do people say that the Son of Man is?' And they said, 'Some say John the Baptist, others say Elijah, and others Jeremiah or one of the prophets.' He said to them, 'But who do you say that I am?' Simon Peter replied, 'You are the Christ, the Son of the living God.' And Jesus answered him, 'Blessed are you, Simon Bar-Jonah! For flesh and blood has not revealed this to you, but my Father who is in heaven. And I tell you, you are Peter, and on this rock I will build my church, and the gates of hell shall not prevail against it. I will give you the keys of the kingdom of heaven, and whatever you bind on earth shall be bound in heaven, and whatever you loose on earth shall be loosed in heaven.' Then he strictly charged the disciples to tell no one that he was the Christ" (Matthew 16:13-20).

Peter's confession was that Jesus is the Christ, the Son of the living God, and this confession is the model confession for all Christians. It is this realization, that Jesus is the Christ, that is the rock or foundation of Christ's church on earth. There is a play of words in the Greek text. First Jesus gave a name to Simon Peter (Πέτρος), which means rock, or a piece of stone, then He said, "upon this rock (πέτρα) I will build my church" (Matthew 16:18). This second variation of the word indicates a solid rock, or a massive stone, and is in distinct contrast to a piece of rock or a rock fragment, which is indicated in the first Greek word. The intention here is to indicate that Peter, who was only a small rock, was actually part of a massive foundation of stone, an idea that Peter would later write about:

> "you yourselves like living stones are being built up as a spiritual house, to be a holy priesthood, to offer spiritual sacrifices acceptable to God through Jesus Christ" (1 Peter 2:5).

The idea suggested by the word play in Greek is that Peter's confession pointed to his membership in something much larger: the Body of Christ—God's Temple. And following Peter's confession, Jesus then began to speak about his impending death. Jesus' death launched this idea of Peter being a member in the soon-to-be-resurrected Body of Christ.

> "From that time Jesus began to show his disciples that he must go to Jerusalem and suffer many things from the elders and chief priests and scribes, and be killed, and on the third day be raised. And Peter took him aside and began to rebuke him, saying, 'Far be it from you, Lord! This shall never happen to you.' But he turned and said to Peter, 'Get behind me, Satan! You are a hindrance to me. For you are not setting your mind on the things of God, but on the things of man'" (Matthew 16:21-23).

Peter is an important disciple because he is so much like we are. He's always getting ahead of the Lord. He was filled with a kind of impetuous self-righteousness as he tried to correct Jesus, and he was often just flat wrong. But he was willing to fully engage with Jesus, and this is his saving quality, the one we need to emulate.

Peter didn't want Jesus to die, but he didn't realize that his desire was in opposition to God's plan. That's usually the way it is: our desires are often not in line with God's plans. We don't want pain and suffering and difficulties. We'd rather avoid them, and we even define such things as being "evil." But they are not evil. They are ordinary elements of life for both the saved and the lost. These things—pain, difficulties, suffering, and sorrow—are not bad or evil in themselves. They can serve the process of redemption or of damnation, depending on how we respond to them. Jesus taught much about suffering and how to use it as an engine of sanctification.

We can set our minds on the things of God by considering the value of Christ's death on the cross. Was it true? Was it honorable? Was it just? Was it pure? Was anything about it lovely, or commendable? Was there any excellence in it? Was it worthy of praise? Rather than thinking about the tragedy of it, or its painfulness, or its travesty of justice, we need to think about its beauty as a masterful solution to the problem of sin and the upgrade to humanity that it has provided.

I'm reminded of the 1944 song by Johnny Mercer and Harold Arlen, and done by Paul McCartney in 2012, "Ac-cent-tchu-ate the Positive." The lyrics are worth repeating:

> You've got to accentuate the positive
> Eliminate the negative
> Latch on to the affirmative
> Don't mess with Mister In-Between
>
> You've got to spread joy up to the maximum
> Bring gloom down to the minimum
> Have faith, or pandemonium's
> Liable to walk upon the scene
>
> (Oh, listen to me children and you will hear
> About the elininatin' of the negative
> And the accent on the positive)
> And gather 'round me children if you're willin'
> And sit tight while I start reviewin'
> The attitude of doin' right

The lyrics fall a bit flat because they emphasize the *positive*, and not the true, honorable, just, pure, beautiful, commendable, excellent, and what is worthy of praise, as Paul taught. But we know that these things are also positive, so keeping Paul's admonition in mind, the song works.

TRANSFIGURATION

In Matthew's gospel Jesus' Transfiguration occurs right after Peter's confession, and its location in the story is important. Peter confessed that Jesus was in fact the long expected Messiah of the Old Testament, the Christ of God. In the story, the Transfiguration provides a divine confirmation of Jesus' identity as the Christ.

Like Peter's vision in Acts 10:9-16 the Transfiguration must not to be taken literally. The dream or vision functions analogically or as a simile. In Peter's dream/vision a great sheet (σκεῦος and ὀθόνη in Acts 10:11), joined at its four corners, was let down from heaven filled with various kinds of land animals. The sheet functioned as a kind of fishing net, which Peter would have been familiar with. The meaning was that God was authorizing for Christians various foods that had been forbidden in the Old Testament. God was changing some of the Old Testament dietary restrictions, which suggested that Christians should be open to some significant changes in what was understood as God's law in the Old Testament. The general idea of a *vision* is that it communicates a deep truth that has serious implications and applications that involve much discussion and study.

The Transfiguration story provides a vision that involved Moses and Elijah talking with Jesus. Moses was instrumental in the receiving of the Ten Commandments, which form the basis for all biblical law, and the allusion to the return of Elijah pointed to the expected fulfillment of the long expected Messiah. The fact that Jesus was talking to these biblical characters put Jesus on par with them. The result of their discussion is the meaning of the vision.

The fact that Peter, James, and John were all there and all witnessed the vision provided legal testimony to its authenticity. Their testimony clearly established that this event, this vision, actually happened. Peter acknowledged that the meeting was *good* (καλός). The Greek word literally means valuable and has both virtuous and aesthetic overtones. It was an important meeting, and would have important consequences for the disciple's understanding of the Old Testament.

Peter immediately wanted to build three tabernacles to commemorate the event. Moses had given instructions for the original Tabernacle that led ancient Israel through the wilderness. Elijah had prophesied against Ahab, who was the worst of the kings, and who had abandoned the law that had been enshrined in Moses' Tabernacle. The implication, then, was that Jesus would inaugurate a new tabernacle through a new giving of God's law. The tabernacle in the vision pointed to God's law because the tablets of Moses had been enshrined in the ancient Tabernacle. And we know today that Jesus made some significant changes in what had become Old Testament law. What Peter did not understand at that point was that Jesus Christ was Himself the Tabernacle (or Temple).

They were then "overshadowed" (ἐπισκιάζω) by a "bright cloud" (Matthew 17:5). This is curious. *Overshadowed* means to cast a shadow upon, but *bright* suggests the elimination of shadows. In the Old Testament Tabernacle God's presence was signified by a cloud. Israel was also led in the wilderness by a cloud by day and a pillar of fire (light) at night. Here the idea of being overshadowed by a bright cloud suggests God's presence and guidance. Then,

> "a voice from the cloud said, 'This is my beloved Son, with whom I am well pleased; listen to him" (Matthew 15:5).

The disciples, believing that they were in the presence of God, were terrified and fell on their faces. They prostrated themselves. Jesus told them to not be afraid, and when they rose from their prostration "they saw no one but Jesus" (Matthew 17:7).

The various elements of this vision are pregnant with significance, particularly when read in light of the rest of the New Testament story. God's command to listen to Jesus in the midst of this vision points to Jesus' role as the new lawgiver. And we find that Jesus' teaching has adjusted, corrected, and augmented various laws of Moses. Dietary restrictions were abandoned, various separation or purification laws were negated, sacrifices became obsolete, etc. But all of this did not happen immediately. It took time. At that moment none of these things had happened yet. So Jesus told them not to tell anyone about the Transfiguration vision "until the Son of Man is raised from the dead" (Matthew 17:9). Why keep it a secret? Because at that point in the story no one would have understood it or believed that Jesus had such authority.

Jesus then identified John the Baptist as the coming of Elijah, because Jesus did not want people to think that He represented Elijah. The coming of Elijah qualified as the fulfillment of the Old Testament prophecy of Malachi 4:5-6. Elijah and John the Baptist represented the call to be reconciled in the Old Covenant. By identifying John the Baptist as the return of Elijah, Jesus closed the Old Testament and opened the New.

I AM STATEMENTS

"I am the bread of life" (John 6:35).

"I am the light of the world" (John 8:12).

"I am the door" (John 10:9).

"I am the good shepherd" (John 10:11).

"I am the resurrection and the life" (John 11:25).

"I am the way, the truth, and the life" (John 14:6).

"I am the true vine" (John 15:1).

When Moses first met God he asked Him His name. To which God replied, הָיָה, which means to be, to exist, to become, to come into being, and is usually translated as *I Am*. Jesus then completed God's identity by identifying Himself as the bread of life, the light of the world, the door, the good shepherd, the resurrection and the life, the way, truth and life, and the true vine. His *I am* statements apply to each of these things. Each of these statements are clarified in various biblical contexts, stories, and parables from the Old Testament and the New.

The importance of all this comes to light when we compare Jesus' identity with something like, "I am Joseph the Carpenter's son, from Galilee." While this latter identity is certainly true, it is not the whole truth. It describes the humanity of Jesus, but not His divinity. Jesus' divine identity provides the solution to the mystery of God's name given to Moses. The mystery of God's name is the majesty of Jesus Christ.

Personal identity must include the various roles that are played during life: child, student, player (of sports or hobbies), brother, sister, parent, worker, etc. And yet we are each more than the sum total of the roles we play. Jesus did in fact play the role of Messiah, but in order to play that role He had to be qualified for it.

Personal identity is developed out of crisis and conflict. Crisis and conflict cause us to reevaluate our understandings of who we are, of what is important to us. People are often not who they think they are when things are going well. Rather, crises and difficulties reveal our deeper selves by striping away our shallow self-images. Conflict reveals character.

THE CONSPIRACY/PLOT

God has created a historical conspiracy with a plot line of some five thousand years. This conspiracy is the plot of the story that weaves human history together, from beginning to end. It's a long story, a convoluted story with many twists and turns. And yet it is an incredibly simple story that can be told in a number of ways.

One way is to talk about God's effort to change human religion from the religion of vengeance, where God's law becomes a tool of revenge, to a religion of forgiveness, introduced by Jesus Christ. Another way is to talk about God's effort to save humanity from extinction, from either destroying itself or being destroyed by a hostile environment. The story of Noah involves such a story. Another way is to talk about the problem of sin and its elimination from the world. The Old Testament is filled with these kinds of stories. Another way is to talk about the civilization or taming of humanity, making humanity fit for Godly culture, domesticity, and service to one another. This is the story of the New Testament, proclaimed by Paul and the apostles. And this story has made much progress in the past two millennia, though the story is not over—not by a long shot.

The biblical conspiracy begins with the Old Testament prophecies about the promised Messiah, first hinted at in Genesis

3:15, and articulated by Moses and the prophets. Think of the Christian Advent lectionary readings that anticipate the birth of Jesus, who then supported the conspiracy as He prophesied His death on the cross. The ancient Jewish Second Temple establishment also lent support to this grand conspiracy:

> "So the chief priests and the Pharisees gathered the council and said, 'What are we to do? For this man performs many signs. If we let him go on like this, everyone will believe in him, and the Romans will come and take away both our place and our nation.' But one of them, Caiaphas, who was high priest that year, said to them, 'You know nothing at all. Nor do you understand that it is better for you that one man should die for the people, not that the whole nation should perish.' He did not say this of his own accord, but being high priest that year he prophesied that Jesus would die for the nation, and not for the nation only, but also to gather into one the children of God who are scattered abroad. So from that day on they made plans to put him to death" (John 11:47-53).

The commentary that begins with verse 51 provides a perspective that was not seen by the High Priest or the council at that time, and tells us how God would use the death of Jesus in human history. Interestingly, Jesus was aware of the plot against Him and "no longer walked openly among the Jews" (John 11:54).

During Passover the Pharisees were actively looking for Jesus in order to arrest Him. A large crowd had gathered during Passover and they marveled at Lazarus, whom Jesus had raised from death (John 11:1-44). Lazarus was evidence that Jesus had worked miracles, so

> "the chief priests made plans to put Lazarus to death as well" (John 12:10).

The next day Jesus made His triumphal entry into Jerusalem.

TRIUMPHAL ENTRY

Jesus was recognized as the King of Israel by a small band of nobodies. The Lord mounted an ass and the people met Him with palm branches, quoting an obscure Old Testament verse. Had you been there, you would have been underwhelmed.

> "His disciples did not understand these things at first, but when Jesus was glorified, then they remembered that these things had been written about him and had been done to him. The crowd that had been with him when he called Lazarus out of the tomb and raised him from the dead continued to bear witness. The reason why the crowd went to meet him was that they heard he had done this sign" (John 12:16-18).

In reality, no one paid much attention to His triumphal entry until much later, well after His crucifixion. But according to the story, when the Pharisees heard about it they used it as another reason to go after Jesus.

Jesus used the opportunity of the crowd that had gathered to teach about His impending death and resurrection. But this idea was so foreign to them, even to those who believed that He was the Christ, that they just didn't understand it. And we shouldn't blame them for not understanding it. It's a wild idea, unique in history, and continues to escape the understanding of many of the most intelligent people today.

> "Although Jesus had performed so many miraculous signs before them, they still refused to believe in him, so that the word of Isaiah the prophet would be fulfilled. He said, 'Lord, who has believed our message, and to whom has the arm of the Lord been revealed?' For this reason they could not believe, because again Isaiah said, 'He has blinded their eyes and hardened their heart, so that they would not see with their eyes and understand with their heart, and turn to me, and I would heal them.' Isaiah said these things because he saw Christ's glory, and spoke about him" (John 12:37-41, *New English Translation*).

LORD'S SUPPER

It is important to pay attention to the series of events that follow. According to John, Jesus washed the disciples feet before supper in the upper room. Then He told them that one of them would betray Him to the authorities. All of this happened during what we usually call the Last Supper in the Upper Room. However, we don't find the institution of the liturgy of the sacrament of the Lord's Supper in John's gospel. V. Taylor said that John's

> "eucharistic teaching, like his conception of faith, centers in the idea of communion with the Living Lord, rather than, as in St. Paul's teaching, the thought of participation in His sacrifice."[7]

John omitted descriptions of the two Protestant sacraments: baptism and the Lord's Supper, and chose rather to expose and discuss the meaning of the reality that these sacraments point to. He didn't oppose the practice of these sacraments as they have been historically practiced in the church. Rather, John's interest was to provide the spiritual realities that these sacraments represent.

> "According to Rudolf Bultmann, Paul gave to the eucharistic meal an expiatory and sacramental significance borrowed from the pagan mystery religions. John, on the contrary, was the first one to realize clearly the meaning of the ministry of Jesus: in Christ, God encounters man. For this reason, in the Fourth Gospel, the idea of forgiveness of sin is practically absent and the death on the cross is subordinated to the incarnation. The Pauline stress on *crucifixion* and *expiation* is replaced by the Johannine assertion of *exaltation* and *glorification*. Christ gives a new *commandment* instead of a new *covenant*. 'The entire salvation drama—incarnation, death, resurrection, Pentecost, the parousia—is concentrated into a single event: the revelation of God's "reality" (ἀλήθεια) in the earthly activity of the man Jesus combined with the overcoming of the offense in it by man's accepting it in faith' (R. Bultmann, *Theology of the New Testament*, I (New York, 1951), p. 144)."[8]

John's concern was not with the choreography of the liturgical practice in church services. Rather, John's concern was the

---

7   V. Taylor, *The Atonement in New Testament Thought*, London, 1958, p. 140.

8   Augsburger, Daniel, *John And The Institution Of The Lord's, Supper*, Andrews University, Berrien Springs, Michigan, 1965.

ongoing reality of Jesus Christ in the world. As such, John's gospel provided much more discussion of the spiritual realities involved. However, John was not trying to point people to the mysteries of the faith, but to the reality of spiritual life in Christ. To get distracted by the mysticism involved detracts from the reality of the spirituality.

John's gospel is much more receptive to the following understanding of the idea of *transubstantiation*. It seems to me that the miracle that happens in the liturgy of the Lord's Supper is not that the bread is miraculously changed into the body of Christ, and/or that the wine is changed into the blood of Christ by the priest or through proper liturgical treatment. Rather, the real miracle comes through simple digestion.[9]

By this I mean that bread and wine which serve as symbols of Christ's body and blood actually become physical elements of the body and blood of communicants through digestion. Here what is symbolized as the body and blood of Christ become real elements of the actual, physical body and blood of the believers as the molecules of the bread and wine are digested and assimilated. Here the miracle is that the symbol actually becomes the reality in the life of the believer through the assimilation (digestion) of the elements and the idea, the symbol, which is described through the spoken words of institution. John's concern was to clarify that the spiritual reality of Jesus Christ actually becomes the physical bodies of believers as the genuine character of Jesus Christ becomes bodily manifest in the lives of individual believers. This is what is symbolized in the eucharist.

John included the story of Jesus washing the disciples feet in the Upper Room as a model for their service among Christians. Then, in the midst of the institution of communion Jesus speaks of His betrayal, chooses Judas to betray Him, and commands Judas to go do it.

After Judas left, Jesus gave them a new commandment to "love one another" (John 13:34), and predicted Peter's denial. Je-

---

9 "To become a butterfly, a caterpillar first digests itself. But certain groups of cells survive, turning the soup into eyes, wings, antennae and other adult structures" (https://www.scientificamerican.com/article/caterpillar-butterfly-metamorphosis-explainer/).

sus then launched into a long teaching session (John 14-17), after which He was arrested.

The Word

"In the beginning, God created" (Genesis 1:1).

"In the beginning was the Word, and the Word was with God, and the Word was God" (John 1:12).

We began this study by discussing what exactly it was that God created in the beginning, and suggested that the creation story is not simply about God creating the physical world of dirt and stars, but that God created language and linguistic categories that genuinely represent various aspects of our human experience. God fused language to humanity.

And the first wrinkle in the story came because the Serpent lied about the integrity of God's Word—perhaps because he was deceived himself. The result of the Serpent's lie damaged our understanding of the integrity between what God said and what God meant. More generally, it damaged the integrity or veracity between words and reality. Did God's words really represent the truth?

The general question that the Bible introduced is whether or not human beings are able to correctly perceive and communicate truth. Do human words rightly correspond to reality? Or does our subjectivity always skew our perception and understanding of reality? When Eve trusted the words of the Serpent, she also doubted the words of God and did what God had forbidden. She trusted her own assessment of the facts.

> "Now the serpent was more crafty than any other beast of the field that the LORD God had made. He said to the woman, 'Did God actually say, "You shall not eat of any tree in the garden"?' And the woman said to the serpent, 'We may eat of the fruit of the trees in the garden, but God said, "You shall not eat of the fruit of the tree that is in the midst of the garden, neither shall you touch it, lest you die."' But the serpent said to the woman, 'You will not surely die. For God knows that when you eat of it your eyes will be opened, and you will be like God, knowing good and evil.' So when the woman saw that the tree was

good for food, and that it was a delight to the eyes, and that the tree was to be desired to make one wise, she took of its fruit and ate, and she also gave some to her husband who was with her, and he ate" (Genesis 3:1-6).

Eve determined that it (the fruit of the tree of the knowledge of good and evil) was eatable, beautiful, and meaningful. Clearly this was not any sort of deciduous or evergreen tree. Rather, the idea of a *tree* is to be understood analogically. The story of the Bible is the story of humanity struggling with the lack of integrity between language and reality. Words and ideas refer to various real things and experiences in the world, and the failure to describe and represent things accurately creates all sorts of problems. And the damnable thing is that we do it willingly, intentionally! The Bible calls this issue Original Sin.

The rejection of God was clearly established in history when Israel asked Samuel to anoint a king like the other nations had. God said that Israel had rejected, not Samuel, but God Himself. This, then, set up the story of the history of Israel as the story of God working with people who had rejected Him and His truth, His Word. God's plan was to bring them back to Him by allowing them to experience the consequences of their own decisions, their rejection of God. And finally, to provide for them the Messiah who would be their King. God's Messiah doesn't merely *represent* truth, but actually *is* Himself Truth itself (John 14:6). The point of all of this is to teach that in Jesus Christ there is complete integrity between Word and reality. Jesus Christ is the הָיָה, the *I Am* (Exodus 3:14) of Truth Itself.

In John's treatment of baptism and the Lord's supper (communion) we find, not justification for liturgical representations that point toward the union of language and reality, or Word and Sacrament, but we find that John's language omits liturgical representation altogether and describes the reality of actual union with or in Christ. This is why John's gospel has been described as mystical. John was not satisfied with linguistic or liturgical representations of reality, and dove directly into the reality that liturgy can only point to.

The New Testament abandons the idea of the Old Testament Temple as an accurate and meaningful analogy for God in order to embrace the reality that the Body of Christ *is* the Temple of God, not just the Body (σάρξ) of Jesus but the corporate body (σῶμα) of His Church.[10] Jesus Christ is not a prophet in the tradition of the Old Testament. He is not a representative of the priestly traditions of Aaron or Levi, which God gave as crutches or helps for disobedient people who had rejected Him.

Rather, Jesus is in the order of Melchizedek (Hebrews 7), which puts Him outside of and apart from the Old Testament Temple and its significance and analogies to God. The advent of Christ means that the crutches and helps of the Old Testament, as genuinely meaningful as they are, must be abandoned in order that people depend, not on what merely represents God, but depend directly on God Himself, on Jesus Christ through the power and presence of the Holy Spirit through regeneration.

And yet, we cannot simply abandon the Old Testament because every individual and every generation must come to see the truth of the long story of humanity and the consequences of the struggle to discern good and evil for ourselves, and the truth, beauty, and goodness of hearing (receiving, accepting, and assimilating) God's Word for ourselves, both personally and socially or culturally. The ultimate consequence portrayed in the long story of the Old Testament ended with the destruction of Jerusalem and the Second Temple in A.D. 70. And the truth, beauty, and goodness of the story has come in the Person of Jesus Christ, which began in the New Testament. The Body of Christ has replaced the Temple of God.

CRUCIFIXION

The crucifixion of Jesus is absolutely necessary to the story of the Old Testament, not because God is some sort of evil monarch. God does not need Jesus to be crucified. His crucifixion is not for God, it's for *us*. It's not because God required Jesus' crucifixion in order to prove His justice. God doesn't need to prove anything. God is not the cause of Jesus' crucifixion, *we*

---

10 Paul plays with these different Greek words in his letters to the Corinthians, but that play is not seen in the English versions. See *Arsy Varsy—Reclaiming The Gospel in First Corinthians*, Phillip A. Ross, Pilgrim Platform, Marietta, Ohio, 2008.

For The Whole World

are. It didn't happen in order to satisfy God's sense of justice regarding human sin, though because it did happen it is able to satisfy *our* sense of justice regarding our sin. God didn't make it happen, *we did*. Humanity made it happen. *We* crucified Jesus. God foresaw it, but it happened because of us. We need it. God doesn't need it, but He was willing to give us what we need.

This is why Jesus' crucifixion is an act of grace and mercy on God's part, though it issued out of human sin and guilt. The cost of the sacrifice was borne by God alone. Jesus didn't benefit from it, nor did God. Rather, *we* are the beneficiaries of the tragedy of Jesus' crucifixion. And because the benefit we receive is great, and because it is real, it turned this very long story of human failure and tragedy into a story of redemption and unrelenting hope. And what is more, it is not just a story, not *merely* a story. Rather, it is history. The story is real, true, and trustworthy. It's a story of truth, beauty, and goodness. In spite of what human beings have made of this story, it is the story of God's truth, God's beauty, and God's goodness—in spite of human sin.

And what is more, this story is both necessary and sufficient to provide redemption for all who understand it, all who stand under it, all who willingly embrace it. This long story (history) of Israel is about God's redemption of humanity in spite of humanity's rejection of God. Israel simply provided a case study, but the case study has universal implications, which in the fullness of time will become increasingly obvious to all.

Resurrection

The resurrection of Christ is the answer to the problem of the Old Testament, the failure of humanity to do the will of God. The actual Person of Jesus Christ actually rose from actual death and is actually seated at the right hand of God Almighty. And as good as that is, it isn't all! The actual Body of Jesus Christ —His Church—actually rose from the dead corpse of the nation of Israel! These two things are different aspects of the same thing by the power and presence of the Holy Spirit! Those who take the name of Christ assume the character of Jesus Christ as manifested and taught in the story of the New Testament. The character of Christ in the lives of believers is provided through the fruits of the Holy Spirit as delineated in the New Testament. Paul has a short list of them in Galatians:

> "love, joy, peace, patience, kindness, goodness, faithfulness, gentleness, self-control" (Galatians 5:22-23).

There are more, but these provide a good start. The genuine manifestation of these character qualities is only possible through the power and presence of the Holy Spirit through regeneration.

Ascension

The ascension of Jesus Christ happened forty days after His crucifixion as He was taken up bodily into heaven.

> "And behold, I am sending the promise of my Father upon you. But stay in the city until you are clothed with power from on high. And he led them out as far as Bethany, and lifting up his hands he blessed them. While he blessed them, he parted from them and was carried up into heaven" (Luke 24:49-51).

Luke repeated the story in Acts:

> "So when they had come together, they asked him, 'Lord, will you at this time restore the kingdom to Israel?' He said to them, 'It is not for you to know times or seasons that the Father has fixed by his own authority. But you will receive power when the Holy Spirit has come upon you, and you will be my witnesses in Jerusalem and in all Judea and Samaria, and to the end of the earth.' And when he had said these things, as they were looking on, he was lifted up, and a cloud took him out of their sight. And while they were gazing into heaven as he went, behold, two men stood by them in white robes, and said, 'Men of Galilee, why do you stand looking into heaven? This Jesus, who was taken up from you into heaven, will come in the same way as you saw him go into heaven'" (Acts 1:6-11).

The disciples asked Jesus this question after he had been resurrected and was meeting with them. At that time the disciples were still stuck in Old Testament categories of thought, and asked about the restoration of the kingdom of Israel. They had not yet realized that the resurrection of Jesus Christ required the

Old Testament system of Temple sacrifices to end. They didn't fully understand that the Temple system had failed, in spite of God's help and guidance. We (human beings) need more than God's Word recorded in the dusty pages of history. We need the dynamic power and presence of the Holy Spirit through personal and social regeneration in order to "hear" God's voice, to rightly understand what we read and what we experience in Christ.

The Holy Spirit provides faithful communication between the Father and the Son of the Holy Trinity, but also between the Trinitarian Godhead and believers. God dispatches His Holy Spirit into the lives of believers to provide fruit-of-the-Spirit character development. That development has a beginning (re-generation or being born-again) in this life, but does not end in this life. Regeneration is both personal and social because human beings are both personal and social beings. Social regeneration is more than the aggregate of regenerated individuals because re-generated individuals are saved into the Body of Christ for a particular purpose. Peter wrote about Christians being living stones that are built by God into a social unit, an οἶκος, house-hold, church, or body.[11]

Thus, we take our godly character with us into heaven. In other words, Holy character in the likeness of Jesus Christ is able to cross the gap between this current life and the next life, or life in heaven. God can—and does—reach down from eternity to establish gospel fruit in the lives of believers today. We can also describe this as God bringing heaven, through the establishment of the character qualities of Jesus Christ into the lives of believers, to earth, as Christians pray in the Lord's Prayer.

This fruit then provides proof to the believer that the bodily resurrection of Jesus Christ is both possible and real. Because the character of Jesus Christ can be emulated in this world by believers, the actual, bodily resurrection and ascension of Jesus Christ is real. And we, then, take that fruit with us into eternity. We become the seeds of the fruits of the Spirit, on earth as it is in heaven. Lord, make it so!

---

11 Body: A group of persons associated by some common tie or occupation and regarded as an entity.

APPENDIX

DISCERNING THE HISTORICAL SOURCE OF HUMAN LANGUAGE

By Edouard Belaga, *FAITH Magazine September-October 2009*

Edouard Belaga, researcher at the Institute of Advanced Mathematical Research, at Strasbourg University, argues that at the origins of the People of God, probably of humanity itself, there was a sudden "inspired" emergence of human language. Dr Belaga was an upcoming Mathematics and Computer Science researcher at the Moscow Institute of Control Problems when he was forced to leave the country in the late 1970's for his dissident loyalties.

The problem of the emergence and evolution of natural languages is seen today by many specialists as one of the most difficult problems in the cognitive sciences, if not of science tout court. As the cognitive scientists Christiansen and Kirby put it:

> "Language is one of the hallmarks of the human species, an important part of what makes us human. Yet, despite a staggering growth in our scientific knowledge about the origin of life, the universe and (almost) everything else that we have seen fit to ponder, we know comparatively little about how our unique ability for language originated and evolved into the complex linguistic systems we use today. Why might this be?"[1]

---

1   Morten H. Christiansen, Simon Kirby. "Language Evolution: The Hardest Problem In Science?," *Language Evolution*, eds. M. Christiansen, S. Kirby,

Human Language

A key, we think, to beginning to unravel this enigma is the close relationship of language to mathematics.

There are some significant linguistic phenomena that are characterized or accompanied by the presence of some clear-cut, non-trivial mathematical structures. This has been observed in ancient, "fossilized" languages—i.e., in languages that fell out of use a long time ago, but which were well preserved in ancient texts. The presence of such structures, for instance in ancient Hebrew, cannot be explained (away) as resulting from the conscious efforts of systematization by savants....

The Source of Language

The sources of mathematical and computational insights have been, we believe, neither biological, nor social, but purely inspirational and intuitional—as a tragedy of Shakespeare or as the Requiem of Mozart. Furthermore systematic language has been at some historical juncture inspirationally created or invented.

The evolution of natural languages, as we know them today, was dramatically affected eight to ten thousand years ago by a linguistic Big-Bang. That is there was a sudden emergence of a radically new language germ, markedly similar to an essentially modern "natural super-assembler," thrown into the "primeval linguistic soup" of its contemporary environment. This emergence was restricted to just a single human family, if not to a single individual, and cannot be accounted for by a previously existing linguistic framework. It is the ancestor of the Semitic family of languages and of some Afro-Asiatic, Indo-European, and possibly other such families.

Language has been described as a vehicle for creating knowledge, for interpretation of meaning or of being, for the construction of identity, of truth, of intangible cultural heritage, etc. Our initial, only oral, proto-language, one would think, was ideally adapted to be a vehicle for a dramatic, prodigiously eloquent, unprecedentedly effective, radically new, previously unthinkable and unspeakable, eminently active vocation of man.

Oxford University Press, pp. 1-15, 2003.

As the well-documented history of this and following epochs witnesses, the germ of these linguistic families has borne extraordinary fruits. On the geopolitical scene, we have seen for instance the emergence of radically different and rich Middle East cultures. In the religious sphere we have the emergence of a dramatically new tradition which, starting with a single man, his family, and then a nation, has spread all over the world forming Judaeo-Christian civilization.

The modern history of language and *belles-lettres* knows analogous cultural upheavals provoked by linguistic or philological revolutions carried by a single person, even if certainly much less radical and influential. Such has been the case, for example, of the Russian poetic genius Alexander Pushkin (1799-1837) who almost single-handedly initiated the modern culture of Russian literature, better "the Russian modern culture tout court."[2]

It is interesting to note that Umberto Eco's book, *The Search for the Perfect Language*, describes the

> "profound influence on European thought, culture, and history [... of] the idea that there once existed a language which perfectly and unambiguously expressed the essence of all possible things and concepts[, which] has occupied the minds of philosophers, theologians, mystics and others for at least two millennia. [...] From the early Dark Ages to the Renaissance it was widely believed that the language spoken in the Garden of Eden was just such a language, and that all current languages were its decadent descendants from the catastrophes of the Fall and at Babel."[3]

Conclusion

Only such a scientifically mature perception of the phenomenon of man and his linguistic abilities can show how the gift of language has its source in the human capacity to be inspirational.

---

2   Edward G Belaga. "Emergence and Evolution of Natural Languages: New Epistemological, Mathematical & Algorithmic Perspectives." LCC-2008 - The International Conference on Language, Communication and Cognition. Brighton, UK, August 4th-7th 2008.

3   Umberto Eco. *The Search for Perfect Language*. Blackwell Publishers, New York, 1997, (Publisher's synopsis). *Faith* I "Discerning the Historical Source of Human Language."

We must be free from popular, infantile determinism. Through such an approach we can grow in understanding of the mystery of human intelligence, and of the noble, mysterious, superhuman and supernatural inspirations of the founders of our civilization and science.

HEAVENS AND EARTH

Another argument that can be made regarding a better explanation of God's creation involves the two primary elements: the heavens and the earth. These terms suggest the human habitat, which is composed of land or earth and atmosphere or heavens. The actual human habitat involves the surface of the earth and several miles of atmosphere. This thin ribbon of reality that extends from the surface of the earth up several miles is the only known place in the entire cosmos that supports life as we know it. Weather is also a major life factor within this global zone. Weather cleans the salt from the oceans and provides water for the land to grow vegetation and life of various forms.

An argument can be made that this thin, global, atmospheric band around the earth is the creation of God intended in the Genesis story. Sure, God created the whole of the cosmos, but the Genesis story is about life on earth, not God's creation of the cosmos. The biblical story speaks of sun, moon, and stars, but not in the sense that we understand these bodies in space today. The biblical story speaks of them in two senses: 1) as being embedded in or part of the atmosphere or canopy of the earth, and 2) symbolically, representing authority and government.

Imagine that the biblical writer of the Genesis creation account had in mind the actual human habitat, the surface of the earth and the atmosphere, and that these were the things in the creation story that God created.

THE CIRCUMCISION PERFORMED BY ZIPPORAH

By Fred Blumenthal

(Fred Blumenthal was educated at the Samson Raphael Hirsch School and the Yeshiva of Frankfort, Germany, and has pursued biblical studies throughout his adult life. Source: Jewish

Bible Quarterly, Vol. 35, No. 4, 2007 http://jbqnew.jewish-bible.org/assets/Uploads/354/354_circum.pdf)

> At a night encampment on the way, the Lord encountered him and sought to kill him. So Zipporah took a flint and cut off her son's foreskin, and touched his leg with it, saying 'You are truly a bridegroom of blood to me.' And when He let him alone she added: 'A bridegroom of blood because of the circumcision' (Ex. 4:24-26).

In the account of Moses' return to Egypt we are confronted with a very short, cryptic story describing the circumcision of one of his sons by his wife Zipporah. The JPS translation of these three verses reads as follows:

The brevity with which this event is reported deserves more attention than the event itself. As it reads, it does not specify who was threatened with death. Was it Moses or one of his sons who was uncircumcised? If one of the sons, was it the older or the younger? Why did Zipporah have to perform the act instead of Moses himself? Last but not least, why was this circumcision of such overriding importance at this moment, when we read in the fifth chapter of the Book of Joshua that all circumcisions had been suspended during the journey in the wilderness, seemingly with the full consent of Moses.

Perhaps we should add that if it was the younger son who was being circumcised at this ceremony, as it appears at first glance, it is surprising that Moses should have had a newborn son at the age of 80, without any mention of this birth in the preceding text. And it appears equally puzzling that he should have taken a newborn child on a perilous trip, together with the mother who could hardly have recovered from the delivery so quickly. All of these questions are left unanswered in this story which is inserted between the account of Moses leaving Midian and his arrival in Egypt. ...

The symbolic story of Zipporah's action and the reality of Moses' acceptance thus foreshadows the prohibition which was later on expressed by Moses himself. In Deuteronomy 13:5 he says: *Thou mayest not put a foreigner over thee, who is not thy brother.*

The allegoric meaning of this brief story becomes even more evident when compared to the symbolism of Lot's wife, who turned into a pillar of salt (Genesis 19:26). Here, too, we find that a wife is used as the symbol of attachment to a strange culture. The nephew of Abraham had lived in an atmosphere far inferior to the ethics and culture he had learned when he had joined his uncle. When fleeing from Sodom, his unnamed wife disobeyed instructions and looked back. The wife can be symbolically seen as Lot's link to his immediate past. Her action, contrary to Zipporah's, represents Lot's inability to disengage totally from the influence of his preceding surrounding. The text hints at this interpretation by saying *She looked behind* **him**, insinuating that the backward glance was his as much as hers. The conversion of the wife into a pillar of salt, salt being a preservative, tells us that Lot failed to cut this link. So he becomes the forefather of two nations, Moab and Ammon, whose names proclaim loudly that they are the fruit of sinful incest.

Zipporah's determined action, portraying the total absorption of the new Torah culture by Moses, is immediately followed by the meeting with his brother, Aaron, as if to demonstrate once more that Moses had no longer any adherence to his past. Aaron, whom he had not seen for many years, is now his brother and confidante. The Israelite slaves have become his brethren.

It was the story of the circumcision, and the ceremony surrounding it, that had completed the appointment of Moses; it made no difference which one of his sons was being circumcised, whether Gershom or Eliezer. The transformation of Zipporah from a symbol of Midianite religion to a companion on their way ahead is the essence of the story told in these three short sentences. Moses becomes her "bridegroom," her newly-acquired husband, because they both were culturally new persons. The expression *hatan damim* [bridegroom of blood] refers to the blood of circumcision which erases any preceding affiliation and allegorically seals the appointment of Moses to the leadership of his people.

SIN

The Hebrew word, סִין, points to the name of an Egyptian town, and/or the name of the adjoining desert. And the ancient mythology of Sin is quite interesting.

Sin or Nanna was the god of the moon in the Mesopotamian mythology of Akkad, Assyria, and Babylonia. Nanna is a Sumerian deity, the son of Enlil and Ninlil, and became identified with Semitic Sin. The two chief seats of Nanna's/Sin's worship were Ur in the south of Mesopotamia and Harran in the north. A moon god by the same name was also worshiped in pre-Islamic South Arabia.

This moon god is commonly designated as *En-zu*, which means "lord of wisdom." During the period (c.2600-2400 B.C.) that Ur (Abraham's homeland) exercised a large measure of supremacy over the Euphrates valley. Thus, Sin was naturally regarded as the head of the pantheon. It is to this period that we must trace such designations of Sin as "father of the gods," "chief of the gods," "creator of all things," and the like. The "wisdom" personified by the moon-god is likewise an expression of the science of astronomy or the practice of astrology, in which the observation of the moon's phases is an important factor.

Source: en.wikipedia.org/wiki/Sin_(mythology)

Because the serpent was already in the Garden when Eve encountered him, we could also say that sin was already involved with God's Creation prior to the creation of Adam. A case could also be made that the sin that Christians struggle against is a product of Original Sin, defined as "doing what is right in our own eyes"—and which could also be related to this ancient Egyptian town and its god, Sin.

METANARRATIVE

The difficulty with using the word "narrative" biblically is that in literary circles narrative is narrowly defined as a fiction-writing mode in which the narrator is communicating directly to the reader, and the Bible is not fiction. The term lends itself to an academic insinuation that the Bible is to be treated as narrative fiction. Until the late nineteenth century, literary criticism as an academic exercise dealt with poetry, i.e., epic poems like the *Iliad* and *Paradise Lost*, and poetic drama like that of Shakespeare. Most poems did not have a narrator that was distinct from the author.

But novels created the possibility of the narrator's views differing significantly from those of the author, lending a number of voices to several characters in addition to that of the narrator. With the rise of the novel in the eighteenth century, the concept of the narrator in opposition to the author made the question of narrator a prominent one in literary theory. It has been proposed that perspective and interpretive knowledge are the essential concerns of the narrative, while focus and structure are lateral concerns of the narrator.

AMALEKITES

The Amalekites play a significant role in the Old Testament, and in order to understand that role we need to know that Amalek, who would become the Amalekites, was a grandson of Esau (Genesis 36:12). The Old Testament describes the Amalekites as a tribe which lived in ancient Israel and in the land called Moab, in what the Romans called Arabia Petraea (Moab and the desert of Sinai), a region depopulated in the fourteenth century B.C. and then occupied by Edomites.

According to the Book of Genesis and 1 Chronicles, Amalek was the son of Eliphaz and the concubine Timna. Timna was a Horite and sister of Lotan. Amalek appears in the genealogy of Esau (Genesis 36:12; 1 Chronicles 1:36) who was the chief of an Edomite tribe (Genesis 36:16). Amalek ruled a clan or territory named after him. In the chant of Balaam (Numbers 24:20) Amalek was called the "first of the nations," attesting to high antiquity. Rashi states: "He was the first of all of them (the other nations) to war against Israel (when they came out of Egypt)." First-century Roman-Jewish scholar and historian Flavius Josephus refers to Amalek as a "bastard" (νόθος) in a derogatory sense.

In Judaism, the Amalekites came to represent the archetypal enemy of the Jews. In Jewish folklore the Amalekites are considered to be the symbol of evil. This concept has been used by some Hassidic rabbis (particularly the Baal Shem Tov) to represent atheism or the rejection of God. Nur Masalha, Elliot Horowitz, and Josef Stern suggest that Amalekites have come to represent an "eternally irreconcilable enemy" that wants to murder Jews, and that Jews in post-biblical times sometimes associate contemporary enemies with Haman or Amalekites, and that some Jews believe that pre-emptive violence is acceptable against such enemies.

During the Purim festival, the Book of Esther is read in the commemoration of the saving of the Jewish people from Haman (who was considered to be an Amalekite), who led a plot to kill the Jews. On the basis of Exodus 17:14, where the Lord promised to "blot out the name" of Amalek, it is customary for the audience to make noise and shout whenever "Haman" is mentioned, in order to desecrate his name.[4]

Reading the New Testament back into the Old Testament through the eyes of Paul's admonition

> "For we do not wrestle against flesh and blood, but against the rulers, against the authorities, against the cosmic powers over this present darkness, against the spiritual forces of evil in the heavenly places" (Ephesians 6:12).

we see that our enemy is not people, but principalities and powers. Principalities and powers refer to cultural structures: values, religions, governments, policies, etc. Paul goes on to contrast the Spirit and the flesh, suggesting an eternal conflict between spiritual things and fleshly things. Thus, we conclude that the Amakekites in the Old Testament represent the flesh. And God's command to eliminate the memory of Amalek becomes for us the command to mortify the flesh,[5] to put to death our own sinful nature as a part of the process of sanctification and maturity in Christ. The primary Christian struggle is not against other people, but is against the values of the flesh, against our own sin. Only as we deal with our own sin can we help others deal with

---

4   Source: https://en.wikipedia.org/wiki/Amalek
5   https://en.wikipedia.org/wiki/Mortification_of_the_flesh

theirs. The death that is called for is the extinction of our old self in the waters of baptism, so that we can rise to the advent of our new self in Christ. And the sin that is traced throughout the Bible is the sin of selective obedience. This was Saul's sin, and David's, and Solomon's, etc. And it is ours! Lord, have mercy.

ISIS

The Islamic State of Iraq and the Levant (ISIL), also known as the Islamic State of Iraq and Syria (ISIS), Islamic State (IS), and by its Arabic language acronym *Daesh* is a Salafi jihadist militant group and unrecognized proto-state that follows a fundamentalist, Wahhabi doctrine of Sunni Islam. ISIS gained global prominence in early 2014 when it drove Iraqi government forces out of key cities in its Western Iraq offensive, followed by its capture of Mosul and the Sinjar massacre.

ISIS follows an extremist interpretation of Islam, promotes religious violence, and regards Muslims who do not agree with its interpretations as infidels or apostates. According to Hayder al Khoei, ISIS' philosophy is represented by the symbolism in the Black Standard variant of the legendary battle flag of Prophet Muhammad that it has adopted: the flag shows the Seal of Muhammad within a white circle, with the phrase above it, "There is no god but God." Such symbolism has been said to point to the belief that it represents the restoration of the caliphate of early Islam, with all the political, religious, and eschatological ramifications that this would imply.

ISIS aims to return the world to the early days of Islam, rejecting all innovations of Islam, which it believes corrupts its original spirit. It condemns later caliphates and the Ottoman Empire for deviating from what it calls pure Islam, and seeks to revive the original Wahhabi project of the restoration of the caliphate governed by strict Salafist doctrine. Following Salafi-Wahhabi tradition, ISIS condemns the followers of secular law as disbelievers, subjecting them to fundamentalist Islamic discipline, which puts the current Saudi Arabian government in that category.

Salafists such as ISIS believe that only a legitimate authority can undertake the leadership of jihad, and that the first priority over other areas of combat, such as fighting non-Muslim countries, is the purification of Islamic society. For example, ISIS regards the Palestinian Sunni group, Hamas, as apostates who have no legitimate authority to lead jihad and see fighting Hamas as the first step toward confrontation by ISIS with Israel.

https://en.wikipedia.org/wiki/Islamic_State_of_Iraq_and_the_Levant

Those individuals who subscribe to ISIS are committed to their death to its beliefs and principles, which cause it/them to be at violent war or jihad with all who do not subscribe to ISIS. They do not believe that ISIS can coexist with any other culture, and are committed to the destruction of all cultures that are not submissive to ISIS.

Alphabetical Index

A.D. 70. 110, 155, 172, 190, 203, 219, 242, 260, 277
Aaron..................92, 111
Abel 37
Abel, sacrifices of.............37
Abimelech..............66, 68
Abishag..........................161
Abraham................63, 206
Abraham's failure.............75
Abrahamic era.................57
Abram's mission...............53
Absalom................159, 177
Accentuate the Positive. 266
Achan............................124
Adam...........................5, 8
Adam, destruction of.......34
Adam, new kind..............21
Adam, second..................22
Adam's sin....32, 33, 46, 113
Adamic Era.....................41
addiction........................76
Adonijah................160, 161
advertising....................108
Agag..............149, 151, 229
agency............18, 19, 23, 33
agreement................45, 102
Agrippa.........................245
Ahab 218, 235, 268
Ahijah...........................189
Ahimelech.....................155
Ai 124
Aleph Null...............28, 230
allegory..................153, 252
alliances...59, 159, 162, 178, 184
Amalek............................95
Amalekites....959, 6, 97, 98,

99, 100, 114, 117, 149, 157, 159
Amaziah........................185
Ammonites...............66, 144
Amnon...................176, 177
ancestry.........................248
ancient elements..............11
ancient myths...................4
annunciation.................235
Antiochus IV.................209
apathy...........................193
Apocrypha.....................210
apostasy..........160, 164, 195
apostate.........................154
apostleship....................248
aprons.............................33
archetype............16, 45, 238
Ark of the Covenant....119, 138, 158, 165
arts 241
Asa 183
ascension.......................279
Athaliah........................184
atmosphere.....................12
atoms...............................9
Augustine........................22
authority.................83, 84
authorship....................194
Babel.........................38, 49
Babylon............................4
Babylonian captivity 7, 191, 194, 198, 204, 210, 211, 213, 217, 234
Babylonian unity.............49
balance of nature............50
baptism....36, 238, 239, 244, 276
Bathsheba..............159, 177

Beatitudes......................257
belief.............................249
Benjamin.......136, 142, 146
Bethel.............................71
Bethlehem.....................232
betrayal.........................274
Bible, inspired...............253
birthright........................69
blessing.........................257
blindness......................202
blood sacrifice.................57
Body v. body.................277
bread..............................73
Bultmann, Rudolf.........273
burning bush................103
Cain 37, 70, 85
Cain, banished................38
Cain, God's mercy...........38
Cain, rejection of............37
Cain, slew Apel...............37
Cain's punishment..........77
calculus..........................16
Canaan, cursed...............48
cartoon..........................30
centralized monarchy....143
chaos........................10, 11
character...1, 26, 69, 75, 81, 85, 95, 115, 225, 245, 246, 247, 278, 280
character & name..........105
character of Israel..........137
Chase, Stuart..................18
Christ, resurrected.........249
Christ's return..............246
church...................231, 280
church membership.......263
circumcision........63, 80, 92
civil war 168, 169, 170, 173,

294

188, 189
clothing technology........36
clouds................12
coexist................99
common origin..............47
communication.......53, 280
conflict....................270
conformity...................228
consciousness.....15, 16, 253
consequences..................218
conspiracy....................270
conversion...................98
Copernican revolution....19
Copernicus....................4
corporate whole..............25
corruption........35, 138, 160, 201, 236, 262, 264
covenant............56, 62, 216
covenant abandonment.217
covenant of grace............91
covenant, first..............44
covenantal eras...............7
creation story..................275
creationism....................4, 6
creatures of habit............106
crucifixion....................277
cultural conflicts..............123
cultural creature.............27
cultural death...................36
cultural identity.................64
cultural maintenance.....253
cultural mandate..............79
culture.....17, 21, 23, 24, 26, 45, 60, 61, 76, 98, 128, 223, 224, 229, 253
culture v. nature..............251
culture v. people............100
culture, two lineages........39
curse.........................227
Cyrus the Great....191, 213, 234
Dagon.........................139
Damascus Road.............248
damnation....................259
Daniel...........209, 233, 234
darkness..........109, 110, 113
David.....................151, 173
David's death.................160
David's sin.............177, 188

day of the Lord.............203
debts................59
deceit..............27, 35, 58
Delilah..............135
desire..............108
Deutero-Zechariah........216
Deuteronomic Reform.191, 198, 199, 202
digestion..........................274
Dinah...................78, 79, 80
dinosaurs..........................40
discipleship.....240, 247, 249
disobedience....................129
distributed network........16
distributed node..........22
divided kingdom...158, 189
divine sanction..............187
divinity........9, 28, 230, 269
divinity & infinity..........231
DNA...................13, 26, 57
double entendre............143
dry bones.............204, 208
dualism..........................227
earth's wobble..............56
ecological periods............7
editorial conflation........217
editors..................191, 193
egoism..........................241
Egypt........57, 162, 179, 232
Egypt, captivity in..........61
Egyptian plunder.............92
Eighth Day sabbath.......107
Ein Gedi..................155, 184
El.............................138
Elijah........218, 235, 237, 267
Elijah, return...................269
environment....................270
environmental factors......41
error..........................35
Esau.............68, 70, 73, 77
evangelism....................260
Eve 24, 26, 31, 276
Eve, helping God..............31
Eve's sin...........................49
evil 29, 40, 266
ex nihilo..........................6
exaggeration..................134
existence of God.................9
extinction..............41, 270
Ezekiel.....................204

Ezekiel's ministry...........208
factual errors....................97
failure.......................7, 160
faith 101, 203
false dichotomy.............171
fear 33, 110
federal head....................46
first blood sacrifice..........36
First Commandment....180, 196
firstfruits........................247
forgiveness......35, 106, 129, 160, 201, 254, 270
fractal..............................16
fraud..............................108
free will..............................33
freedom........................103
fresh start.......................188
fruits of the Spirit..........250
fusion...............................2
future..............................19
genetic variations.............13
genetics..........................72
genocide..................96, 128
Gentile salvation.............47
geometry...........................9
geyser..............................41
Gibeah....................136, 146
Gilboa............................156
Gilgal.....................144, 147
God doesn't change.......215
God's character................28
God's covenant...63, 71, 75, 90, 197
God's curse...........34, 36, 63
God's discernment..........54
God's faithfulness..........130
God's glory............115, 120
God's grand plan............199
God's great plan............212
God's help..............167, 190
God's identity.................269
God's intention........35, 154, 189, 206
God's judgment..45, 64, 97, 126
God's Kingdom.....209, 246
God's law.............258, 268
God's law, change..........267
God's law, supernatural. 251

God's mission.....11, 13, 258
God's original mission...248
God's patience................203
God's perspective.....16, 161
God's presence................219
God's promise..................62
God's sovereignty....93, 200
God's voice....................188
God's weapons................171
God's wrath....................112
godliness..........................32
golden calf............111, 112
Goliath...........................152
gospel..............90, 190, 197
gospel in seed form....52, 57
grace.........11, 213, 218, 261
grace, not race................230
Great Awakening.............10
Great Commission.........248
grudge............................255
Habakkuk......................203
Hagar....................61, 62, 66
Haggai............................212
half-truth.......................178
Hanani...........................183
handlers.........................185
Hannah..........................137
hatred..............................70
Hazael............................185
health & happiness.........106
hear 74, 138, 140, 149, 154, 155, 161, 189, 203, 214, 235, 244, 262, 280
hearing...........................109
hearing God....................51
heaven....................10, 280
Hebron...........................158
hedonism.......................241
Herod.............................231
Herodius........................236
high places....163, 167, 179, 183
higher order......................9
Hiram............................182
historic lessons...............155
historical accumulation. 120
historical-grammatical method..................252
history......15, 172, 224, 278

history, pattern...............193
Holy Spirit....194, 205, 206, 227, 238, 239, 246, 249, 262, 277, 278, 280
hominoid..........................22
homo sapiens..............5, 23
homosexual....................136
hope 6, 194, 204, 246, 257, 278
Hosea.............................194
hosts..............................122
household gods................72
human habitat.....3, 5, 8, 11, 13
human sacrifice........67, 184
humanity, supernatural. 251
I AM...............15, 91, 269
ideational process..............2
identity..........................270
identity, human................10
idolatry..111, 125, 167, 170, 173, 179, 183, 184, 185, 186, 192, 204
idolatry, Temple............172
imagination....................226
imitation........................249
indeterminate growth.....40
individual...................21, 25
infidelity........................196
infinite set.....................230
infinite whole..................17
information.............14, 26
inheritance...............14, 68
injustice.........................149
integrity..........................25
integrity, lack of............276
intellectual catalog............8
interpretation................262
Isaac 63, 64, 68, 75
Isaiah.............................191
Isaiah's prophecy............192
Ish-Bosheth.........158, 175
Ishmael.....62, 63, 64, 66, 67
ISIS 98
Islam........................63, 99
Islamic Caliphate.............98
Israel......................76, 88
Israel's failure.................223
Israel's nationalism.........175

Israelite court system.....102
Jabesh Gilead..........137, 144
Jacob................................68
Jacob became Israel..........74
Jacob's ladder....................70
Jacob's blessing................68
Jacob's vow.......................71
Japheth.............................48
Jehoiakim......................199
Jehoshaphat...................183
Jeremiah................197, 208
Jerico.............................125
Jeroboam.......168, 169, 173, 187
Jerusalem........................59
Jesus' lineage................128
Jesus' temptation...........241
Jethro......................89, 101
Jezebel...........................218
Jezreel............................195
Joash..............................184
John of Damascus..........228
John The Baptist...234, 236, 240, 269
Jonathan................148, 155
Jordan River....................74
Joseph.................72, 83, 86
Joseph's dream................83
Joseph's success...............86
Joshua............................123
Josiah....................191, 202
Josiah's reform...............197
Judas Iscariot................248
judgment.......................258
justice....................241, 255
justice & mercy..............262
justification...................241
kindness........................106
King Hiram...................164
kings of Israel................173
Laban..............................70
Lamb of God.................239
Lamech.....................38, 49
language....2, 4, 8, 9, 12, 13, 21, 23, 26, 30, 52, 53
language, confused..........50
language, corruption of...31
law and order................199
law-based religion.........197
Lazarus..........................271

leadership......111, 115, 121, 135
Leah......71
Levites......113
Leviticus......121
life is dynamic......98
light of Christ......223
likeness......17, 29, 33, 76
likeness, of Noah......45
lineage......226, 228
lineage of the Spirit......229
lineage, parody......230
linguistic catalog......8
linguistic categories......275
linguistic structures......226
liturgy....150, 172, 273, 276
Lo-ammi......195
Lo-ruhamah......195
logos...1, 8, 20, 23, 226, 227
longevity......39
Lord's Prayer......10
Lord's Supper......273, 274
Lot......58, 65
love......26
Luther, Martin......203
lying......108
Maccabean revolt. .210, 211
magi......232, 234
magic......100, 252
Malachi......216
Malachi's prophecy......236
marriage......26, 71, 108
materialism......241
mathematical series......28
mathematical set 11, 21, 230
Matthias......248
Medieval theologians......252
Melchizedek. 8, 59, 73, 203, 221, 230, 277
Mesopotamia......6
Messiah. .225, 236, 267, 276
Michal......153
Midian......89
Milcom......167
military unit......122
miracle......26, 93, 250, 254, 274
miracles, precursor......252
misdirection......27
missionaries......259
Moab......66
moral improvement......47
moral upgrade......105
moralistic platitudes......8
morality......31, 208, 215
Mosaic culture......117, 127
Moses......88, 110, 172, 267
Moses, unable......120
Muhammad......63
mystery......254
mysticism......274
myth......7, 51, 134
name......270
Nathan......158, 159
Nathan's curse......177
Nazarite......131, 138
Nebuchadnezzar...197, 207, 211, 233
Nephilim......40
new creature......76
new heart......204
New Jerusalem......246
new lawgiver......268
new world order......5
Nicodemus......243
Noah......39, 270
Noah, drunk......47
Noah, righteous......43
Noah's flood......12, 46
Noahic Era......41
Noahide laws......47
norms......12, 24
numbered......147
Numbers......121
obedience......105, 182
objective......227
objective perspective......54
objective truth......16
offense......255, 256
one and many......25
oppression......89, 170, 187, 199, 202, 203
order, original......7
orgasm......107
Original Sin......27, 261, 276
overshadowed......268
pagan monarchy......140
paganism......111
Passover......242
patterns & cycles......106
Paul's clarification......99
perfection and perception. 9
perspective......27
Peter's confession......264
Peterson, Jordan......2
Pharaoh's daughter......162, 165, 178
Pharaoh's dream......87
pivotal event......141
Plato......8, 227
poison mouth......31
positive law......251
postmillennial......7
Potipher......85
powers & principalities..128
pride......256
progress......270
Promised Land......123, 126, 128, 129, 188, 223, 229
proof......9, 280
Protoevangelium......221
prototype......21, 28
Psalm 137......200
punishment......255
purpose......23, 258
purpose of law......110
purpose, as cause......19
quadriga......252
quantum physics......10
Queen of Sheba......166
Rabbi Jesus......240
Rachael......71
Rahab......123, 128, 230
rapture......239
reality......9, 69, 226
reality & perception......275
reality, communicable...227
reality, false......262
reality, spiritual......225
Rebekah......68
rebellion......31
Red Sea......94
redemption......44, 46
Reformation......110, 210
regeneration. 239, 240, 244, 245, 247, 249, 262, 277, 280
regeneration & resurrection......245
regeneration, social......244

regurgitated vision of the past..........................202
Rehoboam......168, 170, 173, 187
rejection of God...172, 190, 261, 276
relationship....................249
remnant..........................44
repentance......177, 197, 236
replacement................35, 39
representative............20, 46
resurrection39, 43, 278, 279
revelation..................4, 120
revenge..........................80
riddle...........................132
right questions.............259
righteousness....45, 97, 241, 255
rock, Peter....................264
Ruben.............................85
sabbath........................106
sacraments....................273
sacrifice........................217
sacrifice, end of.............280
salvation..........77, 205, 259
salvation, extent of.........231
Samaria................170, 175
Samson.........................131
Samuel.........137, 154, 276
sapience..................5, 11, 21
Satan.............................35
Saul.......................142, 146
Saul's armor..................153
Saul's death..................157
scam..............................66
science....................54, 241
science & technology........6, 227, 252
seasons..........................12
Second Temple.....212, 213, 215, 216, 218, 233, 234, 236, 271
Seleucid Empire.............210
self-destruction...............230
self-determination............49
self-righteousness............265
self-similar pattern............16
semper reformanda............9
serpent..................6, 63, 69
Serpent's lie....................275
Seth...............................38
sexuality........................108
Shechem..................78, 84
Shechem massacre............81
shekhinah.......................205
Shem..............................48
Shiloh............................140
sin 7, 27, 31, 54, 61, 69, 105, 110, 113, 129, 174, 177, 212, 213, 219, 225, 270
sin, common.................192
sin, foundation of..........225
sin, institutionalize.........261
Sin, moon-god................234
sky................................12
slavery.....91, 141, 144, 164, 166, 200
snake................27, 30, 31, 34
social cohesion................94
social injustice...............197
Sodom.............50, 58, 64, 65
Solomon 162, 167, 168, 178
Solomon's idolatry.........167
species....................12, 36
species, new...................239
straight line......................9
substitution................20, 67
success....160, 178, 181, 193
suffering.........................266
Sunday School mentality..................................171
supernatural............10, 242
supernatural v. natural...250
superstition....................148
surrogate........................62
survival.........................259
swearing.......................105
symbolism..29, 30, 119, 248
syncretism...............180, 182
Tabernacle....119, 121, 138, 187, 223, 268
Table of Nations..............48
Talmud...........................47
Tamar............................176
Tanakh.............................5
taxonomy...................8, 25
Temple..163, 165, 172, 182, 268, 276
Temple, cleansing..........242
Temple, new..........204, 208
Temple, temporary........261
temptation......................27
Ten Commandments.....47, 92, 102, 103, 111, 218, 223, 267
Ten Commandments, rewrite.......................115
Terah......52, 57, 63, 75, 104
theonomy.........................24
thermodynamics............251
thesis.............................190
time......5, 11, 14, 15, 16, 18
time, arrow of..................19
time, secret sauce.............17
tithe...............................71
total destruction.............125
Tower of Babel................49
trade route.....................164
tradition..........107, 188, 205
transcendence..................90
transcendental ideas.....241
Transfiguration..............267
transubstantiation..........274
Trinity....14, 17, 18, 20, 21, 57
triumphal entry..............271
two prostitutes.......163, 181
Tyre...............................182
ultimate author..................4
unbelievers.......................93
understanding....................6
uni-verse...........................2
union........................9, 28
unity......................15, 50
universal..............227, 233
universe........................227
Upper Room..................274
Uriah.............................159
usurp, David.................154
usurped. 147, 148, 149, 163, 193
usury.............................108
Uzziah....................185, 191
veil 118, 199, 204, 205, 216, 222, 262
veil, Paul.......................222
vengeance.......35, 106, 125, 129, 134, 151, 160, 199, 201, 270

vengeance, Saul..............148
veracity..............................44
violence...................126, 255
virgin...............................226
Virgin Birth....................228
visualization...................101
voice................215, 262, 280
voice of God....................74
volcanoes..........94, 103, 109
wanderer..........................49
well-being......................244
Westminster Confession 263
wheat & tares..................263
wholeness...................27, 35
wisdom. 162, 163, 165, 167, 178, 180, 182, 262
wise men.................231, 233
wobble, earth...................12
wooden reading..............188
works righteousness.....163, 165, 250
world-wide ministry.....237
worldly success...............188
worldly wisdom..............163
worldview..................35, 97
worship.......91, 92, 121, 233
Zechariah................213, 235
Zephaniah......................202
Zerubbabel..............213, 214
Ziklag..............................156
Zipporah..........................89
Zoar..................................65
Zoroastrianism........232, 233

SCRIPTURE INDEX

OLD TESTAMENT

Genesis 1:1............2, 3, 275
Genesis 1:2......................11
Genesis 1:3..................2, 21
Genesis 1:3, 6, 9............226
Genesis 1:4......................11
Genesis 1:7......................12
Genesis 1:6........................2
Genesis 1:9........................2
Genesis 1:14......................2
Genesis 1:16-27...............28
Genesis 1:20......................2
Genesis 1:24......................2
Genesis 1:26......................2
Genesis 1:26...14, 17, 20, 21
Genesis 1:28............29, 228
Genesis 1:29......................2
Genesis 2:9.....................24
Genesis 2:17..............34, 41
Genesis 2:19....................25
Genesis 2:21....................32
Genesis 3:1......................31
Genesis 3:1-6.................276
Genesis 3:3......................27
Genesis 3:4......................27
Genesis 3:6....27, 31, 32, 49, 261
Genesis 3:8-9...................32
Genesis 3:10....................33
Genesis 3:12....................90
Genesis 3:14....................91
Genesis 3:15..6, 34, 63, 221, 270
Genesis 3:17....................92
Genesis 3:19....................92
Genesis 3:20....................24
Genesis 4:9......................37
Genesis 4:24....................38
Genesis 6:2.....................40
Genesis 6:5.....................40
Genesis 6:7.....................40
Genesis 6:11-12...............40
Genesis 6:18.............45, 46
Genesis 6:22....................45
Genesis 7:1...............43, 45
Genesis 7:11.......12, 41, 46
Genesis 7:21....................46
Genesis 8:20....................43
Genesis 9:4...................148
Genesis 9:21-23...............47
Genesis 9:26....................48
Genesis 9:27....................48
Genesis 11:4....................49
Genesis 11:4....................49
Genesis 11:7....................49
Genesis 11:7-8.................50
Genesis 11:31..................52
Genesis 12:1-3.........52, 56
Genesis 12:2....................53
Genesis 12:7....................57
Genesis 13:1....................58
Genesis 13:12..................58
Genesis 13:13..................58
Genesis 13:18..................58
Genesis 14:8....................59
Genesis 14:11..................59
Genesis 14:18..................59
Genesis 14:22-24.............59
Genesis 15:1....................60
Genesis 15:6....................60
Genesis 15:17............61, 90
Genesis 15:19-21.............61
Genesis 16:10..................62
Genesis 16:11-12.............62
Genesis 17:4-8.................63
Genesis 17:16..................64
Genesis 17:19..................64
Genesis 18:23..................64
Genesis 20:14..................66
Genesis 21:6, 9................66
Genesis 22:3....................67
Genesis 22:14..................67
Genesis 25:5-6.................67
Genesis 26:35..................69
Genesis 27:41..................70
Genesis 28:9....................70
Genesis 28:13-16.............71
Genesis 28:20-22.............71
Genesis 30:42..................72
Genesis 31:54..................73
Genesis 32:22..................74
Genesis 32:24-30.............74
Genesis 32:25..................75
Genesis 32:29..................76
Genesis 32:30..................77
Genesis 33:9....................77
Genesis 33:10-11.............77
Genesis 33:20..................78
Genesis 34:2....................78
Genesis 34:11-12.............79
Genesis 34:14-17.............79
Genesis 34:21-23.............80
Genesis 34:30-31.............80
Genesis 35:2-3.................81

Genesis 35:10-12...............81	Exodus 32:31-32.............116	Joshua 24:15-15..............126
Genesis 37:2.......................83	Exodus 32:33..................114	
Genesis 37:6-11.................84	Exodus 32:34..................114	Judges 1:27-35................128
Genesis 39:4-6...................86	Exodus 32:35..................114	Judges 2:1-4....................129
Genesis 39:21-23...............86	Exodus 33:1-3.................114	Judges 2:10......................129
Genesis 41:46-49...............87	Exodus 33: 9-20.............205	Judges 2:11-15................130
	Exodus 33:17..................115	Judges 2:16......................130
Exodus 1:17........................88	Exodus 33:19..................115	Judges 2:19......................130
Exodus 2:1-10....................89	Exodus 33:20..................120	Judges 13:3-5..................131
Exodus 3:11........................90	Exodus 33:22-23.............115	Judges 14:3......................131
Exodus 3:14...............15, 276	Exodus 34:1....................116	Judges 14:4......................132
Exodus 3:15........................91	Exodus 34:6-7.................116	Judges 14:7......................132
Exodus 3:21-6....................90	Exodus 34:9....................116	Judges 14:14....................133
Exodus 4:10-13..................92	Exodus 34:17-26.............117	Judges 14:18....................133
Exodus 12:14-17................94	Exodus 34:28..................117	Judges 14:19....................133
Exodus 16:31......................95	Exodus 34:29..................117	Judges 15:6......................134
Exodus 17:4........................95	Exodus 34:29-35.............222	Judges 15:10....................134
Exodus 17:8......................101	Exodus 34:34-35.............117	Judges 15:11-12..............134
Exodus 17:8-13................100	Exodus 40:34-38.............120	Judges 15:18....................135
Exodus 17:14-16.........96, 97		Judges 16:5......................135
Exodus 18: 11-12.............101	Leviticus 1:3....................217	Judges 16:15....................135
Exodus 18:15....................101	Leviticus 2:1-3..................44	Judges 16:20....................136
Exodus 18:23....................102	Leviticus 11:9-10.............258	Judges 16:21....................136
Exodus 19: 3-9.................102	Leviticus 17....................148	Judges 16:28....................136
Exodus 19:10-13..............103	Leviticus 18:3.................179	
Exodus 20:2......................103	Leviticus 27:34................121	1 Samuel 1:3....................122
Exodus 20:3......................103		1 Samuel 1:11..................137
Exodus 20:4-5..................104	Numbers 6:1–21..............131	1 Samuel 2:1-10..............138
Exodus 20:5......................104	Numbers 10:11-13..........122	1 Samuel 3:11-14............138
Exodus 20:7......................105	Numbers 10:33-36..........122	1 Samuel 3:18..................138
Exodus 20:8-11................106	Numbers 10:36................122	1 Samuel 4:11..................139
Exodus 20:12....................107		1 Samuel 4:22..................139
Exodus 20:13....................107	Deuteronomy 18:15-19 221	1 Samuel 5:6....................139
Exodus 20:14....................107	Deuteronomy 22:11.......258	1 Samuel 5:9....................139
Exodus 20:15....................108	Deuteronomy 25:17-19. .95	1 Samuel 5:10-11............139
Exodus 20:16....................108	Deuteronomy 31:10-13 183	1 Samuel 7:3-4, 15-17....141
Exodus 20:17....................108		1 Samuel 7:4....................139
Exodus 20:18-21..............109	Joshua 4:19......................140	1 Samuel 7:15-17............141
Exodus 20:21....................109	Joshua 5:2.......................123	1 Samuel 8:3....................141
Exodus 23:32....................179	Joshua 5:8-10.................140	1 Samuel 8:5....................141
Exodus 32:4......................111	Joshua 5:13.....................124	1 Samuel 8:7....................261
Exodus 32:6......................112	Joshua 6:17, 21...............125	1 Samuel 8:7-9................141
Exodus 32:10....................116	Joshua 7:1.......................124	1 Samuel 8:17-18............141
Exodus 32:10-12..............117	Joshua 8:2.......................125	1 Samuel 8:19-20............142
Exodus 32:14....................112	Joshua 8:22-23...............124	1 Samuel 9:1-2................142
Exodus 32:19....................112	Joshua 10:12...................180	1 Samuel 9:21..................143
Exodus 32:25....................113	Joshua 13:1.....................126	1 Samuel 10:1..................143
Exodus 32:26....................113	Joshua 18:1.....................140	1 Samuel 10:6..................143
Exodus 32:27....................113	Joshua 19:51...................140	1 Samuel 10:17-24..........144
Exodus 32:29....................113	Joshua 22:9.....................140	1 Samuel 11:7..................144

1 Samuel 11:12-15..........144	1 Kings 3:15...........162, 181	2 Chronicles 25:27.........186
1 Samuel 12:20-25..........145	1 Kings 3:28...................181	2 Chronicles 26:3...........193
1 Samuel 13:4..................146	1 Kings 4:20...................181	2 Chronicles 26:18.........193
1 Samuel 13:6-7...............146	1 Kings 4:30...................182	
1 Samuel 13:9..................147	1 Kings 5:5.....................164	Ezra 1:1-11......................234
1 Samuel 13:10................147	1 Kings 5:13-18..............164	
1 Samuel 13:11................147	1 Kings 6:12-13..............165	Job 36:10.........................262
1 Samuel 13:12................147	1 Kings 8:63...................165	
1 Samuel 13:13-14..........147	1 Kings 9:4.....................165	Psalm 8............................251
1 Samuel 13:14................174	1 Kings 9:6-8..................166	Psalm 34:8.......................250
1 Samuel 13:15................147	1 Kings 9: 20-22.............166	Psalm 68:29.....................233
1 Samuel 14:32................148	1 Kings 10:23-24............166	Psalm 72:10.....................233
1 Samuel 14:34................148	1 Kings 11:4-8................167	Psalm 78:60.....................140
1 Samuel 14:45................149	1 Kings 11:11-13............167	Psalm 110:4.......................60
1 Samuel 15:1-3..............149	1 Kings 11:31.................189	
1 Samuel 15:9..................149	1 Kings 11:31-39............189	Proverbs 8:13..................256
1 Samuel 15:11................150	1 Kings 11:34, 36...........190	Proverbs 14:12................132
1 Samuel 15:13................150	1 Kings 12:4...................168	
1 Samuel 15:15................150	1 Kings 12:7...................169	Isaiah 2:12.......................256
1 Samuel 15:22-23..........150	1 Kings 12:10-11............169	Isaiah 9:2.........................110
1 Samuel 15:32-33..........151	1 Kings 12:15.................169	Isaiah 23:9.......................256
1 Samuel 16:1-3..............151	1 Kings 15:11-15............183	Isaiah 35:5.......................262
1 Samuel 16:7..................152	1 Kings 15:14.................183	Isaiah 44:18.....................222
1 Samuel 16:13................152	1 Kings 22:48–49............184	Isaiah 44:28.....................191
1 Samuel 16:14................152	1 Kings 26-33.................170	Isaiah 45:1.......................191
1 Samuel 17....................152		Isaiah 60:3.......................233
1 Samuel 18:10-11..........153	2 Kings 1:8.....................235	
1 Samuel 24:3-4..............155	2 Kings 2:11..........218, 236	Jeremiah 6:16..................198
1 Samuel 26:11................156	2 Kings 3:4–27................184	Jeremiah 29:5-7..............208
1 Samuel 31:1-7..............157	2 Kings 12:2...................185	
	2 Kings 15:5...................193	Ezekiel 37........................208
2 Samuel 1:1-10.............157		
2 Samuel 1:11-16............158	1 Chronicles 12:38..........174	Daniel 1:1-2....................207
2 Samuel 3:3...................175	1 Chronicles 13:8............174	Daniel 1:4........................207
2 Samuel 7:16.................159	1 Chronicles 15:3............174	Daniel 1:15-16................207
2 Samuel 12:10...............159	1 Chronicles 18:14..........174	Daniel 1:17......................207
2 Samuel 12:10-11..........177	1 Chronicles 24:23-24...185	Daniel 1:20......................233
2 Samuel 13:1-14............176	1 Chronicles 28:4............175	Daniel 4:34-37................211
2 Samuel 13:21-22..........176	1 Chronicles 29:9...........175	
2 Samuel 13:28...............177		Hosea 2:14-23.................196
	2 Chronicles 8:16-17.....164	
1 Kings 1:5-53................161	2 Chronicles 16:9...........183	Habakkuk 2:4..................203
1 Kings 2:1-10................160	2 Chronicles 16:10.........183	
1 Kings 2:13-25..............161	2 Chronicles 17:6...........183	Haggai 2:12-14...............212
1 Kings 3:1-15.................178	2 Chronicles 19:4–11.....184	
1 Kings 3:3.....................179	2 Chronicles 20:35–37....184	Zechariah 1:2-6..............214
1 Kings 3:4.....................180	2 Chronicles 25:2...........186	Zechariah 6:15................215
1 Kings 3:9.....................162	2 Chronicles 25:7–10, 13	Zechariah 7:12-14..........215
1 Kings 3:11-14..............162	185	Zechariah 7:13................214
1 Kings 3:12...................180	2 Chronicles 25:14–16...185	

Malachi 1:3.....................98
Malachi 2:11...................217
Malachi 2:17...................217
Malachi 3:16-18.............218
Malachi 3:18...................219
Malachi 4:3.....................218
Malachi 4:5-6.................269
Malachi 4:6............219, 236

NEW TESTAMENT

Matthew 3:13-17...........238
Matthew 3:14-15...........240
Matthew 13:24-13:30....263
Matthew 21:12-17.........242
Matthew 2:11................232
Matthew 2:13-23...........232
Matthew 3:2...................240
Matthew 4:14-16...........110
Matthew 4:17.................240
Matthew 5:3...................257
Matthew 5:3-12.............257
Matthew 5:4-6...............257
Matthew 5:17-18...........258
Matthew 5:17-20...........258
Matthew 6:9-13...............10
Matthew 11:14...............235
Matthew 13:15-17.........262
Matthew 15:5.................268
Matthew 16:13-20.........264
Matthew 16:21-23.........265
Matthew 17:5.................268
Matthew 17:7.................268
Matthew 17:9.................269
Matthew 17:10-13..........236
Matthew 19:28...............244
Matthew 19:28...............244
Matthew 22:37...............241
Matthew 23:33.................30
Matthew 24:15...............210
Matthew 28:18-20..........248

Mark 1:9–11..................238
Mark 11:15–19.............242
Mark 4:3-9....................263

Luke 1:16-17.................236
Luke 3:21–23................238
Luke 19:45–48..............242

Luke 6:20-22.................257
Luke 10:1......................248
Luke 24:49-51..............279

John 2:13–16................242
John 1:1......1, 9, 21, 51, 226
John 1:12......................275
John 1:14...................2, 120
John 1:32-24................238
John 1:35-39................239
John 2:19......................209
John 2:19-21................214
John 2:21......................240
John 3:2........................243
John 3:3, 5....................243
John 3:3-8....................244
John 3:9........................243
John 6:35......................269
John 8:12......................269
John 8:44........................35
John 10:9......................269
John 10:11....................269
John 11:1-44................271
John 11:25....................269
John 11:47-53..............271
John 11:54....................271
John 12:10....................271
John 12:16-18..............272
John 12:32....................228
John 12:37-41..............272
John 13:34....................274
John 14:6..............269, 276
John 15:1......................269

Acts 1:6-11...................279
Acts 1:22......................245
Acts 1:26......................248
Acts 2:38......................249
Acts 4:33......................245
Acts 7:51......................262
Acts 9...........................248
Acts 10:9-16.................267
Acts 10:11....................267
Acts 13:22....................174
Acts 22:6-10.................245
Acts 26:22-23...............245

Romans 1:24.................180
Romans 1:24-27...........142

Romans 3:28.................163
Romans 6:10.................260
Romans 8:29.................247
Romans 9:13...................98
Romans 9:22-26............197
1 Corinthians 3:19.........167
1 Corinthians 5:11.........258
1 Corinthians 9:1...........245
1 Corinthians 11:1.........249
1 Corinthians 15:8.........245
1 Corinthians 15:20.......247
2 Corinthians 3:12-18...118
2 Corinthians 3:13-15..205, 223, 262
2 Corinthians 5:1-5.......247
2 Corinthians 5:17.........245

Galatians 3:27................105
Galatians 5:22-23..105, 244, 246, 279
Ephesians 1:19–20.........245
Ephesians 2:1, 8.............245
Ephesians 2:6.................244
Ephesians 6:11...............171
Ephesians 6:12..........99, 128

Philippians 2:3................256
Philippians 3:20-21........247
Philippians 4:8................264

Colossians 1:15...............247

Titus 3:5.........................244

Hebrews 4:14-16...........214
Hebrews 6:20...................60
Hebrews 7:3.....................60
Hebrews 10:10...............260

James 1:18.....................246
James 4:6......................256

1 Peter 1:3....................244
1 Peter 2:5....................265

1 John 2:16...................241

Revelation 21:1.............246
Revelation 21:5.............244

www.ingramcontent.com/pod-product-compliance
Lightning Source LLC
Chambersburg PA
CBHW071659170426
43195CB00039B/2234